FENCING

ANCIENT ART AND MODERN SPORT

FENCING

ANCIENT ART AND MODERN SPORT

by

C-L. de BEAUMONT, OBE

MEMBRE D'HONNEUR, FÉDÉRATION INTERNATIONALE
D'ESCRIME
PRESIDENT, AMATEUR FENCING ASSOCIATION
PRESIDENT, BRITISH EMPIRE AND COMMONWEALTH
FENCING FEDERATION

Drawings by Miss R. J. Milward

South Brunswick and New York:

A. S. BARNES & COMPANY

First American Edition 1971
A. S. BARNES AND CO., INC.
Cranbury, N. J. 08512

Library of Congress Catalog Card Number: 77-155733

ISBN 0 7182 0898 6

Printed in Great Britain by
Lowe & Brydone (Printers) Ltd., London

Contents

List of Illustrations

DRAWINGS

PLATES

Between pages 112 *and* 113

Preface

THIS book has been written in order to provide an answer to the questions which fencers, and aspiring fencers, habitually ask me.

Fencing cannot be learned from a book. Its technique must be acquired by lessons from a qualified master or leader. Nevertheless it is hoped that the chapters dealing in detail with the technique of each weapon may help beginners to understand the reasons for the various fencing movements, which they learn from their instructors, and their tactical application.

In the belief that this book will be used as a work of reference by practical fencers, an attempt has been made to make each section, as far as possible, self-contained, and a certain amount of repetition has proved to be unavoidable.

Thus I hope that this small book may prove useful to the increasing numbers of people already fencing or becoming interested in this ancient and fascinating art. I hope that it may help them, each and every one, to a better understanding of fencing and that this 'ancient art and modern sport' may bring them the lifetime of happiness and enjoyment which it has given to me.

C-L. de BEAUMONT

I

Fencing as a Modern Sport

FENCING is an art with a long and fascinating history and with its roots in the traditions of chivalry.

Swords existed long before the dawn of recorded history, and throughout the centuries much attention was devoted to their development and to the study of a wide variety of schools and systems for their use. The swords in use today have been evolved from these ancient weapons, and the basic movements and indeed many of the fencing terms currently employed in the present-day fencing rooms have been used for centuries by generations of swordsmen.

While preserving much of its romantic background of history and tradition, fencing is today a very modern and athletic sport. During the past fifty years it has been increasingly practised by persons of every class and calling throughout the world.

In Britain a revival of interest began about the middle of the nineteenth century and this led to the foundation in 1902 of the Amateur Fencing Association as the governing body for the sport. It remained the sport of the few up to the First World War and was confined to a few London clubs, the larger universities and public schools and the services. It was more widely practised between the two wars and clubs were formed in many of the larger provincial towns. By 1939 the Amateur Fencing Association had 109 affiliated clubs and had established area organizations for Scotland and for the North and Midlands.

The Second World War disrupted this progress and in 1945 only fifty-one clubs remained active. Since then there has been a dramatic upsurge of interest in fencing throughout the United Kingdom. By 1969 there were some 638 affiliated clubs, besides a large number of evening-institute classes in which fencing was taught and the Association had established fourteen Sections or area organizations covering every part of Great Britain and Northern Ireland.

This remarkable expansion in numbers has happily been accompanied by an equal advance in technical excellence. Today British fencers have reached the first flight in international competition, especially at foil and épée. British teams have reached the finals of Olympic and World Championships, Miss Gillian Sheen became the first British fencer to win a Gold Medal at the Olympic Games when she won the ladies' individual title at the 1956 Olympic Games and

two years later Mr H. W. F. Hoskyns won the Épée Championship
of the World at Philadelphia, while in 1959 Mr. Allan Jay won the
World Foil Championship in Budapest.

The main factor which has led to the striking development of
fencing in Britain has been the success of the National Training
Scheme launched by the Amateur Fencing Association in 1949.
This has been ensured by the devoted work of the National Fencing
Coach and of the hundreds of leaders, or amateur instructors, which
the scheme has produced.

Fencing has also made great progress throughout the British
Empire and Commonwealth since 1950 when, at the instigation of
New Zealand, it was first included in the British Empire Games
held that year at Auckland. At Auckland the British Empire and
Commonwealth Fencing Federation was founded to co-ordinate
and develop fencing in the Commonwealth. This Federation was
founded by Great Britain, Australia and New Zealand and now
includes eight nations with the addition of Canada, South Africa,
Rhodesia, Hong Kong and Singapore. There are now flourishing
associations in these countries and the marked improvement in the
standard of their fencers has been manifested in the Vancouver and
Cardiff Empire Games.

THE NATURE OF THE SPORT

The growth of interest in recent years, not only in Britain but
throughout the world, is probably due to a wider recognition of
the many advantages of fencing as a modern sport. Many people
are first attracted by its romantic appeal but they soon realize that
it is the perfect relaxation, especially for those dwelling in towns. It
provides concentrated physical exercise in a short space of time,
independent of the weather, without excessive cost, the need for
large numbers of players or expensive venues and apparatus. Fencing
develops co-ordination of mind and body in the highest degree and
exercises every part of the body. However tired or worried one may
be, half an hour or so spent at the *salle d'armes* will bring a wonderful
sense of freshness and well-being. This is because it is impossible to
fence and to think about anything else at the same time and the
hard physical exercise is therefore accompanied by complete relaxation of the mind. The value of fencing, especially for young people,
in the development of quick thinking, poise, balance and muscular
control and for strengthening the limbs and back has long been
recognized.

There is no advantage in mere brute strength in this game of
speed and finesse. Control of movement and quickness of thought
and execution can, in great measure, overcome lack of height or
reach or strength which would be a severe handicap at other sports.

Foil fencing is equally suitable for women as for men and both sexes can fence together on far more level terms than is possible at most other sports.

Fencing, while providing concentrated physical exercise, does not put excessive strain on heart or lungs. It can be started at an early age, say thirteen to fifteen, and can be continued practically all one's life. There are many examples of fencers who have remained in the championship class well into their fifties and of people in their sixties and seventies and even older who can still give far younger fencers an excellent bout. Possessed of a sound technique, experience often enables a trained fencer to outwit a much younger and faster opponent.

In recent years competition fencing has become less artistic and more athletic than it was before the last war. In this respect it has followed a tendency noticeable in a number of other competitive sports. Nowadays it is not uncommon to find World Champions in their early twenties or even in their teens—a thing which would have seemed impossible a couple of generations ago.

Fencing is a complex and difficult art to master. Anyone who aspires to becoming a complete fencer must be prepared to devote much time and effort to lessons and to gaining competition experience. It is, however, well worth making the not inconsiderable effort required to acquire a sound technique because, by so doing, one masters a game which will be a fascination and a source of great satisfaction for the rest of one's life.

Besides the stance, the lunge and footwork which are peculiar to fencing, the use of light weapons at close quarters and at great speed requires a considerable discipline of muscular and reflex actions, if the wide variety of fencing movements available are to be used to the full. During a bout the correct stroke has to be chosen and executed within a fraction of a second. It is necessary to practise assiduously the various fencing movements and combinations of fencing movements until they are done automatically in the correct way at the correct time. Only then will the mind be free to analyse the opponent's game and devise the strategy and tactics required to outwit him.

Much of the interest of a fencing bout lies in the fact that you have not only to induce your opponent to misjudge your intentions so that he leaves some part of his target unprotected for your hit to land, but to anticipate his reactions correctly.

A simple example will suffice to illustrate this. Unless you are much superior to your opponent in speed and sense of distance it is unlikely that you will be able to hit him, except occasionally by a surprise attack, with a direct thrust. His natural reaction will be to deflect your threatening blade with his sword, which is called a simple parry. To make this parry successfully, his sword-hand has to travel only a few inches across his body while your point is travelling forward several feet to reach his target. You must obviously find a way to overcome this handicap if you are to hit him.

The simplest way to make an opening for an attack is to straighten your arm so that your point threatens an opening in your opponent's guard, as if you were going to make a direct thrust at the target. When your opponent moves his sword across to parry this thrust, a slight finger movement, called a disengagement, will carry your point out of the path of this parry towards the other side of his target which has been exposed by the parry. Thus a lateral parry from one side of the target to the other is deceived by a simple disengagement and you have gained time and distance for your attack by causing your opponent to misjudge your intention.

Your opponent can, however, parry a direct thrust in two ways, either by a lateral parry made by moving his blade from one side of his body to the other or, keeping his sword-hand in its original position, he can sweep away the threatening blade by a circular movement of his own blade.

If your opponent chooses this circular form of parry, then you cannot make your disengagement passing below his blade because your blade will be collected by the circle performed by his. Your correct stroke after your feint will be to describe a circle with your point in the same direction and just ahead of your opponent's circular parry. Your blade will thus avoid being caught up and will end on the 'open' side of your opponent's target, towards which you made your original feint. This movement is called a *doublé*.

When, therefore, you launch even this simple form of attack—a feint followed by a deception of the parry—you must anticipate which form of parry your opponent will take if you are to succeed.

The quicker and more complex the actions which a well matched pair of experienced fencers attempt, the greater the speed of anticipation and execution that will be required. It has been well said that fencing is like a game of chess played at lightning speed.

HOW TO START

Fencing cannot be learned from a book, although books on fencing may help materially to the understanding of the purpose of the various movements and tactics. Lessons from a qualified teacher are the only way to learn the essential technique and constantly to perfect it.

Non-fencers are often surprised to find that established fencing champions continue to have regular lessons from their masters each week. Regular lessons throughout one's fencing life are necessary because all fencing movements have to be made very accurately, with a definite rhythm and with perfect co-ordination of hand, body and footwork. Only by regular lessons can one maintain one's technique at concert pitch and correct the faults and loose movements which inevitably appear during practice bouts and matches.

A fencing lesson is much more than a routine repetition of fencing movements. A good master must develop co-ordination and rhythm in his pupil's movements, and give knowledge of and practice in their tactical application. A great master will give inspiration to his pupils.

There are many professional masters in clubs in London and the larger towns, and these are supplemented throughout the country by the coaches or qualified amateur instructors trained under the Amateur Fencing Association's National Training Scheme. It is wise to seek the best instruction available—and which you can afford.

In many areas fencing can be started very inexpensively by joining an evening-institute fencing class. At many the initial equipment is made available on loan, and an instructor is always provided. In London alone there are over ninety such classes. Particulars can be obtained from the local education office.

Although these classes are a good way to start fencing, their standard of instruction is not usually very advanced. It is as well therefore, when possible, to join an established fencing club. Particulars of the clubs available can be obtained from the Section of the Association covering the area in which you live. If there are a number of clubs available, your choice will probably be dictated by the friends that you may have among the members of a particular club, or by financial considerations. If these factors do not apply you will be well advised to examine the results obtained by the club team and members in competitions and to join the club which has the best current record at the weapon which you favour.

A great deal of the pleasure obtained from membership of a fencing club is derived from friendly bouts with fellow members which are called loose play. During such bouts one can practise and perfect the strokes learned from the master during lessons and obtain competitive experience by fencing for a definite number of hits. It is wise for beginners to heed the advice of their instructor as to when they are ready to begin loose play. If it is attempted before a sufficient basic technique has been acquired from lessons, many bad habits may be formed which will be difficult to eradicate and may seriously retard the aspiring fencer's progress.

Fencing is a sport with a special tradition of friendliness. A fencer is always welcomed at any club he may visit anywhere in the world. In a fencing club everyone, champion and novice alike, fences everyone else. When a beginner is invited to have a bout by an experienced fencer, he should try to *fence* to the best of his ability and not just try to score hits in any unorthodox way he can. Much can be learned by studying the way the established fencer deals with the novice's efforts—even if the latter is regularly and soundly beaten.

Fencing has also a special tradition of courtesy, as one might expect from its long connection with chivalry. A fencer should be punctilious about saluting his opponent before putting on his mask to commence a bout, and should salute again, remove his mask and shake hands, when the bout is finished. In a competition it is customary to salute the President and judges before saluting one's opponent. When fencing bouts with one's friends in a club, hits should always be acknowledged but never claimed. A fencer is not, however, expected to acknowledge hits received during a competition, since it is the function of the judges or the electrical apparatus, as the case may be, to establish the arrival of hits. He may, of course, acknowledge a hit under such circumstances if he wishes to do so and this frequently occurs. A fencer engaged in a competition must, however, remember that the rules only permit him to make an acknowledgment immediately he receives a hit and before the jury have debated it. To acknowledge a hit after the President has awarded it is regarded not only as bad manners but as a possible reflection on the competence of the jury.

DRESS AND EQUIPMENT

Fencing equipment is not particularly expensive and it lasts for years. Initially the beginner will only require a foil, mask, jacket and gloves, which will involve him in a total cost of between £8–10. Flannel trousers or a short, wide skirt or gym tunic can be worn with rubber-soled gym shoes. Later on this outfit can be completed by the purchase of canvas breeches, white stockings and fencing shoes.

Jackets and breeches should be made of a strong, closely woven white canvas, but stiff cloth which restricts movement should be avoided. A fencing jacket can be bought ready-made, but for comfort it is well worth incurring the small extra expense of having it made to fit. A lighter-weight material can be used for a foil jacket than for one for épée or sabre. A short jacket ending just below the waist is favoured by many fencers for foil and sabre, with rather widely cut breeches. For épée close-fitting breeches or jodhpur-type trousers are worn, with a full-length jacket covering the whole trunk and secured by a strap passing between the legs, attached to a buckle at the back. All fencing clothing should be white and many fencers like to wear their club buttons on their jackets. British international fencers have the right to wear gilt Tudor-rose buttons.

It is important to ensure that there is a stout inner sleeve in all jackets, reaching from shoulder to elbow of the sword-arm, and that a strong double lining covers the armpit and the breast on the same side. A separate plastron made of two thicknesses of hemp cloth and covering the under side of the upper part of the sword-arm, the armpit and breast down to the waist must always be worn. These precautions will prevent a serious accident when a blade breaks.

Ladies' jackets must always be fitted with breast-protectors made of steel mesh or other rigid material which fit into pockets in the jacket. Ladies can avoid painful and unsightly bruises which can occur, especially with the rigid blades used for electrical foil, by wearing a quilted waistcoat under their jackets.

Ribbed woollen stockings should be worn, especially at épée, and the self-supporting type of stocking is the most comfortable to wear. At foil and sabre many people prefer ankle socks. An extra pair of socks of a thinner material worn over socks or stockings and rolled down to the ankle will prevent sore feet, especially during competitions.

It is essential to wear light-soled shoes without heels. On a cork or linoleum *piste*, speci fencing shoes with canvas or soft-leather uppers reinforced with strap across the toes and with a flat raw-hide sole, give the best grip when rubbed with resin. They provide an excellent foothold on that type of floor and enable the fencer to 'feel' the *piste*, which helps balance and gives security in the lunge. Nothing is more disconcerting during a bout than to find one is slipping when lunging. On any other type of flooring, such as wood or the copper-mesh *pistes* used at épée and electrical foil, rubber-soled shoes must be used. A strong, light plimsoll with an ordinary ribbed-rubber sole is the best shoe for this purpose. Crêpe rubber is inclined to grip too firmly and to prevent quick, light footwork; it is usually too thick to enable one to feel the *piste*.

It is important to remember that resin must never be used with rubber-soled shoes, it will cause them to slip on any type of flooring. If one finds that one is slipping when wearing rubber-soled shoes, the remedy is to wet the soles of the shoes by rubbing them in a very wet cloth between bouts.

Because of the difference in the method of preventing slipping according to the type of shoe worn, a fencer is well advised always to carry both leather- and rubber-soled shoes when fencing ordinary foil or sabre. If one is called upon to fence on a linoleum *piste*, one's opponents who wear leather-soled shoes will use resin and this will soon impregnate the flooring so that it becomes slippery for anyone wearing rubber-soled shoes. On the other hand one often arrives at a competition to find that the *piste* is marked out on a wooden floor, when rubber-soled shoes are the best to use.

An all-wire mask may be used for foil and épée and is light and cool. Extra protection from sabre cuts, which can often whip round painfully at the back of the head, can be obtained by using a mask with the sides and top covered with leather. Masks for universal use should be white. The use of an eyeshade inside the mask is helpful when fencing in sunshine or under glaring lights. It is as well to get used to wearing an eyeshade at all times because it can be disconcerting when first used.

It is obviously important to ensure that masks are strong and light. A mask should be frequently examined to see that the mesh

B

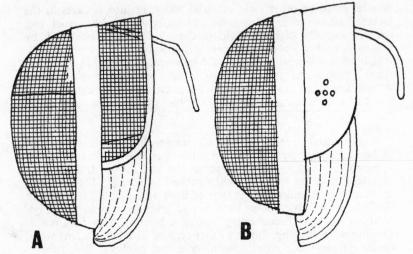

Fig. 1 The Mask
A. Foil or Épée Mask   B. Sabre Mask

has not rusted or become dented or broken. It should be discarded as soon as the mesh can be pressed in with the thumbs.

Gloves should be close-fitting when new, as they will take the shape of the hand in use. For foil the best gloves are made of chamois or soft hide, slightly padded at the back of the hand and with a soft gauntlet. Épée gloves should be made of strong doeskin, with reinforced canvas back covering the fingers and a close-fitting canvas gauntlet with an elastic insertion inside the wrist. For sabre the glove should be made of soft hide, well padded at the back and with a padded or quilted, close-fitting gauntlet. A separate, narrow padded strap is often added to protect the wrist.

A light canvas fencing bag piped with leather should be used for carrying weapons and equipment. Such bags are banjo-shaped and should have a sufficiently wide 'throat' to allow a number of weapons to be packed together without the blades being constricted. The bag may be made with a separate division at the widest part, in which clothing can be placed. This will prevent the clothing being soiled by contact with the weapons. A small pocket sewn on the outside of the bag is useful for carrying such small items as spare *pointes d'arrêt*, waxed thread, a roll of plaster, sandpaper and other oddments.

During fencing competitions it is important to keep warm between bouts. A dressing-gown or warm overcoat with wide sleeves is useful for this purpose and is better than a blazer which does not cover the thighs and lumbar regions. Some fencers prefer to wrap themselves in a rug or blanket. If a track-suit is used, the whole front of the blouse should open, being fitted with a zip-fastener running its whole length. This type of blouse can be put on like a coat and is much more practical than the normal type of blouse which has to be pulled on over the head, which is not very easy when wearing a fencing jacket. Similarly a thick cardigan-type woolly is more practical than a sweater when one is dressed in fencing kit.

THE FENCING WEAPONS

Modern fencing is practised with three weapons—the Foil, the Épée and the Sabre.

The foil is a light weapon with a tapering quadrangular blade and a small bell-shaped guard. Evolved from the short court sword of the seventeenth and eighteenth centuries, it is the basic weapon for the practice of fencing and is not a duelling sword. Valid hits are restricted to those which are made with the point on the trunk only. Hits which arrive on the head, arms or legs are not counted as good.

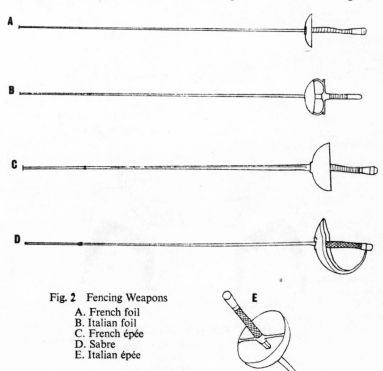

Fig. 2   Fencing Weapons
    A. French foil
    B. Italian foil
    C. French épée
    D. Sabre
    E. Italian épée

Foil fencing is governed by rather complex rules and conventions which are described elsewhere.

The épée is the duelling sword and was developed in the mid-nineteenth century to train people for actual duels. It is a heavier weapon than the foil, with a stiffer, fluted triangular blade to which is affixed a three-pronged *pointe d'arrêt*. It has a large bell-shaped

Fig. 3   Silhouettes of the Targets

A. Target: foil
B. Target: épée
C. Target: sabre

guard. Épée fencing conforms as closely as possible to the conditions of a duel. Hits made with the point are valid wherever they arrive on the opponent's person or equipment. There are no conventions and priority between hits on both fencers is established entirely as a matter of time. If no difference of time between two hits exists, a hit is scored against each competitor, which is called a double hit, on the principle that in a duel both combatants would be wounded—or dead.

The sabre is the cut-and-thrust weapon. It has a flattened V-shaped blade, with a blunted cutting edge and with the point folded over to form the button. There is a half-circular guard to protect the sword-hand from cuts.

Hits at sabre may be made with the whole of the front edge or the last third of the back edge ('cuts') as well as with the point. The target consists of the head, arms and trunk down to just below the waist. Although the sabre is a duelling weapon, it is fenced in schools and competitions according to similar rules and conventions as for the foil.

Each weapon consists of a blade and mounting. The parts of a weapon are shown in the accompanying diagram (Fig. 4). It can be seen that the mounting consists of a guard within which there is a small cushion to protect the fingers and a handle or grip through which passes the tang of the blade; the pommel or locking nut is screwed to the end of the tang. The stronger part of the blade, nearest to the guard, is called the forte and the remainder of the blade is called the foible.

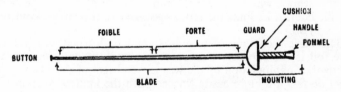

Fig. 4   Parts of the Sword

There are two main schools at foil and épée, differentiated basically by the form of the mounting—they are the French and the Italian schools.

The French foil or épée has a simple bell guard and a plain, slightly shaped handle which lies lightly in the hand and is manipulated entirely by the fingers.

The Italian foil or épée has a cross-bar affixed to the inner edges of the guard, sometimes with two rings through which the first fingers are slipped, while the pommel of the shorter handle is bound to the wrist by a strap or long leash. This gives much more strength in holding and manipulating the weapon, but there is a corresponding limitation in finger play.

The basic difference in holding and manipulating the weapon has produced the different styles and methods of fencing of the French and Italian schools. Each was evolved through the centuries to suit the different temperament and approach to combat of these two nations. Neither school is superior to the other. A fencer should adopt the one which is best suited to his physique and temperament.

The beginner will probably be taught the method which his instructor favours or which the master considers will suit him best. It is possible later to change from one school to the other, since the difference between them is one of application of the same basic technique. It is wise, however, to learn one method completely before attempting to adopt the other school.

A wide variety of specialized handles are available for foils and épées, with transverse bars, pistol grips, grooves, or handles moulded to the form of the hand. These are usually known as orthopaedic grips and, although they are generally fitted with the French type of guard, in use they approximate more to the Italian style and are often combined with a flattened extension strapped to the wrist.

Orthopaedic handles are mostly used by people with weak fingers or wrists and many fencers favour them for manipulating the heavier electrical weapons. The writer considers that these specialized handles, while undoubtedly useful to certain fencers, are generally inferior to the orthodox French or Italian handles: while they combine elements of both, they detract from the effectiveness of either. A beginner should learn his fencing with the orthodox handle of the school which he adopts and only change to a specialized handle later, if he finds the latter necessary to the proper control of the weapon.

The basic technique of fencing should be learned with the foil. The foil is the cheapest weapon to use and the body movements, footwork, manipulation of the weapon and feel of the blade (*sentiment du fer*) are more easily learned with the lightest weapon. Foil fencing provides the most complete game, because all fencing movements can be made with the foil but some are not practicable with the épée or sabre. Further, the rules and conventions applicable to foil fencing teach appreciation of fencing time, distance and phrasing.

It is true that excellent results have been obtained by masters who have taught their pupils from the beginning with épée or sabre; but for the reasons given above, it is generally wiser for the beginner to lay the foundations of his basic fencing technique with the foil before adapting this technique to another weapon. If you have mastered the elements of fencing with the foil you can easily graduate to another weapon of your choice, but the reverse is much more difficult.

CHOOSING A WEAPON

The choice of a weapon and the 'setting' of the blade in the weapon require a good deal of experience. For the normal type of French foil or épée, the length and thickness of the handle is a matter of individual taste. If it is found that the hand tires quickly even when the handle is held correctly, this can often be cured by choosing a slightly thicker handle.

The metal pommel or locking nut at the end of a weapon is used both for securing the handle to the blade and to balance the weapon. The weight of this pommel can therefore be varied to alter the point of balance of the weapon. Normally this point of balance should be between one and two inches along the blade from the outer face of the guard, but some fencers favour a weapon which comes more into the heel of the hand, while others prefer the balance slightly nearer the point.

The most serviceable type of pommel at foil and épée is the universal model, which screws on to a slotted and threaded piece of brass which fits into a groove at the end of the tang of the blade and obviates the cutting of a special thread on each blade.

A foil blade should be light, flexible and well balanced. While bending easily it should spring back when released. Avoid stiff, heavy blades, or soft blades which remain in any shape in which they are bent. Excessively light or whippy blades do not give sufficient opposition when parries are made and detract from accuracy of point. More rigid blades are necessary at electrical than at ordinary foil, to counteract the weight of the point and to ensure that hits arrive as directly as possible in order to depress the spring in the electrical point.

Electrical épée blades should be as strong and rigid as is compatible with essential lightness and balance. A sufficiently rigid blade will ensure that the spring-loaded point is depressed when a hit is made, and that a legitimate stop hit is not made into a double hit by the opponent forcing his attack through the bend of the defender's blade.

All competitive épée is now judged with the electrical apparatus, but it is costly and quite unnecessary always to use an electrical épée for loose play in the *salle*. However, it is desirable to choose ordinary épée blades similar in strength and weight to the electrical blades one uses in competitions and to balance the ordinary épée used for practice, by adjusting the weight of the pommel, so that it conforms to the balance of the competition épée which is of course affected by the heavier spring-loaded point.

A sabre blade should be light and flexible, but should retain its rigidity after it is bent. Soft or whippy blades reduce the accuracy of cuts and do not provide sufficient resistance when a parry is formed. On the other hand a thick, heavy blade tires the sword-hand and causes the user to make wide, slow and clumsy movements.

Foil and épée blades, especially when the electrical apparatus is being used, should be kept as straight as possible. A curved blade, particularly at foil, will cause the spring-loaded point to land rather flat on the target and prevent the quality of penetration in a hit, which is essential if the apparatus is to register. At sabre, a slight but even curve downwards, when the hand is in third position, will assist in 'carrying' the blade. No curve in the direction of the cutting edge is allowed.

At ordinary foil the flattened end of the blade or 'button' must always be covered with waxed thread or plaster or with a plastic button. This has a twofold purpose. It prevents the point penetrating between the meshes of the mask and helps in 'fixing' the point when a hit is made.

The electric foil or épée is fitted with a cylindrical, spring loaded point which is either flattened at the top or step-cut and forms a *pointe d'arrêt*. At ordinary épée a triple-pronged metal *pointe d'arrêt* is affixed to the flattened metal button at the end of the blade with waxed thread. Dental floss is an excellent material to use for this purpose. This triple point is designed to catch in the clothing and establish when a hit arrives. Without it, it is very difficult to be sure whether a hit has actually arrived or is flat, especially when the hit is made on the arm.

When fencing épée regularly in the *salle*, the triple point causes considerable wear and tear on jacket and gloves and for this reason many fencers prefer not to use the *pointe d'arrêt* for practice. This is a mistake because without the triple point one cannot be certain whether one's hits are landing correctly and loose play loses much of its value in training accuracy of point and correct angulation of the hits at wrist.

All *pointes d'arrêt* should be protected when carried in a fencing bag. This not only prevents excessive wear on the bag but, in the case of electrical foils and épées, prevents the points damaging the thin wires which run along the blades, when the weapons are put into the bag. For this purpose small metal screw caps may be used. An even better method is to use narrow-gauge aluminium tubes cut half an inch longer than the blade. These are slipped over the blade before packing and give complete protection to blade and point— and to the bag.

ESSENTIAL PRECAUTIONS

The question is often asked whether fencing is a dangerous sport. As in all sports, accidents occasionally occur and, when they do, they generally attract undue publicity, probably because fencing has for so long been associated with duelling. In fact the risk today is negligible, provided reasonable precautions are taken to ensure adequate protection by the use of regulation clothing and equipment *in good condition.*

To obviate serious accidents the following elementary safety rules should be strictly enforced, not only in competitions but in every club:

(*1*) Never fence at any time without a mask, even when merely practising strokes with a friend. This may seem obvious, but a number of serious accidents have occurred in recent years when this elementary rule has been disregarded.

(*2*) Never fence in clothing which is unsuitable for the weapon used. For example, it is dangerous to fence épée in a foil jacket, or in flannel trousers, or without wearing a plastron under the jacket. It is equally dangerous to fence foil in a sweater or track-suit without a fencing jacket, or with a jacket which is so short that it allows a gap between jacket and breeches. Accidents usually occur when a blade breaks and only proper clothing will prevent the penetration of the broken blade. A painful injury can be sustained at sabre unless an elbow-guard is used.

(*3*) Never fence in clothing which is torn or badly worn. This applies particularly to masks, which in time become rusty and may have the meshes of the trellis broken or opened by dents.

(*4*) If you are a left-hander never fence in equipment made for a right-hander—or vice versa. A fencing jacket has the necessary reinforcement over the upper arm, armpit and breast on the sword-arm side only and the buttons on jacket and breeches are turned away from that side. None of these safeguards are available if this clothing is worn by a fencer using the opposite arm as sword-arm.

(*5*) Discard a blade which has been badly kinked, it is obviously more liable to break.

(*6*) Ladies should wear breast-protectors of metal or rigid material at all times. A padded jacket will prevent unsightly bruises, but without protectors is not sufficient to prevent the danger of injury to the breasts which may cause serious complications later in life.

II

The Foil

THE foil has been used since the seventeenth century and has existed far longer than the other two weapons.

It was long regarded merely as a practice weapon. Luigi Barbasetti wrote during the present century: 'Fencing with the foil is too much a recreation to be looked upon as fencing in the strictest sense of the word. It is not real training for serious combat, but a healthy sport, serving its purpose as a fine introduction to the more intricate and advanced forms of sword-play.'

Foil fencing was but rarely included in international fencing programmes until after the First World War. For example, there was no foil event in the 1908 Olympic Games and foil did not appear in the European Championships until 1926. Ladies' foil was not included in major international competitions until the 1924 Olympic Games. Today the foil is well established as a competitive weapon for ladies and for men, indeed the individual foil title at the Olympic Games and World Championships is regarded by many as the blue riband of the event.

VARIATIONS IN TECHNIQUE

The description of foil technique in this book is confined mainly to the French school of foil, because that school has been adopted by the National Training Scheme for Great Britain and is the most widely practised in this country. This should not be taken to imply that the Italian school is in any way inferior to the French. The French school is more widely used in Britain probably because most of the masters who taught fencing with foil and épée in this country in the late nineteenth and early twentieth centuries were Frenchmen or had been taught in France.

The details of foil technique described in this chapter follow the method adopted for the British National Training Scheme, which was founded in 1949. It must, however, be clearly understood that although this method represents the most modern thought and development on the subject, it in no way invalidates alternative or more traditional details of technique.

Take, for example, the method of holding a foil. We have adopted the grip with the weapon in the palm of the hand, because it is considered that this facilitates 'carrying' the weapon while relaxation of the sword-hand is maintained, which avoids strain and counteracts any tendency to muscular contraction of the arm and shoulder.

Many great masters have, however, taught and continue to teach what is called the finger-tip grip, because they consider that it gives greater accuracy of point and a better control of the weapon. Many champions have achieved equal fame with either one grip or the other—to adopt one, as we have done, in no way implies that the other is wrong.

The description of the technique of fencing with each weapon in this and the two succeeding chapters is intended as a guide for fencers and will, it is hoped, enable them the better to understand the lessons which they receive in their schools. The descriptions included here must be regarded as explanatory of, and supplementary to such lessons.

The basic fencing position, the stance and footwork must be acquired correctly before the beginner attempts to learn the various attacks, parries and other blade movements which complete his technique.

These basic positions, the body and foot movements and the lunge, do not come naturally to most people and some muscular stiffness will be experienced until the right muscles have been developed. The stance and footwork have been evolved through the centuries (the lunge, for instance, dates from the sixteenth century) as the position of perfect balance and the most effective way to be prepared at all times for attack or defence, while moving rapidly towards or away from the opponent.

The beginner is strongly advised to persevere with the considerable (and initially painful) practice which is necessary to acquire a good basic on-guard position, lithe and light footwork and a smooth and well controlled lunge and recovery—without these he cannot hope to reach championship class as a fencer.

HOW TO HOLD THE FOIL

It will be observed that the handle of a French foil is slightly curved to the shape of the hand. To hold the foil, lay the handle with the curved side in the hollow of the hand, so that it lies against the palm just under the fleshy base of the thumb. ·

Place the second phalanx of the index finger under the handle, just inside the guard, so that the edge of the handle fits into the first joint of the finger, which is then hooked round the handle with the end phalanx of this finger resting on the outer face of the handle.

Now place the thumb *flat* along the top of the handle so that this is firmly held between thumb and first finger. Wrap the remaining fingers lightly round the handle so that the first phalanx of each finger rests along the outer side of the handle. ·

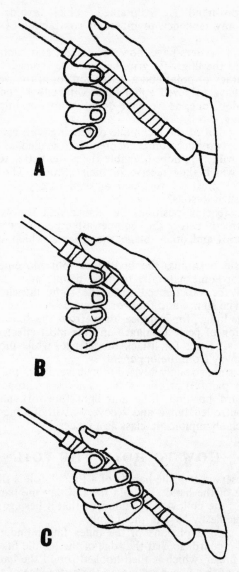

Fig. 5 The Grip

A. Position of the index finger
B. Position of index finger and thumb (manipulators)
C. The grip assisted by closing the last three fingers (aids). Note that the hand
   is relaxed and the foil is 'carried' rather than gripped

As mentioned above, a common variation of this grip is to hold the handle between the tips of the forefinger and thumb, that is to say without having the thumb flat along the handle, which is known as the finger-tip grip. This grip has the merit of giving considerable accuracy and control of the point, but is more tiring because the foil does not lie in the palm of the hand and there is a gap between the thumb and the base of the index finger which causes the muscles of the hand to be constantly contracted.

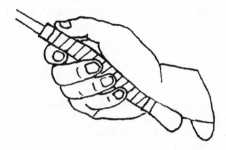

Fig. 6   The Finger-tip Grip

The grip has been treated in some detail because of its importance for finger play, which is the basic factor in manipulating the foil in the French school.

We have favoured the method of holding the foil first described above because the method of carrying the foil in the hand rather than constantly gripping it brings relaxation to the sword-hand, arm and shoulder and helps to develop that ideal of all foil fencers—the light hand. The famous French master, Lafaugère, has said: 'Hold your foil as if you had a little bird in your hand, firmly enough to prevent it escaping and yet not so firmly as to crush it.'

The foil should be manipulated rapidly and accurately by the fingers and not by wrist movements. Lateral or circular movements of the blade in any desired direction should be effected by the fingers alone. The blade is controlled by the forefinger and thumb, which are called the manipulators, assisted by the opening and closing of the last three fingers of the sword-hand, which are called the aids.

Raising or lowering of the point of the foil is achieved by alternately pushing with the thumb and pulling with the forefinger and vice versa. Semicircular or circular movements are imparted to the blade by rolling the handle between the forefinger and thumb while the pulling and pushing movements are made.

The importance of strength and dexterity of finger play cannot be overstressed, because on it depends the speed and accuracy of most fencing strokes. Further, through his fingers a fencer can feel the blade actions and reactions of his opponent, while controlling any desired part of his own blade. This feeling of the blade or *sentiment du fer* is an essential part of the foil fencer's technique.

The rules permit a fencer to hold the handle of an ordinary French foil at any point he pleases, provided he does not throw the weapon during a thrust or have any device, such as a strap, which helps him to get a better grip. It is, however, wise to form the habit of holding the foil in the orthodox position, that is to say with the end of the thumb about three-quarters of an inch from the inner face of the guard. To hold the foil nearer the pommel may add a few inches to one's reach, but has the serious disadvantage of limiting finger play and therefore reducing the speed and dexterity of fencing movements. On the other hand, to hold the foil with the tip of the thumb nearer the guard cramps the hand and may lead to a painful blow on the thumb-nail, if the guard comes into violent collision with the opponent's guard as sometimes happens during a bout.

The hand holding the foil may be in three positions: with the palm upwards, called supination; with the palm downwards, called pronation; or in half-supination, that is with the thumb uppermost and the palm facing to the side, in a position half-way between the other two positions.

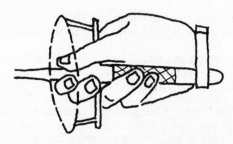

Fig. 7   The Grip with the Italian Foil

The grip of the Italian foil is entirely different. The *ricasso*, which is the flattened portion of the tang of the blade between the inner face of the guard and the cross-bar, is gripped between the thumb and first finger. The thumb lies on top of the flat side of the *ricasso* and the two end joints of the first finger below it are bent and pressed against the cushion inside the guard. The middle finger is passed through the outer ring between guard and cross-bar, so that it lies in the angle between the *ricasso* and the cross-bar. The last two fingers are wrapped round the handle, which is bound to the wrist by a long leash or a strap.

Normally with the Italian foil the hand remains in supination and this grip gives great strength and authority over the weapon. The blade movements are guided by the manipulators.

THE ON-GUARD POSITION

The on-guard position is the basic position of a fencer's arms, body, legs and feet which places him in the best balanced position for attack or defence, for advancing or retiring, or for making a lunge in the course of a bout (plates I and II).

Throughout this book, unless otherwise stated, all descriptions of movements and positions will apply to a right-handed fencer. Obviously for a left-hander the positions and movements must be reversed.

To come on guard, a fencer should stand erect with feet at right angles and with the right shoulder and right toe pointing towards the opponent. The leading foot should then be advanced until there are approximately two foot lengths between the heels, which remain in the same line so that the front foot hides the heel of the rear foot from the opponent. The distance between the heels will vary according to the height of the fencer, but two lengths of his feet or approximately eighteen inches is an average guide. The body is then balanced evenly between the feet.

The sword-arm is then raised, half extended with the hand in half-supination, until the sword-hand is level with the right breast and the elbow about a hand's breadth from the body. The foil follows the line of the forearm.

The other (unarmed) arm is then raised in a graceful arch, so that the upper arm is level with the left shoulder, and the hand in a relaxed position to the left and a little higher than the head.

At the same time the trunk is turned so that the chest half faces the opponent, with the head erect and both eyes looking straight at the opponent. The legs are bent so that the fencer 'sits' well down with the trunk erect and bent *very slightly* forward.

The position of the legs and feet in the on-guard position is known as the stance and is of great importance to ensure balance and mobility. Each fencer must find by trial and error the distance between the heels which best suits his height and weight. If this distance is too short there will be a lack of balance and if too wide the lunge will be correspondingly reduced and there will be lack of mobility.

The heels must always remain in line, whatever foot movements such as advancing or retiring, lunging or recovering, are made. If the leading foot is to the right of the rear heel, there will be a tendency to fall inwards during such movements, while placing the leading foot opposite the instep of the rear foot causes the body to fall outwards. The weight of the body must be balanced evenly between the feet. Any tendency to keep the weight predominantly on one or other of the feet will reduce mobility and cause fatigue.

It is particularly important to keep the knee of the leading leg always pointing towards the opponent, that is to say in line with the toe of the foot. The position of the knee is governed by the position adopted by the shoulders and hips. If the body is turned too far to the side from the hips, the front knee will automatically turn inwards and this will cause a lack of balance, especially when lunging. Such lack of balance will probably also cause inaccuracy in the direction of the point of the weapon.

Considerable practice is required to develop the muscles of the legs until the 'sitting down' position when on guard is acquired comfortably and naturally. The fencer must not crouch down on his heels, as this places too great a strain on the legs and ankles. The ideal position is one of relaxation, so that the legs can act as swiftly and lightly as springs when an attack is launched and footwork becomes mobile and smooth. The beginner will be well advised to spend quite a lot of time practising his on-guard position and footwork before a long mirror, so that he can correct his stance and check the various details mentioned above.

When fencing, the left arm helps to maintain balance and, when correctly placed, it helps to give direction to the lunge. If the rear arm is allowed to swing to the side or is held stiffly, it will pull the shoulders round and displace the direction of the sword-arm.

While the trunk is inclined very slightly forward when in the on-guard position, this must not be exaggerated or it will throw the weight of the body on to the leading leg and hinder footwork and the lunge as much as if it were leaned backwards.

The orthodox on-guard position, described above, must be varied slightly to suit the muscular structure of each individual fencer. The position adopted should be the one which is found to give the maximum ease and relaxation, combined with smoothness of movement.

The foregoing description of the on-guard position applies primarily to the French school but is basically the same as for the Italian school. In the latter, however, it is usual to efface the target rather more than in the former school; thus the body is turned sideways to the opponent by keeping the left shoulder well back, but without turning the hips unduly. In the Italian school the thighs are almost at right angles and the fencer bends the legs rather more when on guard, relying on extra spring from the legs and ankles when launching an attack.

THE SALUTE

From its long association with chivalry fencing has retained a special tradition of courtesy. Before any bout in the *salle d'armes*, fencers salute each other before putting on their masks, and when the bout finishes they again salute, take off their masks and shake hands with the unarmed hand.

In a competition bout the fencer salutes the President and the two judges opposite him before saluting his opponent.

Before beginning a bout a fencer takes up his position on the *piste*, standing erect, half facing his opponent, holding his mask in his left hand and with his sword-arm extended, the point of the weapon being a few inches from the ground. The sword is then raised in a graceful movement until the guard is level with the chin, the blade pointing vertically upwards and the elbow close to the body. After a momentary pause the sword-arm is lowered to the former position, the mask is put on (usually by drawing it over the face by the tongue which grips the back of the head) and the fencer assumes the on-guard position.

Similarly, at the conclusion of a bout the same salute is given, the mask is removed and tucked under the sword-arm and the fencer shakes his opponent's hand with his unarmed hand.

Beginners are usually taught a more elaborate method of coming on guard, combined with the salute. This movement is often used in galas or displays of fencing and a line of young fencers carrying it out gracefully and rhythmically is a most attractive sight. The movement is carried out in the following stages:

(*1*) Each fencer stands erect, at attention, with feet at right angles and the body half turned to the front, with the toe of the leading foot pointing in that direction. The mask is held in the crook of the unarmed arm and the sword-arm is extended to the front, slightly to the right of the foot, away from the body and with the point of the weapon a few inches from the ground.

(*2*) The sword-arm is then raised slowly, without bending the elbow, until it is pointing diagonally upwards at an angle of approximately forty-five degrees from the shoulder.

(*3*) The elbow of the sword-arm is bent until it rests lightly against the body, with the hilt of the weapon close to the chin and the blade pointing vertically upwards.

(*4*) After a momentary pause the sword-arm is again extended forward and downwards to the original position as in (*1*) above.

(*5*) The mask is now drawn over the face. It should be held by the tongue at the back with the unarmed hand and the chin inserted first.

(*6*) The sword-hand is then swept round to the left side, bending the elbow and the wrist so that the sword is pointing to the rear, level with the thighs and parallel to the ground, with the blade lightly held by the tips of the fingers of the unarmed hand which is extended slightly to the rear.

(*7*) Both arms are now raised upwards, contact being maintained by the unarmed hand on the blade until the hands are just above the head, with elbows slightly bent and the sword lying horizontally between the hands.

(8) The fencer then lowers the sword-arm forward and, advancing the leading foot, assumes the on-guard position with graceful unhurried movements.

At the conclusion of an academic assault, a fencer 'reassembles' or returns from the on-guard position to the erect or 'prepare' position described in (1) above. He then removes his mask by holding it by the tongue at the back and drawing it down over his face to hold it in the crook of the unarmed arm, after which he carries out the salute described in (2), (3) and (4) above, slowly and gracefully.

ADVANCING AND RETIRING

Advancing and retiring, called in fencing parlance gaining and breaking ground, is done by taking short steps on the *piste* in order to achieve or maintain the desired distance from the opponent. The way this is carried out ensures that the balance of the body is always maintained, so that any offensive or defensive movement required is not limited or impaired as the fencer moves up or down the *piste*.

To advance, the leading foot is carried forward a short step, at the same time raising the toes slightly, and the rear foot is then brought up an equal distance by lifting it from the knee. These actions are exactly reversed when retiring.

When making these movements the feet are only slightly raised, the leading foot gliding forward and just skimming the *piste*, so that a smooth, even, cat-like step is achieved which in no way disturbs the poise and balance of the body.

The length of the step forward or backwards will obviously depend on the height of the fencer and his distance from his opponent, but care should be taken not to make excessively long strides, or to raise the leading foot too much which will give a rising-and-falling action: either of these faults will upset the balance of the body. It is better to take two medium steps rather than one long one to cover the same distance.

The feet must not be stamped or dragged when advancing or retiring. A tendency to drag the rear foot in advancing is generally the result of lifting it from the hip instead of from the knee. It is important not to move the hips during these movements, because if they are turned or swung the fencer will move diagonally across the *piste* instead of in a straight line.

Besides the normal method of advancing and retiring just described, there are the following ways of gaining and breaking ground:

(a) **The Balestra**. This is a short jump forward, generally followed by a lunge. It is widely used by the Italian school at foil and sabre. It is an alternative to the step forward as a means of getting within distance to launch an attack and often surprises the opponent.

The short jump forward is taken from the balls of both feet together, care being taken neither to jump too high off the ground nor to attempt to spring too far forward. The fencer should land after his jump with the weight of the body *slightly* on the rear foot, so as to anchor that foot as a firm foundation for the lunge which must follow immediately.

The *balestra* should be made from immobility, without disturbing the balance of the on-guard position. A *balestra* followed by a lunge should be made as a very crisp, staccato movement and as rapidly as possible.

Fig. 8   The *Balestra*

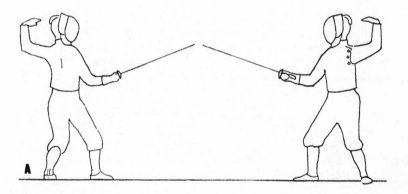

Both fencers are out of distance

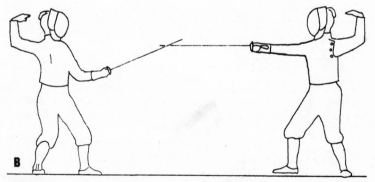

Fencer on right extends his arm to attack and jumps forward with both feet

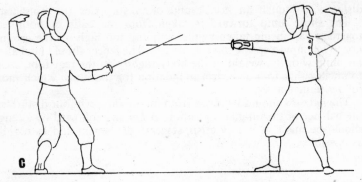

Fencer on right completes his jump forward (*balestra*), landing with weight
on rear foot

Fencer on right begins his lunge into the low line

The attack is completed

(*b*) **The *Flèche*.** The *flèche* is used to reach an opponent who is out of distance for a lunge, by means of a short quick run. A *flèche* depends entirely on speed and surprise for its success. If a fencer fails to hit his opponent with his *flèche* attack he is very vulnerable to a riposte or stop hit, because not only is he momentarily off balance and lacking control, but he cannot recover out of distance as he can from the more orthodox lunge. To achieve success with a *flèche* attack, the correct choice of time is of the first importance and the hit must land at the first possible moment after the *flèche* is launched.

In order to gain speed and momentum as quickly as possible, the *flèche* initially involves a loss of balance. A *flèche* is therefore best prepared by shifting the weight of the body forward on to the front foot while in the on-guard position.

To make a *flèche*, extend the sword-arm and at the same time throw the weight of the body forward over the front leg. This will cause a loss of balance and, to save one from falling forward, the rear leg leaves the ground and is swung past the front foot. This is followed by a series of quick running steps past the opponent.

Maximum penetration and length is achieved by consciously swinging the rear leg as far past the leading foot as possible in the initial step, by a sharp turn of the hips. The aim should be to land the hit on the opponent as the rear foot reaches the ground in this initial movement.

A *flèche* made from a position on the *piste* which is too far from the opponent will necessitate several steps before the point can reach the target, and is unlikely to be successful. It gives the opponent ample time to form a parry or launch a stop hit, or to take avoiding action, and thus loses much of its essential quality of surprise. Since surprise is so important, it is obvious that the *flèche* should be used sparingly in a bout or pool as a method of attack.

Under the technical rules a fencer is penalized if he jostles his opponent during a *flèche* attack. At foil and sabre he is penalized if a *flèche* attack results in his forcing a *corps à corps*, even without jostling. It is therefore important to form the habit of passing the opponent, should a *flèche* attack not result in a hit.

Success with the *flèche* can thus only be achieved by a correct choice of time and distance and by rapidity in swinging the rear leg forward in the initial step. Used sparingly it is a most effective stroke, especially at épée and sabre, but it requires considerable practice (Fig. 44, page 116).

(*c*) **The Spring Backwards.** The spring backwards is an effective method of getting rapidly out of distance after an attack made with a lunge has failed. It is much used in the Italian school, particularly at épée and sabre.

From the lunge, the fencer springs backwards so that he lands on the ball of the leading foot, as far as possible behind the position occupied by the rear foot during the lunge. He then rocks back on to the rear foot, which causes the leading foot to leave the ground, and assumes the correct on-guard position as the leading foot again reaches the ground. The sword-arm is kept extended until the on-guard position has been resumed.

The balance of the body must be controlled throughout the spring backwards, care being taken not to swing the hips unduly. The length of the spring to the rear depends on the strength of the 'kick' which is made with the leading foot, and the rapid shifting of the weight of the body backwards so as to attain maximum length rather than height in the spring.

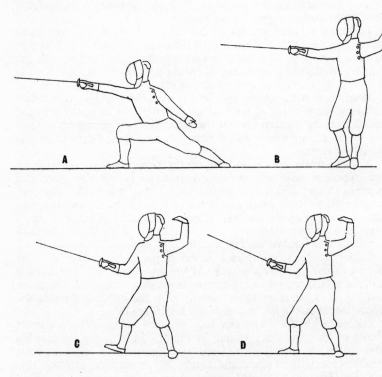

Fig. 9 The Spring Backwards

A. The fencer on the lunge
B. The fencer springs back as far as possible, landing on the leading toes. Note that the arm remains extended
C. The fencer rocks back on to the rear foot
D. The fencer returns to the on-guard position

The spring backwards is a valuable exercise for developing a sense of balance and for strengthening the ankle and thigh muscles. With practice it is possible to spring back from the full lunge over half the length of the *piste* and to maintain perfect balance in the final on-guard position.

THE LUNGE

The lunge is the rapid extension of the arm, body and legs, which is made from the on-guard position in order to land a hit on the opponent's target. The lunge and the recovery from the lunge to the on-guard position are called the development and the return to guard.

There are two distinct parts of the development: the extension of the sword-arm which establishes the attack and directs the point of the weapon, and the lunge which carries the point on to the target as rapidly and directly as possible.

The extension of the sword-arm initiates and establishes the right of attack. It directs the point towards the target and, at the same time, covers or protects the attacker during his lunge. The sword-arm should be extended swiftly and smoothly until it is slightly higher than the shoulder, with the arm and weapon forming one straight line. The arm and shoulder muscles must remain relaxed, in order to avoid a jerky, punching movement which would impair point control and accuracy. Fordham, who was my first master at Cambridge, used to say: 'Imagine that you are reaching for an apple which is the other side of the dining table—you wouldn't snatch at it but reach for it with a relaxed, cat-like movement.'

Indeed, this is but the first example of the timing and relaxation which is the ideal to be aimed at in performing most fencing movements. Italo Santelli, the famous Italian master who founded the peerless Hungarian sabre team, illustrated this to his pupils by drawing their attention to the ways of catching a fly. Imagine a fly sitting on a table: a man cups his hand, tenses his muscles and becomes a picture of concentration as he seeks to sweep up the fly with every ounce of speed he can muster—generally the fly flies happily away. In similar circumstances a monkey, scarcely appearing even to look at the fly, reaches out with a relaxed, almost lazy movement, picks up the fly and eats it.

The technical rules lay down that only a straight arm, with the point of the weapon threatening the target, constitutes an attack. To lunge with a bent arm does not therefore constitute an attack. The fencer who is hit while making such a movement by an opponent who has maintained a straight arm, even if the latter has made no movement of the body or legs and even if both are hit simultaneously, will have the point scored against him at foil or sabre.

In attack, and indeed in most movements with the foil, the factor of primary importance is the point of the weapon. The fencer should try to concentrate his brain on the movements of his point, to which all his other actions are subsidiary, in the sense that they are designed to direct the point on to the target if a hit is to be scored. Following the same train of thought, the extension of the arm is made to place the point on the target and if the target is still out of reach, then the point is carried forward by the lunge.

To lunge, the toes of the leading foot are raised and that foot is carried well forward, with the heel just skimming the ground, by a fast but smooth extension of the rear leg acting as a spring and thrusting from the rear foot, which remains flat on the *piste* throughout. This action will have the effect of thrusting the body forward over the thigh of the front leg as that leg bends at the knee. As the rear leg extends, the rear arm is dropped down with the palm of the hand turned slightly upwards, until the arm is parallel to and just above the rear leg.

During the lunge the body remains in the on-guard position; it is not twisted or turned although, of course, it leans well forward as the action develops to give maximum reach. The head remains erect and the sword-hand is kept up, so that it finishes about level with the face and is allowed to rise as the point arrives on the target.

At the completion of the lunge, the front knee should be just above the instep of the leading foot. If the foot is in front of the knee, one is over-lunging, and if the knee is so bent that it is in front of the toes, then the lunge has been too short. In either case it will be difficult to achieve a smooth, rapid recovery from the lunge.

The rear leg should be fully extended and not bent at the knee, while the rear foot must remain flat on the ground. A slight dragging of the rear foot can be tolerated, so long as the foot remains flat on the ground and there is no tendency to lunge from the toes by raising the heel.

Common faults when lunging, besides those already mentioned, include falling forward at the completion of the lunge, which is often due to not carrying the front foot far enough forward and not keeping the body erect and the sword-hand high enough; not fully extending the rear leg, which is usually caused by lunging from the toes of the rear foot; falling inwards or lunging out of a straight line, which is generally caused by swinging the rear arm or the hips to one side or the other.

The lunge will only be accomplished smoothly and rapidly if it is made with maximum relaxation. To tense the muscles will generally result in a short, jerky development.

Speed in the lunge comes from the drive imparted from the rear foot, assisted by the downward swing of the rear arm. The aim should be to attain the maximum acceleration at the end of the lunge, in order to give maximum penetration to the point as it lands on the target.

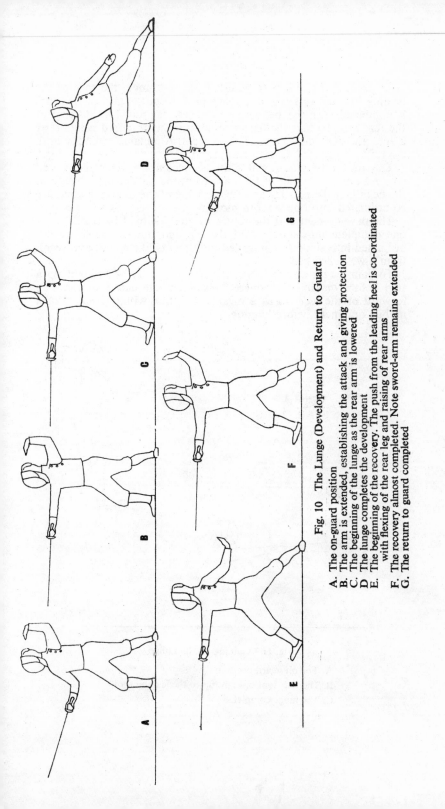

Fig. 10 The Lunge (Development) and Return to Guard

A. The on-guard position
B. The arm is extended, establishing the attack and giving protection
C. The beginning of the lunge as the rear arm is lowered
D. The lunge completes the development
E. The beginning of the recovery. The push from the leading heel is co-ordinated with flexing of the rear leg and raising of rear arms
F. The recovery almost completed. Note sword-arm remains extended
G. The return to guard completed

To recover, or return to guard, from the lunge, the toes of the leading foot are raised and a sharp push from the heel of this foot is combined with the bending of the rear leg and the upswing of the rear arm, so that the fencer returns to the on-guard position by a smooth, swift movement. The sword-arm remains extended until the return to guard has been completed.

The return to guard will only be accomplished correctly and without muscular strain if the push from the heel of the front foot, the flexing of the rear leg and the upswing of the unarmed hand are co-ordinated into one smooth movement.

The development and the return to guard should be practised as one complete movement, until the leg and body actions are co-ordinated into smooth, controlled movements like a shot and recoil from a well oiled gun.

To gain length on the lunge, the rear foot may be brought up a step before making the lunge. This is an alternative to the step forward or the *balestra* as a means of getting within distance of a mobile opponent before lunging.

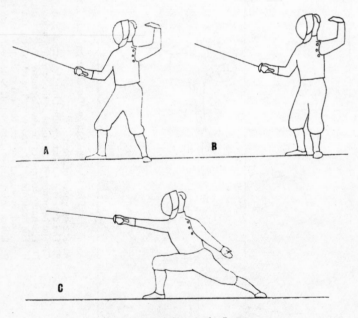

Fig. 11   Gaining on the Lunge

A. The on-guard position
B. The rear foot brought up to the leading foot
C. The lunge completed

This method of gaining length on the lunge is used particularly in the Italian and Hungarian schools. It has the advantage of masking the advance from the opponent, since it can be effected after several similar displacements of the rear foot have been made.

THE HIT

The technical fencing rules emphasize that to count as a hit the point of the foil must arrive clearly and distinctly on the opponent. Flat hits are completely disregarded wherever they arrive. To be counted as good, a hit must not only reach the target but be sufficiently definite, in the sense that it would penetrate if the swords were sharp.

A hit, therefore, has two distinct prerequisites: firstly, the point must fix on the target clearly and distinctly and, secondly, the hit must have the quality of penetration.

The most carefully devised action will come to nought unless the fencer who makes it is able to fix his point on his opponent's target. The fixing of the point is achieved by the fingers of the sword-hand. From the normal position of the foil when on guard, the point is brought down by pressing on the handle with the thumb, while contracting the index finger and thus directing the point so that it fixes on the target. Once the point has fixed on the target, 'penetration' comes from the smooth extension of the sword-arm which is allowed to rise as the blade bends, until, at full extension, the sword-hand is above the level of the shoulder.

The fixing of the point by finger play is common to all weapons and is essential whether a hit is made from a bent arm or from an extended arm position, during an attack, as a riposte or as a stop hit—in fact whenever a hit is made with the point.

The fixing of the point and the extension of the sword-arm as one smooth, co-ordinated movement should be practised first at close quarters, then with a half-lunge and finally with a full lunge and from a variety of angles. In this way the essential control of the point can be acquired.

To obtain maximum speed and accuracy in placing one's hits, it is necessary to direct the point by the fingers alone, while keeping the arm and shoulder muscles relaxed. As the Italians say, 'a hand of steel on a rubber arm'. Tensing of the shoulder muscles will cause a jerky, punching movement which will probably cause the point to miss or arrive flat. A faulty grip, or lack of elasticity in the fingers, or directing the point with the aids instead of the manipulators, will have the same effect.

Accuracy of point and sufficient penetration are of paramount importance when fencing with the electrical weapons, in order to depress the spring in the electrical point sufficiently to enable the apparatus to register a hit.

THE FENCING MEASURE

The distance maintained between two fencers during a bout is known as the fencing measure. The fencing measure is not determined solely by the physical distance, but is relative to the reach of the fencers concerned.

At foil, the distance normally maintained when on guard is such that neither fencer can land a hit on the other's body unless he makes a full lunge, yet not so far apart as to prevent a hit made with a lunge reaching the target. It is therefore obvious that the fencing measure largely depends on the relative height and length of arm of the fencers.

The sense of fencing measure is essential for a fencer. It seems to come more naturally to some people than to others, but it must in any case be developed by observation and experience during practice bouts.

Gaining and breaking ground, gaining on the lunge and the *balestra* are all movements made to maintain or alter the distance from the opponent. By such constant, rapid foot movements, a fencer seeks to place himself at the correct distance to launch an attack and, if possible, to deceive his opponent regarding the measure which he has achieved, or conversely obtain the measure that will make it most difficult for his opponent's attacks to succeed.

THE TARGET

At foil the target is restricted to the trunk, back and front, including the collar of the jacket but excluding the head, arms and legs. At the back the target goes down to a line joining the prominence of the hip-bones, and in front includes the V-shaped part of the trunk bounded by the folds of the groin. The bib of the mask, which of course covers part of the target area, is not included in the target, but the length of the bib is regulated.

Under normal conditions of fencing, only hits which arrive on the target are counted as good and hits which arrive on any other part of the fencer or his equipment are not scored against him. However, a hit which arrives off the target will be counted as good in two cases: firstly, if the fencer receives the hit on some part of his person which is not included in the target, but which he is using to shield the valid target; secondly, when by some displacement or alteration of position, the fencer receives on some part of his person which is not part of the valid target a hit which, but for his displacement, would have arrived on the target.

A common example of the first condition is the fencer who places his arm across his body to shield his target or who ducks, when his attack with lunge has failed, to shield his target from the riposte with his mask. In these circumstances a hit arriving on the arm or head will be counted as good. Of course, when a fencer parries quarte his sword-arm is in some measure shielding his target, but in these circumstances a hit on the arm would not be counted as good, because he is making a legitimate fencing movement and not seeking to obstruct his target.

As regards the second condition, an example of this would be a short fencer who crouches down on his heels when attacked by a taller man, so that a hit which would normally have hit his target arrives on the mask. In this case the hit on the mask is counted as good, because the short fencer has substituted a part of his person not normally included in the target for his valid target.

For convenience the target is divided by imaginary lines into parts which are related to the position in which a fencer places his sword-hand when on guard (see Fig. 12).

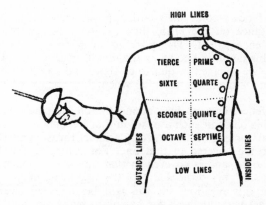

Fig. 12   Parts of the Target

When a fencer comes on guard, the parts of his target which his opponent can see above his sword-arm are called the high lines and those below are the low lines. The parts of the target farthest from the sword-arm (bounded by a vertical line) are the inside lines, while those on the same side as the sword-arm are the outside lines. There will thus be 'high outside lines' and 'low outside lines', 'high inside lines' and 'low inside lines'. With a left-handed fencer, the outside and inside lines are of course the reverse of those of a right-hander.

There are eight theoretical lines, named after the parries which are designed to protect them. Two cover each quarter of the target. When a fencer is on guard his sword-hand will be covering or protecting one of the lines of his target; this is known as his fencing position and he is said to be 'on guard in quarte' or some other line.

The four basic positions of quarte, sixte, septime and octave are the most commonly used. In all four positions the sword-hand is in supination or half-supination. Quarte and sixte protect the high lines and septime and octave the low lines.

The four remaining positions of prime and tierce (high lines) and seconde and quinte (low lines) are less generally used at French foil. In all four the sword-hand is in pronation.

When adopting these various fencing positions, the fencer alters the angle of his blade from high to low, or moves his sword-hand from one side of his body to the other. Throughout these movements, which may include turning the sword-hand from pronation to supination or half-supination, the hand remains at approximately the same level—that is to say, breast-high.

THE ENGAGEMENT

When two fencers come on guard opposite each other at correct fencing distance on the *piste*, they usually cross swords—this is called the engagement. The position of a fencer's sword-hand relative to his target is known as the line of engagement. Thus two fencers may be engaged in quarte or sixte, and so on according to the position of their sword-hands when they engage each other's blade.

When a fencer engages his opponent's foil, he places his sword-hand with his blade in such a position that his opponent cannot hit a certain part or line of his target by a direct thrust. This is what is meant by being covered in that line. For example, if a fencer is engaged in sixte, and is covered in that line, his opponent's blade will be 'outside' his own blade. If the opponent makes a direct thrust from this position, his foil will be deflected clear of the fencer's target without the latter having to make any movement of his foil or his sword-hand or his body.

The object of being covered when on guard is to limit the possible actions your opponent can make if he wishes to hit you, or to ensure that he must do more than make a simple direct thrust to achieve this result. This has been likened to the position of a man who has to watch two adjacent doors through one of which he may be attacked. If he tries to watch both doors he may be surprised and he may not be quick enough to slam the door through which the attack is launched. If he locks one door, he can then concentrate on the only one through which he can be directly attacked. By covering in one line (rather than adopting a central guard position) a fencer knows that he is completely secure from direct attack in that line, and if his opponent wishes to hit him he must attack in some other line.

When two fencers are engaged in a certain line, if one is covered, his opponent must be uncovered and therefore more vulnerable to a

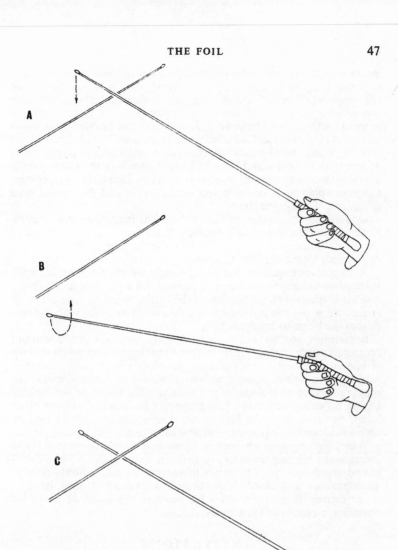

Fig. 13   Detail of Finger Play for the Change of Engagement
A. The engagement in sixte
B. The blade is lowered by the manipulators while relaxing the aids
C. The opposite finger actions raise the blade to engagement in the opposite line

direct thrust. To regain the covered position in these circumstances, it is necessary to change the engagement, that is to say to engage the opponent's blade on the opposite side. To achieve this the fencer who finds himself uncovered must pass his blade under or over his opponent's blade, so that he gains the covered position—when his opponent will, of course, be uncovered in that line.

Such blade movements are executed entirely by finger play, although the sword-hand may be moved across at the same time if a new line of engagement is adopted. When changing engagement, the finger play must be crisp and authoritative and there must be a minimum of blade movement.

One of the advantages of the engagement is that, by maintaining contact with the opponent's blade, a fencer can acquire the feel of the blade (*sentiment du fer*) which will help him to anticipate his opponent's intentions and reactions.

A double engagement, or two changes of engagement in rapid succession, is sometimes made to prevent the opponent ascertaining one's intentions through the feel of the blade. When making a double engagement, the last movement should always be made with opposition of the blade to cover the line.

Sometimes, for tactical reasons, fencers come on guard without crossing swords and therefore without making an engagement. This is known as fencing 'with absence of blade'. It is used, especially at épée and sabre, against a fencer who has a predilection for making attacks on the blade, or for taking the blade, or for making strong pressures or beats when preparing his attacks. On the other hand, by uncovering the line by absence of blade a fencer may be able to induce his opponent to attack in a certain line.

When fencing with absence of blade it is usually wise slightly to increase the fencing measure, to make it more difficult for a determined attack to land. Fencing with absence of blade should only be attempted as a premeditated tactical movement. It can be very disconcerting to a fencer who has formed the habit of using his opponent's blade for his attacks.

INVITATIONS

An invitation is the intentional opening of a line so as to expose some part of the target. Its object is to induce the opponent to attack into the open line, in order to score with a parry and riposte or to provoke a reaction which may be used when launching an attack.

An invitation may be made with absence of blades, or by opening the line by a pressure on the opponent's blade, thus exposing the opposite line to a disengagement.

Usually invitations are confined to the lines of quarte and sixte or septime and octave. They are used to test the reactions of an

Fig. 14   The Direct Thrust

A. The fencers engaged in sixte
B. Fencer on right begins to extend his arm as his opponent opens the line
C. The straight thrust completed with a lunge

opponent, or to induce him to react in a desired way so that such reaction can be anticipated correctly.

An experienced fencer will always regard any obvious invitation as a trap and try by his reactions to circumvent his opponent's intentions, but they may be very effective for drawing a less experienced opponent into the required position for a successful conclusion to a movement.

At foil invitations are mostly used by the Italian school. They are more widely used at épée and sabre and are frequently the prelude to a counter-time or second-intention attack at these weapons.

When making an invitation it is obviously desirable to conceal the intention from the opponent, as he is unlikely to react unless he thinks that the opening of the line or the pressure out of line is unintentional. For example when engaged in sixte covered, a slight relaxation of the covered position, so as to expose the high line to a *coulé* or direct thrust, is more likely to provoke these movements than if the opponent's blade is completely quitted by dropping the hand or by moving across into quarte. As with so many fencing movements, subtlety is the secret of success when making an invitation.

ATTACKS

The object of fencing with any weapon is to land a hit on the opponent's target. Attacks are offensive movements made to achieve this object. There are two main types of attack:

(1) A simple attack is made by a single blade movement, either in the line of engagement or in the opposite line.

(2) A compound attack is one made with several blade movements. In a compound attack the final thrust is preceded by one or more false attacks, which are called feints.

By the rules of fencing, an attack must be made with the sword-arm straight and the point of the weapon threatening some part of the opponent's target. This definition is of particular importance at foil and sabre because, by the conventions of these weapons, an attack is given the right of way between simultaneous hits. Thus an offensive movement made with a bent arm, or with a straight arm but with the point of the weapon not threatening the target, does not constitute an attack and would not be given the right of way. On the other hand, if a fencer has his arm straight and the point of his weapon directed at his opponent's target, this constitutes an attack even if the fencer remains absolutely immobile, and the opponent must deflect the threatening blade by a beat or other movement before he in his turn can gain the right of attack.

SIMPLE ATTACKS

Simple attacks can be made in one of the following ways:

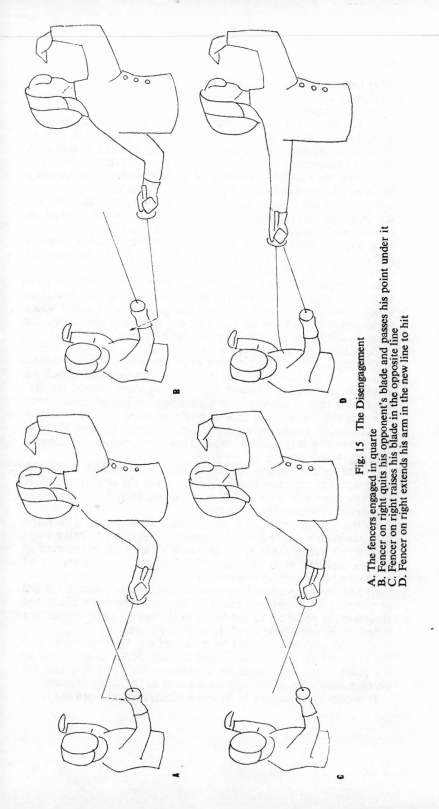

Fig. 15 The Disengagement

A. The fencers engaged in quarte
B. Fencer on right quits his opponent's blade and passes his point under it
C. Fencer on right raises his blade in the opposite line
D. Fencer on right extends his arm in the new line to hit

(*a*) Directly—by a straight thrust or a *coulé*.

(*b*) Indirectly—by a simple disengagement, a cut-over, or a counter-disengagement.

(*a*) **The Direct Attack.** The direct attack is a straight thrust made in the line in which a fencer is engaged. A direct thrust can only be made when the opponent is uncovered in any line. If the opponent, through negligence or a faulty position, is only partially covered in some line, the attacker's blade can be glided along his opponent's blade without pressing on it, which is called a *coulé*.

A direct attack is made by extending the sword-arm and carrying the point on to the target by a lunge. Its success will depend on speed of execution and on seizing the correct opportunity.

In order to limit the risk of impaling himself on his opponent's point when making a direct attack, a fencer must cover by a correct elevation of his sword-hand.

It is obvious that such a simple movement as a straight thrust is very easily parried, and that the greater the fencing measure from which it is launched, and therefore the greater the distance which the attacker's point has to travel before it reaches the target, the easier it will be for the defender to form his parry.

To achieve the momentary surprise which is essential if such a simple movement is to be successful, the attacker must 'lodge' himself, that is place himself at the correct distance, and launch his attack at the precise moment when the opponent leaves the line open. This may occur when he is changing his line of engagement, or opens the line with absence of blade, or when he is returning to guard without extending his arm. A direct thrust is more likely to be successful if it is made as the line is opening rather than when it is being closed.

(*b*) **The Indirect Attack.** An indirect attack is an attack made with a single blade movement which passes under the opponent's blade (disengagement) or over it (cut-over), or by deceiving a change of engagement (counter-disengagement).

By the rules governing foil fencing, an indirect attack, if correctly executed with a single blade movement, is regarded as being equal to a direct attack; that is to say, each is made in one period of fencing time and each has the right of way if both fencers are hit in the course of such movement.

(i) *The Disengagement.* It is made by passing the point of the foil in a broad U-shaped movement under the opponent's blade and thrusting the point on to the target in the open line by means of a lunge, at the same time covering in the new line.

The disengagement should be made entirely by finger play, with the arm and shoulder relaxed, and the size of the U described by the point of the foil should be adjusted so that the point does not become caught up in the opponent's arm as the lunge develops.

It is equally important to weld the disengagement with the lunge

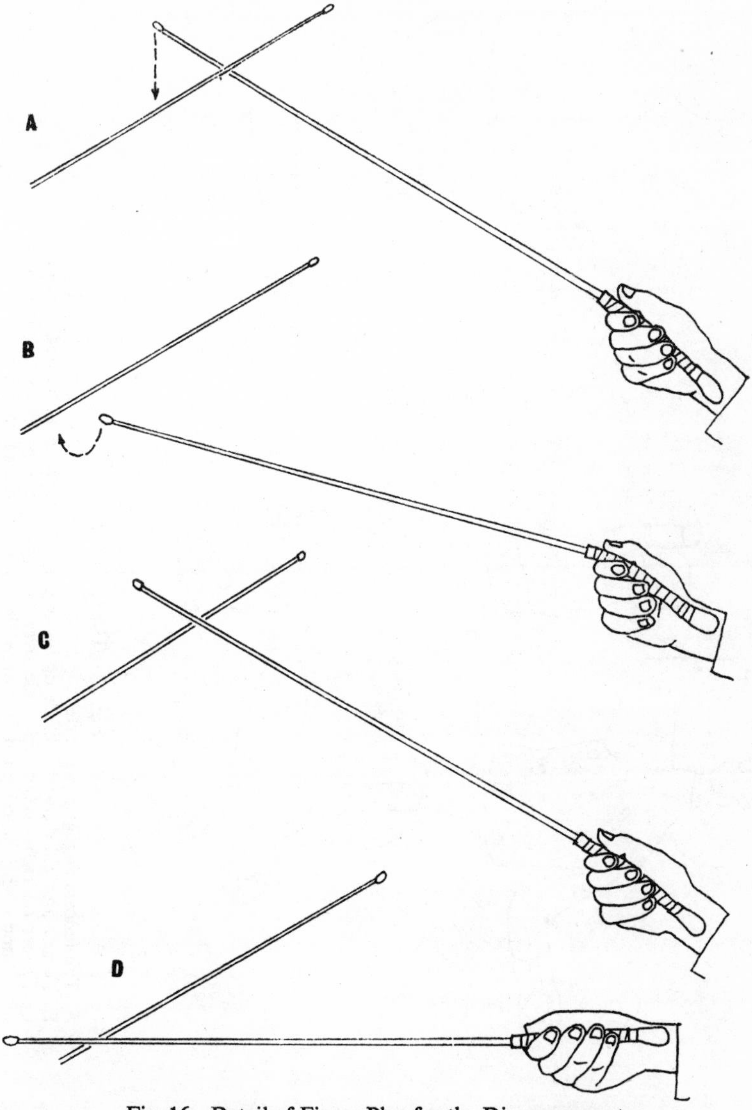

Fig. 16   Detail of Finger Play for the Disengagement

A. The engagement in quarte
B. The blade is lowered by pressure of the thumb and pull of index finger, while relaxing the aids
C. The blade is raised in the opposite line by opposite action of the manipulators, while closing the aids
D. The thrust is made in the new line

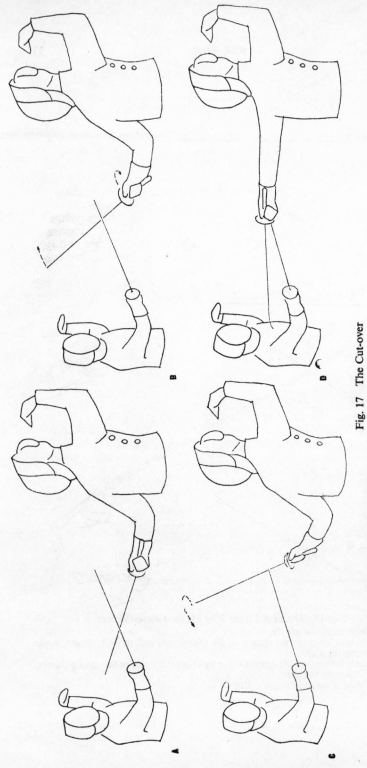

Fig. 17 The Cut-over

A. The fencers engaged in quarte
B. Fencer on right draws his blade up his opponent's blade, maintaining contact
C. Fencer on right passes his blade over his opponent's point by turning his hand slightly into pronation, while slightly bending his forearm
D. Immediately the fencer on right has passed his blade over his opponent's point, he extends his arm to hit, while his hand returns to the normal

into one smooth progressive movement, in order to gain time and distance on the opponent.

When an attack of this nature is made from the normal distance maintained when on guard, the attacker's point has to travel about three feet before it can reach the target, while the defender merely has to carry his foil some six to nine inches to one side in order to form his parry. By welding the disengagement and the lunge together into what is called a progressive attack, rather than first making the disengagement and following it by the lunge, the attacker seeks to cut down this disparity in time and distance between his movement and that of his opponent.

When a fencer is covered in any line, a disengagement into the opposite line is easily parried by him. It is therefore important to time the disengagement so that it is made into an opening line, rather than when the opponent is static in a covered position or when he is closing the line. For example, a disengagement may be made with advantage when the opponent exerts pressure on the attacker's blade, or when he is changing engagement and covering in the new line, or when he is returning to engagement after fencing with absence of blade.

The disengagement is a basic movement for most composed attacks and its execution and timing should be carefully practised.

(ii) *The Cut-over.* This is a simple disengagement, in the course of which the attacker's blade passes over, instead of under, the opponent's blade.

To cut over, the blade is slipped up the opponent's blade by a swift raising and slight withdrawal of the forearm. Immediately the blade has cleared the opponent's point, the sword-arm is extended in the new line. During the initial movement the wrist is bent slightly downwards from the line of the forearm, to avoid making a wide movement by raising the point unduly.

When commencing a cut-over a fencer is vulnerable to a stop hit and this stroke should therefore be used sparingly, so as to preserve the essential element of surprise. The cut-over is particularly effective where the opponent is exerting pressure on the blade when engaged.

The disengagement and the cut-over are strokes which can only be used successfully against an opponent who moves his blade laterally in defence.

(iii) *The Counter-disengagement.* A simple indirect attack made to deceive a circular instead of a lateral movement of the opponent's foil. It is designed to deceive the opponent's change of engagement or his circular parry. Unlike the disengagement and the cut-over, which are completed in the opposite line to the line of engagement, the counter-disengagement ends in the same line as that of the original engagement.

When a fencer changes his line of engagement, probably to obtain a covered position, the counter-disengagement is made by following the blade round while extending the arm into the original line of engagement, thus deceiving the opponent's attempt to take the blade.

The counter-disengagement is made by finger play alone and should be co-ordinated with the extension of the arm and the lunge into one progressive movement.

The success of a simple attack depends on the correct timing of the movement, which must naturally be related to the cadence of the opponent's movements if it is not to be caught up in them.

All simple attacks can, of course, be completed in the low lines as well as in the high lines and this is often very effective, especially against fencers who keep their sword-hand in an exaggeratedly high position. When making a simple attack into the low line, care must be taken not to lift the point on the completion of the blade movement and it is often helpful to turn the hand slightly into pronation, in order to pass the point under the opponent's arm.

Attacks into the low line are effective when using the electrical foil, because the angle at which the point reaches the target helps to ensure a fix and penetration and therefore causes the apparatus to register the hit.

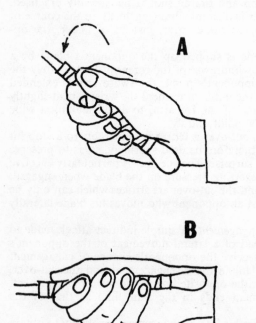

Fig. 18 Detail of Hand Movement in a Cut-over

A. The hand rotated into pronation as the blade travels up the opponent's blade to his point

B. Having passed over the opponent's point, the hand returns to the normal half-supinated position when extending the arm to thrust in the new line

Fig. 19   The Counter-disengagement

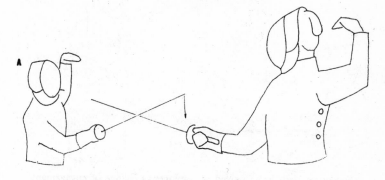

The fencers engaged in quarte

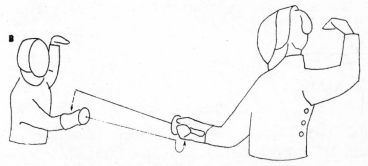

Fencer on left begins to change the engagement

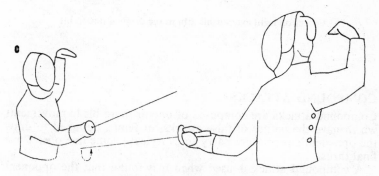

Fencer on right follows his opponent's blade round
in its change of engagement

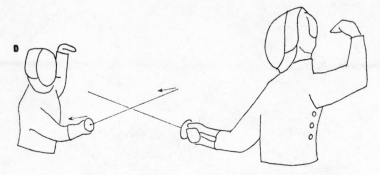

Fencer on right has deceived his opponent's change of engagement
by his counter-disengagement

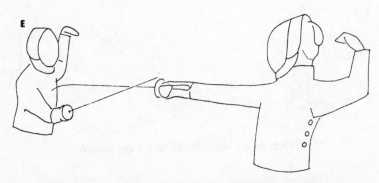

Fencer on right extends his arm in the original line to hit

COMPOUND ATTACKS

Compound attacks are composed of one or more blade movements
which have the nature of false attacks, or feints, designed to draw
the opponent's premature parry so as to leave some line open for a
final thrust.

A compound attack is used when it is found that the opponent
cannot be hit by a simple attack, which he is able to parry. The
complexity of the compound attack used is therefore directly related

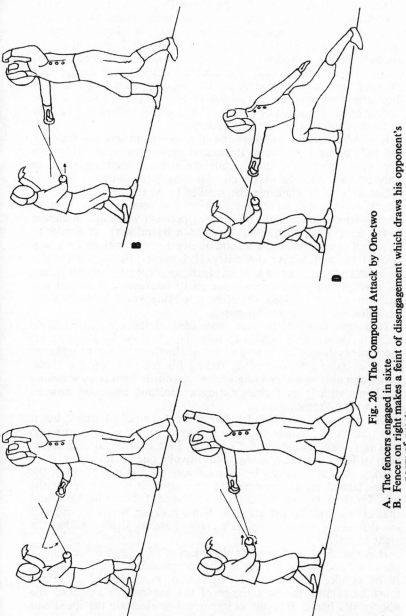

Fig. 20 The Compound Attack by One-two

A. The fencers engaged in sixte
B. Fencer on right makes a feint of disengagement which draws his opponent's parry of quarte
C. Fencer on right deceives his opponent's parry by a second disengagement
D. Fencer on right completes his attack

to the opponent's ability to parry the offensive movements made.

Basically, compound attacks are a combination of the four forms of simple attack—the straight thrust, the simple disengagement, the cut-over and the counter-disengagement. For example, two disengagements constitute a 'one-two' attack; a disengagement followed by a counter-disengagement is a *doublé*; a disengagement followed by a counter-disengagement which is then followed by a disengagement makes up a *doublé dégagé*. There are thus a wide variety of combinations of the four simple attacks which can be used to form compound or composed attacks.

It will be remembered that the disengagement and the cut-over can only be used to deceive the lateral blade movements which the opponent makes in defence, while the counter-disengagement can only be used when he makes circular movements with his blade.

Similarly when choosing the strokes to be used in a compound attack, success will depend on a correct anticipation of the form of parry—lateral or circular—which the opponent will make in answer to the feint. Thus if an opponent takes a lateral parry in answer to a feint of disengagement, a second disengagement (making up a one-two attack) will deceive this parry. If, however, he takes a circular or counter-parry, then a counter-disengagement (making an attack by *doublé*) will alone deceive this parry because, if a second disengagement is attempted, the attacker's blade would be swept aside or 'collected' by the circular parry.

It is thus essential to gain some idea of the opponent's likely reaction before an attack is chosen. This is done by studying his movements during the bout and his instinctive reaction to tentative feints or false attacks and by feeling his reactions on the blade. Much can also be learned of a fencer's favourite strokes by watching his bouts with other fencers during a pool and observing how he deals with different attacks.

The correct strokes may be chosen for a compound attack, but it will not succeed unless they are delivered with the correct timing, that is to say, in the correct cadence. In a compound attack, the feint or feints are made in order to provoke one or more premature parries, so that these can be deceived and the last movement of the attack landed on an open part of the target. It is essential for the attacker to make sure that there is no contact between his blade and that of the defender during these feints because, under the rules, if the defender finds the attacker's blade, however lightly, he has the right to riposte.

It is therefore necessary for the attacker's blade to move slightly ahead of his opponent's during the compound attack, if contact is to be avoided. The timing of the strokes made during the attack must be related to the cadence of the movements made by the opponent's blade. It is just as important to ascertain the speed and cadence of one's opponent, as to discover his reaction to a feint.

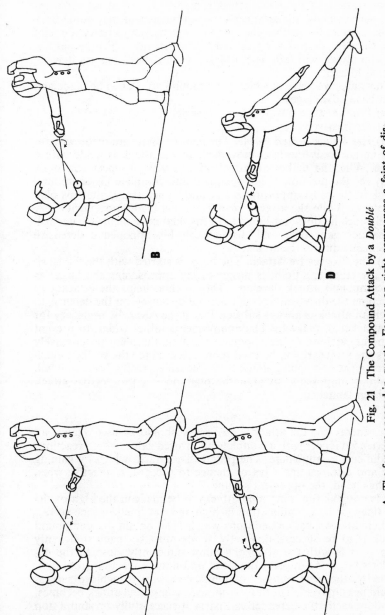

Fig. 21   The Compound Attack by a *Doublé*

A. The fencers engaged in quarte. Fencer on right commences a feint of disengagement into sixte

B. Defender (on left) begins a parry of counter-quarte

C. Attacker (on right) deceives the counter-parry by a circular movement of his
   blade (by finger play)

D. The counter-parry is deceived and the *doublé* thus completed

For example, if a one-two attack is made very fast on an opponent who reacts slowly, the attacker's second movement may come back to the original line before the defender has moved to parry the feint and, since the defender is still covered in that line which he has not left, the attack will fail. The attacker by his speed has, as it were, parried himself.

There are two ways in which a compound attack can be made and both have advantages:

(a) From a static position (*à pied ferme*).

(b) Progressively.

(a) **The Attack à Pied Ferme.** The feint or feints are made without lunging and only the final movement of the attack is made with a lunge. When he makes an attack in this way, a fencer can more easily see the reaction of his opponent and complete his compound attack in the most appropriate way and, if necessary, alter his plan of attack. While the attacker can make his blade movements very small, since he does not lunge until his final movement is launched, he cannot gain time and distance on his opponent's defensive movements during the attack.

(b) **The Progressive Attack.** The lunge is started with the feints, so that the attacker's point is progressively approaching the target as the compound attack develops. This method helps the attacker to overcome the disadvantages of time and distance over the defence, to which an attack is always subject. It will, however, be necessary for the attacker to make his blade movements rather wider, to prevent his point catching in the opponent's arm as the point progressively nears the target. It will be even more essential for the strokes which make up the compound attack to be chosen correctly, because it will be almost impossible to alter the plan once a progressive attack has been launched.

As a general rule the attack *à pied ferme* should be used against an experienced fencer with a complete and varied game, whose reactions are difficult to anticipate. The progressive attack, which by gaining time and distance has a better chance to succeed, is effective when one has 'read' the opponent's game.

It is possible for compound attacks to be made in the high or the low lines, or in a combination of high and low lines, or vice versa.

There are two basic conditions which must obtain if a compound attack is to be successful. Firstly, feints must be made sufficiently deep, that is with the attacker's point sufficiently close to the defender's target, to impress the latter and draw a reaction from him. Secondly, the least number of feints necessary to achieve success should be employed. The more complex a compound attack becomes, the more easily the defender can parry it successfully or land a stop or time hit.

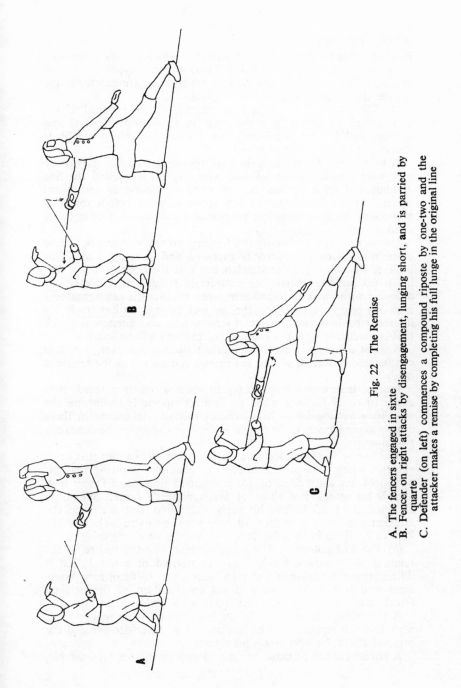

Fig. 22 The Remise

A. The fencers engaged in sixte
B. Fencer on right attacks by disengagement, lunging short, and is parried by quarte
C. Defender (on left) commences a compound riposte by one-two and the attacker makes a remise by completing his full lunge in the original line

RENEWED ATTACKS

Renewed attacks are offensive movements which are made immediately the original attack has failed. There are three types of renewed attack, differentiated by the way in which they are executed: the remise, the redoublement and the reprise.

(*a*) **The Remise.** A remise is a continuation or renewal of the attack, made immediately, in the same line as the original attack and without withdrawing the sword-arm, making any additional blade movement or returning to guard.

A remise can be made against an opponent who has parried or otherwise avoided an attack and who has either opened the line without making a riposte, or has made a delayed or compound riposte. In the latter case, a remise must arrive before the final movement of the compound riposte is commenced, if it is to be valid in time.

Under the rules governing foil fencing, no renewed attack can be given priority over a correctly executed and immediate direct or indirect riposte, since the attacker has lost the right of way when his attack has been parried or completely avoided. If, however, the defender withdraws his sword-arm, when making the disengagement after his parry which forms the indirect riposte, he has made his indirect riposte in two periods of fencing time and a renewed attack that is made during the withdrawal of the arm will be valid.

Against a properly executed indirect riposte, however, a remise can be made covered, so that the riposte is deflected as the remise is made.

Indeed, it is wise always to try to make a remise covered. It is easier to cover the line when an indirect riposte is ending on the attacker's outside lines. It is difficult to cover in quarte in these circumstances, because the riposte is liable to slip under the attacker's sword-arm.

The remise is often used as an opportunist stroke, but it is most effective when it is premeditated. For example, knowing that his opponent has a predilection for compound ripostes, a fencer may launch his attack just short of his opponent's target. When, as expected, the latter follows his parry with a first feint of riposte, the attacker need only lean forward, using the few extra inches he has kept in hand on his original lunge, to score with a remise.

(*b*) **The Redoublement.** The redoublement, like the remise, is the renewal of an attack which has been parried or avoided; but it differs from the remise in that it includes a new blade or arm movement and is therefore not a direct continuation of the original attack, but a new form of attack made while still on the lunge.

A redoublement can only be made successfully on an opponent who does not riposte after he has parried or otherwise avoided the original attack, or who delays his riposte.

A remise cannot be made against an opponent who, for example,

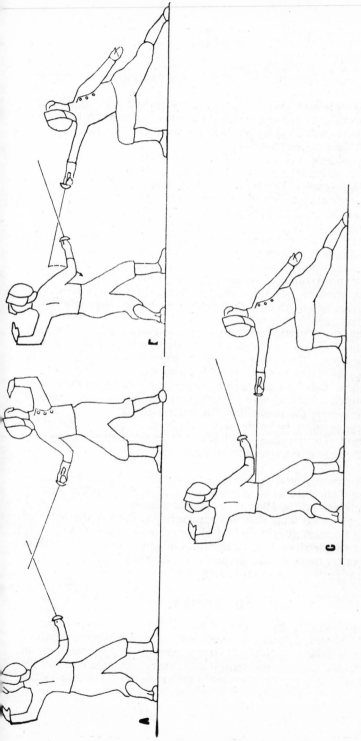

Fig. 23 The Redoublement

A. The fencers engaged in sixte
B. Fencer on right attacks by disengagement and is parried by quarte
C. As the defender does not riposte but remains covered in quarte, the attacker
   makes a redoublement by disengagement into the low line

parries and keeps the line closed; a disengagement or a cut-over, in other words a redoublement, is necessary successfully to renew the attack.

A redoublement may be simple or compound according to the reactions of the opponent. Since the attacker remains on the lunge, both fencers will be close together and a cut-over is often easier to perform than a disengagement.

A redoublement is usually a premeditated stroke, although it can, of course, be made as an opportunist move.

(c) **The Reprise.** The reprise is a renewal of the attack which differs from the remise and redoublement in that it is made after a return to the on-guard position. It has, therefore, the quality of a new attack.

The return to guard from the lunge made with the original attack is generally only momentary and may be made either backwards, as the usual recovery, or forwards by bringing up the rear foot to assume the on-guard position, thus gaining distance, before lunging again.

Often when an attack has been parried, the attacker returns to guard. Noting the absence of a riposte he immediately launches a new attack, which constitutes a reprise.

The reprise is particularly effective against an opponent who steps back out of distance when attacked—indeed, it is generally the only effective means of renewing the attack against this type of fencer. In this case the return to guard is made forwards.

A reprise may be made with a simple or a compound movement and is often combined with a preparation on the blade or a *prise de fer* to minimize the possibility of a counter-attack.

A reprise must be made very rapidly, as a smooth controlled movement. This requires suppleness and perfect balance, especially when the return to guard is made forwards.

All the renewed attacks depend to some extent on the element of surprise if they are to be successful. They should therefore be used sparingly and not be allowed to become a habit.

A fencer who finds that his opponent has formed the habit of making renewed attacks instead of parrying the riposte, need only make a simple riposte, when the rules of foil fencing will give him the priority, or he can be prepared to parry twice before riposting (which is perhaps the safest tactic).

DEFENCE

Fencing is said to have been so named because it was the art of defence. Indeed, defence is in many ways the most important part of a fencer's technique. Not only does it prevent the opponent scoring a hit. As we have already seen, it also controls in large measure the choice of stroke for the opponent's attack, because few attacks can

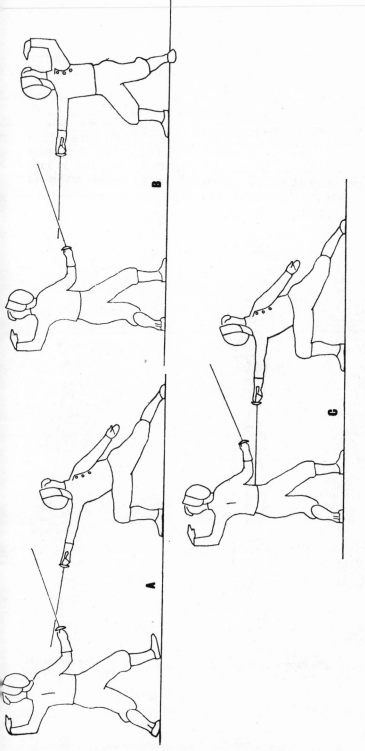

Fig. 24 The Reprise

A. The attack is parried by quarte, as the defender (left) steps back out of distance but does not riposte
B. Attacker (right) returns to guard *forwards*
C. Attacker delivers his renewed attack in the low line

succeed unless the form the defence will take is correctly anticipated.

A fencer defends his target by deflecting the attacker's blade with his own blade—this is called a parry.

The basic principle of defence is to oppose the forte of the defender's blade to the foible of the attacker's blade—in other words, to oppose strength to weakness. If a parry is taken with the foible, or weakest part, of the blade, a determined opponent will be able to force his attack through the parry on to the target and the defender will not have sufficient strength in his blade to prevent this. In such a case the attack has not been completely parried and an 'insufficient parry' results.

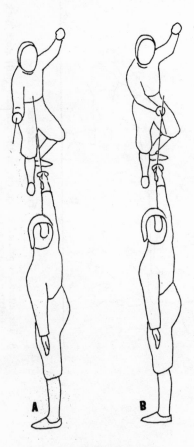

Fig. 25   The Parry of Quarte

Fig. 26   The Insufficient Parry of Quarte

When forming a parry, a fencer is not seeking to strike the attacker's blade aside, but to place a barrier with his blade in the path of the line into which the attack is launched. If then the attacking blade is forced on, it will be deflected clear of the target. To attempt to strike an attacking blade aside will result in wide movements in which control of the blade will soon be lost, making it easy for the attacker to deceive such attempts to parry.

When a parry is made it is essential that the whole blade covers the target in the line of the parry. It is not sufficient for the sword-hand alone to be placed in the proper position to form the parry, while the blade remains at an angle to it; the whole weapon must form a barrier against penetration by the attacker's blade in that line.

When a fencer is on guard with his sword-arm in the correct position, that is with the hand breast-high and the elbow about a hand's breadth from his body, the foil is in the best position to oppose the forte to the foible of an attacking blade. From this position all the lines can be covered by lowering or raising the point of the foil, without altering the level of the sword-hand or arm.

There are eight parries at foil, two to protect each of the four quarters into which the target is theoretically divided (see Fig. 27). Four of these parries, namely quarte, sixte, septime and octave, are made with the sword-hand in supination or half-supination; the remainder—prime, seconde, tierce and quinte—are made with the hand in pronation. The last four parries are rarely used today, probably because the turning of the hand entails a loss of time. In practice, quarte and sixte protect the target adequately against attacks directed into the high lines, while septime and octave similarly protect the low lines (see Fig. 12).

The easy way to remember the sequence of parries is to start with prime as the position in which the hand immediately finds itself when a sword is drawn with the right hand from a scabbard worn on the left hip, therefore with the sword-hand on the left side of the body. Thereafter the sequence is right-right-left-left-right-left-right.

There are two distinct schools of thought regarding the position of the sword-hand when the parries of sixte and quarte are taken. The traditional school taught that sixte should be taken with the hand completely in supination (finger-nails uppermost) and that when moving to the parry of quarte the hand should be rolled into rather more than half-supination. With the hand in either position, the point of the foil points towards the centre of the opponent's target and about level with his eyes.

The modern school teaches that parries of both sixte and quarte should be taken with the hand in half-supination (with the finger-nails to the side). It is not necessary to roll the hand when moving from quarte to sixte or vice versa, but the whole foil and sword-hand is carried from one side of the target to the other by a movement of the forearm and flexing of the wrist. The point of the foil

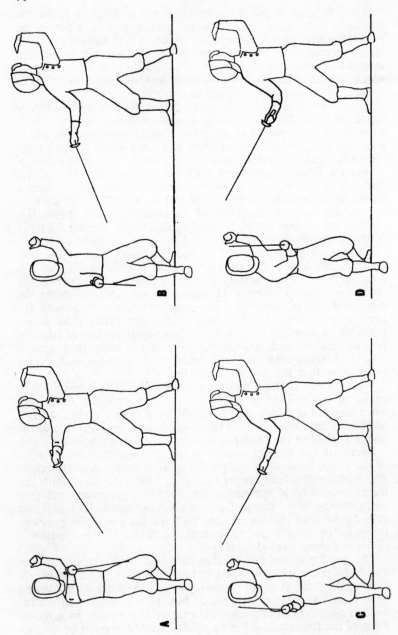

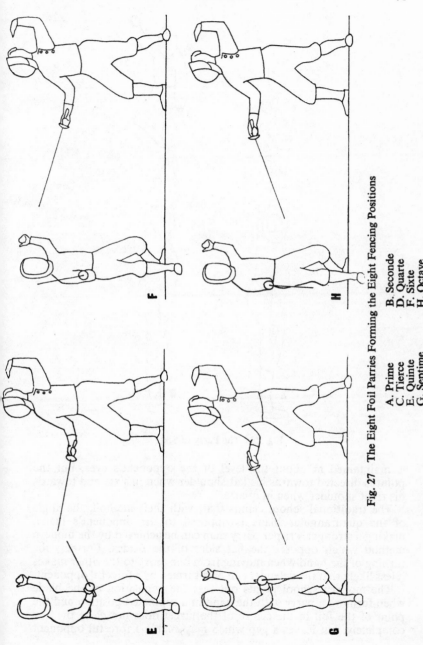

Fig. 27   The Eight Foil Parries Forming the Eight Fencing Positions

A. Prime   B. Seconde
C. Tierce   D. Quarte
E. Quinte   F. Sixte
G. Septime   H. Octave

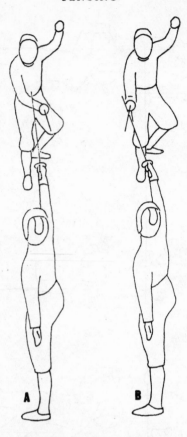

Fig. 28   The Parry of Sixte

is maintained at about the level of the opponent's eyes, but the point is directed towards his left shoulder when in sixte and towards his right shoulder when in quarte.

The traditional school claims that, with their method, the angle of the quadrangular blade is opposed to the opponent's blade, making a stronger, crisper parry than can be achieved by the modern method which opposes the flat sides of the blades. Further, the turning of the hand when moving from one parry to the other makes it less likely that the defender can be disarmed by a forceful opponent.

The modern school points out that the angulation of the blade when forming a parry with the hand in a supinated position and the point of the foil in the centre of the target does not close the line completely, but leaves a gap which may enable a forceful opponent to force his attack through over the top of the blade when the parry is formed. Further, the riposte does not come as such a natural, spontaneous movement when the hand is in full supination as when it is in half-supination. The position of the point and the moving of the sword-hand and weapon 'in one piece' across the target is a more natural movement, which ensures that the line is completely closed and reduces a tendency for the point to fly out of line when several parries are taken in rapid succession.

As with most differences of technique between different schools, each method has its advantages and disadvantages and it is a mistake to be dogmatic and to assume that the method which one has not been taught is useless.

On balance the writer recommends the modern school, on the grounds that it is a more natural way of forming a parry, especially in sixte where there is less strain on the muscles of the forearm. It conforms more closely to the ideal of offering a completely closed barrier to the path of the attack and facilitates the riposte from sixte.

There are three basic types of parry:
(1) Simple or direct parries.
(2) Semicircular or indirect parries.
(3) Circular or counter-parries.

SIMPLE PARRIES

When a fencer is attacked by a direct thrust, his instinctive reaction is to deflect the attacking blade with his own blade—this is a simple parry.

Simple or direct parries are made by moving the foil laterally across the target, in order to cover the line into which the attack is approaching. Thus from the half-supinated position of the hand when on guard in sixte covered, the foil and sword-hand are carried laterally to the quarte position. Similarly the hand may be carried from left to right when moving from the position of quarte to the parry of sixte.

It is stressed again that the object when forming a simple parry is not to strike aside the threatening blade, but to oppose the foil as a barrier in its path to the target. Hence it is essential that the lateral movement of the sword-hand and foil when passing from one parry to the opposite one should be carefully controlled, so that the hand and blade are stopped exactly in the position in which that side of the target is covered, regardless of how wide the opponent's point movements may be. A tendency to follow the opponent's blade from side to side, or lack of hand and blade control, will result in wide, slashing movements which can easily be deceived and which are aptly described as 'sugaring strawberries'.

Considerable practice in lessons is required if the wide, instinctive movement of the blade, when forming a succession of lateral parries, is to be canalized into the controlled blade movements which are so essential, and the necessary lightness but firmness of hand acquired.

Simple parries can be made in two ways:

(a) By detachment.

(b) By opposition.

(a) **The Parry by Detachment.** The opponent's blade is quitted as soon as it has been met, either to make a riposte or to move into another line.

(b) **The Parry by Opposition.** Contact is maintained with the opponent's blade after it has been met, the defender either remaining covered in that line or riposting along the blade.

The parry by opposition has the advantage that the defender retains possession of the attacker's blade and can feel the latter's reactions through the contact of the blades. It is particularly valuable at épée and electric foil, because it minimizes the chance of a renewal of the attack in the same line.

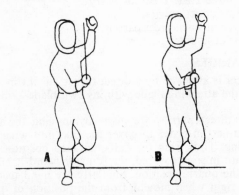

Fig. 29   The Semicircular Parry: Quarte to Septime

SEMICIRCULAR PARRIES

Semicircular, or indirect, parries are parries taken from a high-line engagement to deflect an attack directed into the low line, or vice versa. They are so called because the foil describes a half-circle, for example, from the engagement of sixte to the parry of octave, or from the engagement of quarte to the parry of septime.

When making a semicircular parry, the sword-arm is maintained in its original position and the semicircular movement of the blade is made by a rotation of the wrist, assisted by a slight opening and closing of the last three fingers of the sword-hand, which remains in the half-supinated position throughout the movement.

As for simple parries, it is important that the whole foil should cover the line of the parry. When the parry of septime or octave is made, the line is closed by ensuring that the point of the weapon is placed slightly outside the sides of the opponent's body.

Semicircular parries should always be made with opposition and should be taken from high to low line or from low to high line *on the same side* of the target, for example, from sixte to octave or from quarte to septime or vice versa, but *not* from sixte to septime. This is to ensure that the opponent's blade is gathered away from the target and is not deflected on to the body or legs or missed altogether.

CIRCULAR OR COUNTER-PARRIES

Circular parries, also called counter-parries, are made by a circular movement of the defender's blade which envelops the attacker's blade and brings it back to the original line of engagement, while deflecting it off the target. There is a circular parry corresponding to each simple parry, such as counter of sixte, counter of quarte and so on.

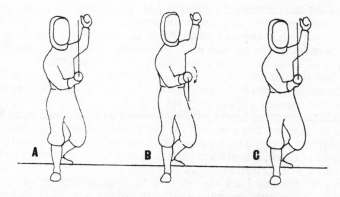

Fig. 30   The Counter- or Circular Parry of Quarte

As an example, let us take two fencers engaged in sixte. If one fencer attacks by a disengagement, the defender may take a counter-parry of sixte instead of a simple parry of quarte. The counter-parry of sixte will, by its circular blade movement, collect the attacker's blade and bring it back to the original line of engagement in sixte covered. If, therefore, the attack is pressed home, the blade will be deflected off the target in the same way as it would have been had the attacker attempted a direct thrust into the closed line of sixte, when both fencers were on guard in the original line of engagement in sixte.

When making a counter-parry it is obviously necessary to sweep the opponent's blade away from the target by the shortest route. Thus counter of sixte is taken by moving the blade clockwise, while counter of quarte will require an anti-clockwise rotation of the blade.

The counter-parries of quarte and sixte are made by rotating the foil entirely by finger play, but in making counter-parries of septime or octave, some slight wrist action is usually necessary. Excessive use of the wrist when making a counter-parry will result in wide, slow movements and loss of direction of the point of the foil. The most common fault is to raise the sword-hand or draw back the forearm when making a circular parry, which is likely to result in the parry being late or missing the opponent's blade altogether.

One should aim to make a counter-parry by rolling the foil handle in the hand with the fingers, without moving the wrist or sword-arm and with the arm and shoulder muscles completely relaxed. In this way the attacker's blade can be gathered cleanly, so that the counter-parry results in a completely covered position, with the opponent's blade firmly held by the forte of the defender's foil.

Against most attacks the defender has the choice of the three forms of parry to deflect any single offensive action from his opponent. For example if engaged in quarte, a disengagement into sixte can be parried by the circular parry of counter of quarte, by the direct parry of sixte, or by the semicircular parry of septime.

Semicircular parries are, of course, generally used against attacks into the low lines; but it should not be forgotten that they are often effective against attacks into the high lines, where the opponent tends to lower his hand by falling forward when lunging, or to keep his sword-hand too low with his point directed at a high line.

Against a very fast fencer or one with a marked superiority of height or reach, it is often necessary to step backwards when making a parry. It is preferable to do so rather than commit the common fault of drawing back the sword-arm, in an attempt to gather the blade. When parrying with a step backwards, the parry should be taken as the rear foot moves backwards in the course of breaking ground; in other words, the parry should be formed with the step back and not after it has been completed.

Inexperienced fencers, who are not confident of their ability to parry, often form the bad habit of retreating every time they are attacked and thus generally find themselves out of distance for the riposte. The step back as a defensive movement should always be adjusted to the length of the opponent's attacking movements, to ensure that the required measure is maintained for a successful parry and riposte.

A fencer must remember that his opponent is always seeking to ascertain his likely reaction to attacks because, as we have already seen, this knowledge is essential if the form of the attack is to be chosen correctly. The habit of always reacting to attacks with the same type of parry will obviously play into the hands of an observant opponent. It is therefore wise to vary the type of parry taken as much as possible during a bout, in order to keep the opponent guessing.

Fencing is, however, a game of tactics and cunning, and it is possible to show intentionally an apparent predilection for a certain type of parry, in order to induce one's opponent to use a desired form of compound attack. To lay a trap in this way in the heat of battle requires considerable experience and control but, when successful, it brings great satisfaction and is part of the fascination of fencing tactics.

SUCCESSIVE PARRIES

Against a compound attack it is often necessary to take a series of parries, in answer to the opponent's feints. These are called successive parries.

Here again, when taking successive parries, it is wise consciously to vary the type of parry used, as far as conditions allow, in order to make it as difficult as possible for the attacker to choose his strokes successfully.

It has already been noted that a circular parry provides a surer way of gathering the attacker's blade than the simple parry, especially against an opponent who makes wide blade movements, or who varies the height of his hand when making feints. When taking successive parries against such opponents, there is a danger that a series of simple or lateral parries may pass over the top of the attacker's blade. In such circumstances it is useful to follow a simple parry by a counter-parry, when the former has been deceived.

Controlled hand and blade movements are essential when taking successive parries; the blade must be checked exactly when the correct covered position of each parry is reached, or the movement will quickly degenerate into wild slashing with the blade. The commonest faults are overrunning the parry position by attempting to follow an opponent's wide blade movements in his feints, and withdrawing the sword-arm as the opponent's point nears the target, which usually results in the parry being made too late. The correct level of the sword-hand and of the point of the foil must be maintained throughout a series of parries—to raise the hand may result in missing the attacker's blade altogether, while lowering the hand or point may result in an insufficient parry.

THE RIPOSTE

The offensive movement made by a fencer after he has successfully parried an attack is known as the riposte.

Normally the riposte immediately follows the parry, in order to hit the opponent before he can recover from attack to defence. This also takes advantage of the rule of foil and sabre fencing that the immediate riposte has priority over the continuation of an attack after a successful parry.

Sometimes a riposte may be delayed, that is to say, delivered in broken time or after a short pause. The variation of cadence is used to disconcert the opponent, or to make him disclose his reaction to the riposte prematurely. Much of the success of a delayed riposte stems from its unexpectedness, and it follows that it is a tactic which should be sparingly used.

A riposte may be made from the static position in which the parry has been made, that is to say *à pied ferme*, or it can be delivered with a lunge or *flèche*. Which method of delivery is adopted will naturally depend on the distance between the two fencers, which is usually governed by the opponent's speed of recovery from the lunge.

Basically a riposte is an attack (or more accurately a counter-attack) following a parry. As one might expect, the various forms a riposte can take conform exactly to the different types of attack. Thus a riposte may be:

(*1*) Simple—either direct or indirect.

(*2*) Compound.

The choice of the riposte, like the choice of the attack, is determined by the type of defensive movement one thinks that the opponent is likely to adopt against it. The opponent's reactions can only be ascertained by observation of his usual blade movements when recovering from an unsuccessful attack.

Whatever type of riposte is used, it should be made as a continuous, supple movement, without contracting the muscles of the sword-arm or shoulder; this avoids any tendency to deliver the riposte as a punching movement, which will probably cause the point to miss the target. The point is placed on the target by the use of the fingers, as already described for the hit, and the arm should be fully extended.

As with most fencing strokes, the timing is all-important. A parry and riposte is most effective if it is made as the attack is completing its course. At this point the time available to the opponent to change from attack to defence is cut to the minimum, and consequently the riposte has the best chance to succeed before the attacker can parry it.

Ripostes may, of course, be made in the low line as successfully as in the high line, and the choice of which of these is used will depend on the position of the opponent's arm after his attack has failed, or the line which he covers when he is returning to guard.

Whatever type of riposte is made, the line in which it ends should, whenever possible, be closed or covered to reduce the risk of a continuation of the attack landing if the riposte should miss. When making a riposte in the high lines, covering is best achieved by

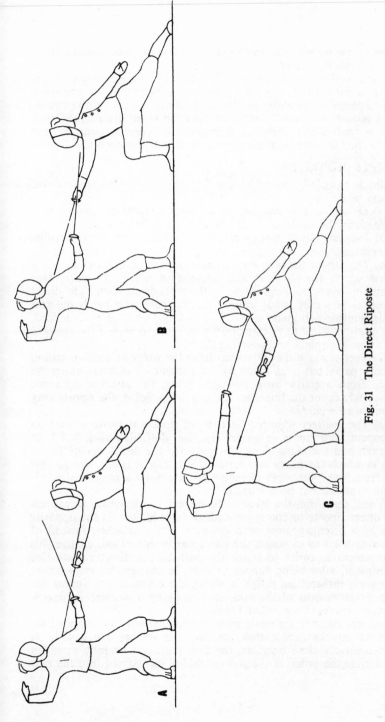

Fig. 31 The Direct Riposte

A. The attack parried by quarte
B. Defender lowers his blade as the attacker withdraws his arm
C. The riposte is delivered

allowing the sword-hand to rise as the arm is extended when following through the riposte.

It is sometimes rather more difficult to obtain accuracy of point when riposting in the low lines than it is in the high lines. The point will be placed more easily on the target in the low lines if the sword-hand is turned into full supination and the knees are slightly bent. This is particularly useful at electrical foil, where a clean fix and penetration is essential if the apparatus is to register a hit.

SIMPLE RIPOSTES

A simple riposte is one which consists of a single blade movement. It may be either:

(a) Direct—in the same line as the parry by a direct thrust or by a *coulé* along the blade, if the line is only partially covered.

(b) Indirect—by a disengagement, a cut-over or a counter-disengagement.

(a) **The Direct Riposte.** As its name implies, a direct riposte is a thrust which travels from the position in which the parry was formed to the opponent's target by the most direct route. The direct riposte is generally made against an opponent who bends his arm while returning to guard after his attack has been parried; indeed, it is rarely possible to riposte directly and immediately if the attacker maintains a straight arm covering the line.

A direct attack either rebounds from the parry as a reflex action, when a parry has been made by detachment, or is made along the blade from a parry by opposition. When the attacker does not completely cover the line after his attack has failed, the riposte may be made by a *coulé*.

(b) **The Indirect Riposte.** An indirect riposte is made against an opponent who closes or covers the line after his attack has been parried, and therefore blocks the path for the direct riposte in the line in which the parry was formed. Similarly it is effective against the fencer who attempts to renew his attack by a remise, after his original attack has been parried.

When, therefore, the attacker covers the line in which he expects the direct riposte to come, the defender can hit him in the opposite line by a disengagement or a cut-over. If the attacker, instead of covering the line in which the parry has been formed, changes his engagement in order to block the path to the direct riposte (for example if, after being parried in sixte, he changes his engagement to quarte rather than cover in sixte), the defender can follow the circular movement of the attacker's blade by a counter-disengagement to riposte in the original line.

Indirect ripostes are made by finger play, exactly as described for indirect attacks except that, because the fencers are usually at comparatively close quarters, the arm must not be fully extended until *after* the point of the defender's foil has passed into the new

Fig. 32 The Indirect Riposte

A. The attack is parried by quarte
B. Defender passes his blade under the attacker's blade as the latter covers the
   quarte line. Note that the defender's arm remains bent
C. The riposte is delivered in sixte

line. If the arm is extended prematurely the point of the weapon will probably catch in the opponent's arm. On the other hand, care must be taken to ensure that the arm is not withdrawn when making an indirect riposte. This is a common fault and indeed there is always a temptation to withdraw the arm to find room to riposte, especially against a forceful opponent or a left-hander who maintains a straight arm and presses on with a remise or continuation of the attack, after the original attack has been parried.

Under the rules governing foil fencing, an indirect riposte has priority over the continuation of the attack or remise only if it is made immediately and *without withdrawing the arm*, that is to say, in one period of fencing time. If the arm is withdrawn even momentarily when making an indirect riposte, the latter is considered to have been made in two periods of fencing time and would then not be valid over an immediate remise.

This rule was evolved by the International Fencing Federation to solve a heated controversy which arose in 1925, during a series of three matches between the famous Italian professional, Nedo Nadi, and the equally famous French master, René Haussy.

Haussy was a left-hander and an extremely fast and forceful attacker. Nadi was a right-hander. Noting that his opponent had a predilection for the indirect riposte, Haussy scored with an immediate remise, keeping his arm straight, as soon as his attack had been parried. His supporters claimed that this remise was good in time.

Nadi and his vociferous Italian supporters claimed, however, that an indirect riposte was a movement made in one period of fencing time and should be counted as valid over any remise, however swiftly and accurately made.

After passionate debate, the International Federation ruled that an indirect riposte must be made entirely by finger play and without being assisted by a withdrawal of the arm, if it was to be considered as being made in one period of fencing time and therefore given priority over an immediate remise.

The writer recalls that during the match in this series which he witnessed in Milan, Nedo Nadi certainly appeared to make a distinct arm movement to get round his left-handed opponent's blade, when making his favourite riposte by disengagement. He remembers this match between these two famous and complete fencing champions as one of the greatest he has ever seen.

The riposte by cut-over is used against an opponent who covers the line after his attack has failed, but who is too close for the defender to pass the point under his arm by disengagement.

Slight pressure should be exerted on the opponent's blade when making the cut-over, in order that it should spring back as the cut-over is completed and thus leave more room for the riposte to land. When making this form of riposte at close quarters, the arm must not be extended until the cut-over has been completed. Even then, considerable blade control is required to place the point accurately on the target.

Naturally, when a riposte by cut-over is made, some withdrawal of the arm is necessary to clear the opponent's blade. This should as far as possible be confined to bending the elbow, while keeping the point of the foil down by slight bending of the wrist so as to avoid wide movements. During the cut-over the fencer is more vulnerable than during a disengagement and it is therefore particularly important to cover the line as the hit is placed on the target.

Unlike the riposte by disengagement or by cut-over, the speed and timing of the riposte by counter-disengagement is dependent on that of the opponent's counter-movement, which it is designed to deceive. Care must be taken not to start this movement until the opponent initiates his change of line and therefore this form of riposte is often a delayed riposte.

Like all indirect ripostes, the riposte by counter-disengagement must be made entirely by finger play, without any arm or wrist movement and with the point action completed before the arm is extended to hit.

It is particularly effective against left-handers, many of whom have the habit of returning to guard in quarte after an attack has failed, because in that line they obtain more authority over the top of a right-hander's blade. Such fencers are often vulnerable to the counter-disengagement into sixte.

All forms of indirect riposte can, of course, be completed in the low line instead of in the high line, against an opponent who keeps his hand high or who withdraws his hand when recovering from the lunge.

When completing a riposte in the low line, the sword-hand cannot be raised to cover the line. Indeed, it is necessary to keep the hand low and angulate the blade to direct the point on to the target, and it is often helpful to bend slightly at the knees when making this stroke, turning the hand into full supination, which will help to place the point.

COMPOUND RIPOSTES

A compound or composed riposte is one which includes one or more feints.

The feints and combinations of feints used in making a compound riposte are exactly the same movements as those which are used in compound attacks; they are based on the four simple offensive movements—the direct thrust, the disengagement, the cut-over and the counter-disengagement.

There is, however, one important difference. The feints during a compound attack are made with the arm straight; whereas during a compound riposte, owing to the closeness of the fencers, the feints must be made with the sword-arm bent, in order to have room to

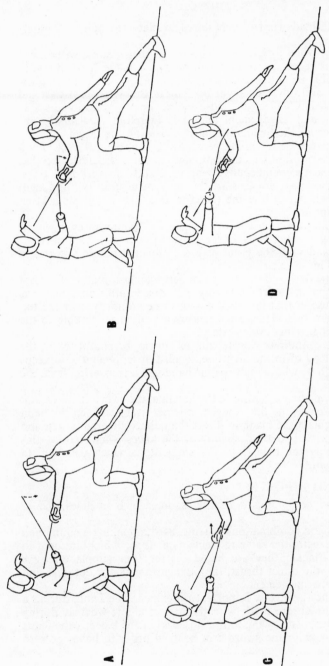

Fig. 33 The Compound Riposte (with Two Disengagements)

A. The attack (from right) is parried by quarte
B. Defender (on left) has made a disengagement (keeping his arm bent to pass the point) which the attacker attempts to parry in sixte
C. Defender has deceived this attempt to parry with a second disengagement and is extending his arm.
D. Defender completes his compound riposte

pass the point without it getting caught up in the opponent's arm. The arm must only be extended on the final movement of the compound riposte.

The types of feints used in a compound riposte will, of course, depend on a correct anticipation of the opponent's reaction to them. Tactically the feints may be made continuously or with a pause, that is in broken time. The compound riposte may be made *à pied ferme* or may conclude with a lunge or *flèche*, depending on the speed of recovery of the opponent and the measure between the fencers.

Of necessity this riposte must be made in several periods of fencing time, and the more complex it is made, the more vulnerable it is to a renewed attack, such as a remise or redoublement.

As a general rule, the simplest fencing movements are the most effective and the safest. A compound riposte must therefore only be used when it is impossible to score with a direct or an indirect riposte and, when it is used, it should include the least possible number of feints necessary to achieve one's aim.

To form the habit of making unnecessarily complicated compound ripostes merely invites the opponent to score with a premeditated remise or redoublement.

COUNTER-RIPOSTES

A counter-riposte is the offensive movement made by a fencer after he has successfully parried a riposte or a counter-riposte.

In a fencing phrase containing a number of offensive and defensive movements, after the first riposte all subsequent ones are called counter-ripostes and are numbered in the sequence in which they occur. For example, if an attack is parried, the offensive movement made by the defender is called the riposte; if this riposte is parried by the original attacker, his next offensive movement is the first counter-riposte; should this counter-riposte be parried by the original defender, his next offensive movement is the second counter-riposte, and so on. Therefore in a fencing phrase, the riposte and the even-numbered counter-ripostes (second, fourth etc.) are always made by the original defender, while the odd-numbered counter-ripostes (first, third etc.) are always made by the original attacker.

Counter-ripostes may be simple or compound. They may be made while on the lunge, while recovering, *à pied ferme*, or with a new lunge according to the distance which happens to exist between the fencers.

A light hand and accurate blade control are essential when engaged in a series of counter-ripostes, or these will rapidly develop into a series of wild, slashing movements. A common fault is to withdraw the arm when parrying instead of adjusting the distance, to assist in gathering the opponent's blade, by footwork. Excessive arm movement will cause the following counter-riposte to arrive late and help the opponent to parry or avoid it.

A series of counter-ripostes is often made spontaneously by reflex action, but the counter-riposte can also be used tactically as a premeditated movement. For example, the original attack may be launched with no intention of hitting, but to draw a parry and riposte in a certain line, with the object of parrying the riposte and scoring with a counter-riposte. This form of second-intention attack is often effective against a fencer with a very strong defence, who can be surprised and disconcerted by a counter-riposte. Similarly, an intentional change of cadence in a series of counter-ripostes often proves an effective tactical move.

When it is intended to use the counter-riposte as a premeditated movement, it is often wise to remain on the lunge after the original attack has been parried, in order to score with the counter-riposte before the opponent can get out of distance. At such close quarters it is important to bend and lower the elbow, while being careful not to take the blade out of line when parrying the riposte.

COUNTER-ATTACKS

A counter-attack is an attack made when the opponent launches an attack. There are two basic types of counter-attack:

(*a*) The stop hit, which seeks to land a hit on the target sufficiently before the opponent's attack arrives to be valid.

(*b*) The time hit which seeks to land a hit on the target in such a way that it succeeds in neutralizing the opponent's attack at the same time.

(*a*) **The Stop Hit.** At any rate in theory, a stop hit is designed to arrest the development of an attack. With sharp swords, a properly executed stop hit would have a similar effect to 'beating the opponent to the punch' at boxing—the attack would not arrive or, if it did, it would have no power of penetration behind it.

We are not, however, using sharp swords and at foil, which is a conventional weapon, the rules provide that the attack has priority if it arrives simultaneously with the stop hit. In order to have priority over the attack, a stop hit must arrive clearly before the last movement of the attack; i.e. to be counted as good, a stop hit must arrive on the target at least one period of fencing time before the arrival of the attack.

A period of fencing time (*temps d'escrime*) is the time taken by a fencer to perform one simple fencing movement. Such simple fencing action may be a single blade movement, an arm movement, or a movement of the foot such as a step forward.

It must be clearly appreciated that a period of fencing time bears no direct relation to a fixed period of time as may be measured by a watch. The time taken to make a simple fencing movement will vary according to the speed of execution of the movement by each individual fencer.

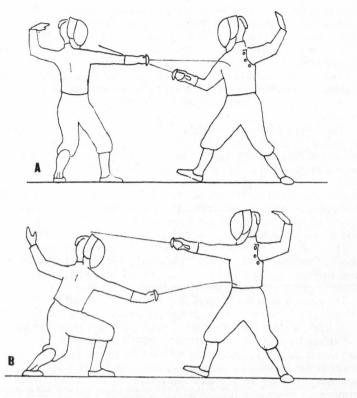

Fig. 34   The Stop Hit

A. Stop hit in the high line on a bent-arm attack
B. Stop hit in the low line on a step forward

Thus a straight thrust or a disengagement requires one period of fencing time; two blade movements, as in a one-two attack, are made in two periods of fencing time. A step forward is one period of fencing time; a step forward followed by a one-two attack equals three periods of fencing time; if the step forward is combined with the feint of a one-two attack, this attack is then made in two periods of fencing time.

According to the rules governing foil fencing, if an attack is made which comprises several periods of fencing time, a stop hit, to be valid, must arrive at latest during the movement which constitutes the penultimate period of fencing time. Thus in a one-two-three attack, which is an attack comprising two feints and is made in three periods of fencing time, the last moment when it is possible for a stop hit to be valid is during the execution of the second feint.

Stop hits are particularly effective during the preparation for an attack made with a step forward, or against an opponent who attacks with a bent arm or who makes feints with wide blade movements.

Correct appreciation of time and distance is essential to the making of an effective stop hit which, while usually made with a straight thrust, may also be made with a disengagement or counter-disengagement.

It is often an advantage to lean forward when making a stop hit, or to bend the legs when making a stop hit in the low line. The stop hit should have the character of an offensive movement and not be a mere straightening of the arm to allow the opponent to fall on the point, as this will probably occur on the last movement of his attack and therefore be out of time. While the stop hit is often an instinctive or opportunist stroke, it is most effective when used as the result of observation of an opponent's faulty execution in his attacks or his predilection for complex movements in attack.

The stop hit depends for success on an element of surprise and should therefore be made sparingly during a bout. Its indiscriminate and habitual use can easily be used by an observant opponent to score by counter-time, as described below.

The *passata sotto* is a form of stop hit much favoured by the Italian school. It is generally used against an attack directed at the outer high lines, and its purpose is to remove the target from the path of the attack by ducking below the opponent's blade, while leaving the foil in line so that he impales himself on the point. The *passata sotto* depends for its success on surprise, and to perform it correctly it is necessary to wait for the final movement of the attack, when the opponent's lunge is in full flight. At that moment the defender ducks as low as possible, by stretching back the rear foot with the leg straight as far as he can, while maintaining equilibrium by placing the unarmed hand on the *piste*. At the same time the sword-hand is turned into seconde, with the arm straight and the point of the weapon directed upwards at the opponent's flank.

Perfect timing is essential in carrying out the *passata sotto* to ensure that the attacker's point entirely misses the defender. As this is a case of displacing the valid target and in some measure of replacing the valid target by the head, under the rules of foil fencing, should the fencer who performs the *passata sotto* be hit on the head, it will be scored as a valid hit.

The *in quartata*, or side-step, is another form of displacement of the target often used with a stop hit. It is more frequently used at épée than at foil. The object of the *in quartata* is to remove the target from the path of the attacker's point, while leaving the point in line to score a stop hit. The important difference between the *in quartata* and the *passata sotto* is that in the former movement the fencer is removing the target and not replacing it or covering it by any other part of his body. If, therefore, while performing this movement the fencer is hit on the mask or the legs, such a hit, at foil, would not be counted as valid.

The *in quartata* must be performed on the final movement of the opponent's attack when he is making his lunge or *flèche*, preferably towards the inside lines. As the defender extends his arm to make his stop hit, he pivots on his leading foot by swinging his rear foot as far to the right as possible, which has the effect of swinging the body out of line with the opponent. As it also has the effect of displacing the sword-arm to the side, it is necessary to co-ordinate this side-step with angulation of the wrist, so that the point of the weapon remains directed on to the opponent's target. The swinging of the body is assisted by swinging the rear shoulder and the unarmed arm to the rear. These movements, and the length of the side-step, which is performed entirely by the rear foot, must be controlled to maintain equilibrium.

(*b*) **The Time Hit**[1]. The time hit is a counter-attack, made by anticipating the line in which the opponent's attack will finish, and closing that line so as to hit the attacker while at the same time carrying his blade clear of the defender's target. It may be described as a stop hit made while closing the line, or as a parry and riposte made in one movement.

The time hit is the safest form of counter-attack because, when correctly executed, a hit is scored without the possibility of the attack landing. It has eliminated the necessity to land the counter-attack a period of fencing time before the attack, because it prevents the attack landing at all. On the other hand, since the time hit can only be executed on the final movement of the attack, it is essential that the attacking blade be deflected completely—if it lands anywhere it will, under the rules, annul the counter-attack, which will in fact have become a stop hit made out of time.

The time hit is one of the most difficult strokes to perform correctly. It requires a correct anticipation of the opponent's intentions, exact placing of the blade in the path of the final movement of the attack and timing and precision in placing the point on the target. The anticipation of the form of the opponent's attack and the line in which it will be completed may be the result of observation of his habits. It may, however, be achieved by inducing the opponent to adopt a certain line of attack by intentionally repeating a certain form of parry to his feints.

To make a time hit the parry must be formed with strong opposition, while the point of the blade remains lower than is usual when parrying so as to be directed on to the opponent's target as the arm is extended. The time hit may be made with a simple or a circular parry and it is generally helpful to make some angulation of the wrist, in order to dominate the opponent's blade.

---

[1] Since 1967 the 'Time Hit' has been more accurately termed the 'Stop Hit made with opposition' in the Rules.

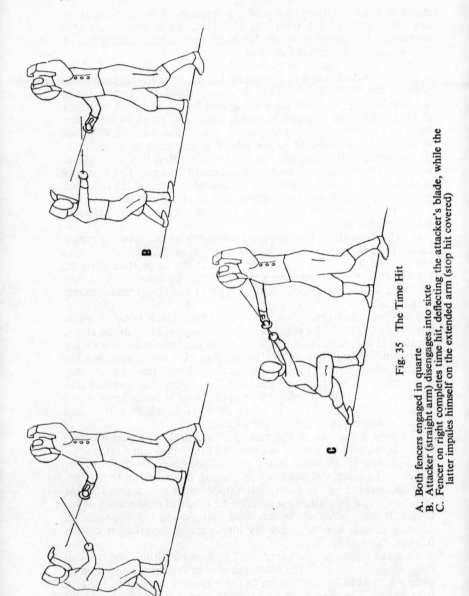

Fig. 35 The Time Hit

A. Both fencers engaged in quarte
B. Attacker (straight arm) disengages into sixte
C. Fencer on right completes time hit, deflecting the attacker's blade, while the latter impales himself on the extended arm (stop hit covered)

A correctly executed time hit has a demoralizing effect on the most confident opponent. Like the stop hit, it must be used sparingly and as a movement of surprise, or an alert opponent will use it to score with a second-intention attack.

Time hits are most easily made against a fencer who keeps his hand low when attacking, so that the defender can dominate his blade when making the time hit over the top of his blade. They are best attempted against attacks on the outside lines, that is in the lines of sixte or octave, and are very effective in the low lines. When made on the inside lines of quarte or septime there is difficulty in deflecting the opponent's blade, which has a tendency to slip over or under the opposition of the defender's blade.

A time hit can be usefully combined with the *in quartata* movement described above, particularly when the opposition is taken in the low line.

COUNTER-TIME

Counter-time, or the second-intention attack, consists of drawing a stop hit or a time hit, parrying it and scoring with a riposte.

The second-intention attack is, as its name implies, a premeditated movement, generally used against a fencer who has formed the habit of continually attempting stop hits or who attacks into the attack, that is to say one who launches an attack as soon as his opponent makes any offensive movement.

The success of a counter-time movement largely depends on concealing one's real intentions and inducing the opponent to make his stop or time hit with conviction, so that he has little opportunity to recover when it is parried before the riposte lands.

The stop hit may be drawn in a variety of ways: by use of invitations, by intentionally uncovered feints, by making false attacks with a half-lunge or merely by stepping forward. Once it has been drawn and parried, the riposte may be direct, indirect or compound.

Fencing is a game of subtlety and finesse and the reader will by now have appreciated that many movements can be used or combined in a number of ways to outwit the opponent, or to bluff or counter-bluff him. The second-intention attack is a good example of this. By invitations, preparations and attacks intentionally made incorrectly and other means, the opponent is induced to launch his counter-attack, so that it may be parried and followed by a riposte. On the other hand, if the opponent realizes that a second-intention attack is intended, his stop hit may be launched as a feint, so that he can parry the riposte and score with a counter-riposte. A fencer can even induce his opponent to make a second-intention attack by showing an apparent predilection for the stop hit. These are examples of the ways in which an intelligent fencer can impose his game on his opponent, inducing him to make the strokes as he wishes. As we have seen, knowledge of the movements one's opponent is going to make is of the greatest assistance in devising the means of his undoing. This bluff and counter-bluff is the essence and fascination of fencing.

PREPARATIONS OF ATTACK

A preparation of attack is the action taken by a fencer to make an opening for his attack. It usually consists in making some movement which will either deflect the opponent's blade, or obtain a desired reaction from it, but it may consist merely of a change of distance. A preparation may equally be used to obtain an opening for a riposte and may precede a simple or a compound attack or riposte.

The various forms of preparation described below may be used singly, repeated, or combined together. For example, a beat may be preceded by or used with a step forward, or two *prises de fer* may follow each other to disconcert the opponent.

Any preparation of attack requires a period of fencing time to perform, which is usually distinct from the period or periods of fencing time required for the attack itself. The use of a preparation will usually, therefore, increase the possibility of a successful counter-attack. Thus a correctly executed attack consisting of a straight thrust cannot be nullified by a stop hit. If, however, the straight thrust is preceded by a preparation consisting of a step forward, in order to get within distance for the attack, then the movement is made in two periods of fencing time, and a stop hit can be made in time on the step forward. There are three types of preparations of attack:

(*1*) Attacks on the blade—the beat, the pressure and the graze (*froissement*).

(*2*) *Prises de fer* (taking the blade)—the envelopment, the bind and the *croisé*.

(*3*) The step forward or the step back.

ATTACKS ON THE BLADE

Attacks on the blade are made either to deflect the opponent's blade in order to force an opening for a direct attack, or to induce him to react so as to obtain an opening in another line.

Attacks on the blade, whether based on strength or subtlety, must be made with authority and decision and must be followed immediately by the attack. Their success largely depends on the element of surprise, which momentarily disconcerts the opponent and they should therefore be used judiciously and sparingly during a bout.

(*a*) **The Beat.** A beat is a sharp blow delivered crisply on the opponent's blade. It is made by opening the last three fingers of the sword-hand, which causes the blade to quit contact with the opponent's blade, and then swiftly closing these fingers to make a crisp beat on the opponent's blade.

There are two types of beat, the direct beat and the change beat,

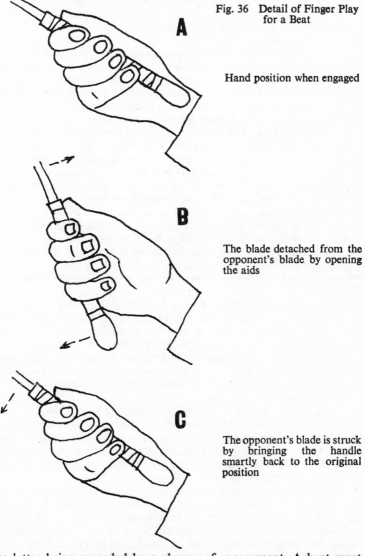

Fig. 36   Detail of Finger Play
for a Beat

A

Hand position when engaged

B

The blade detached from the
opponent's blade by opening
the aids

C

The opponent's blade is struck
by bringing the handle
smartly back to the original
position

the latter being preceded by a change of engagement. A beat must
be made crisply and neatly, by using the fingers only with the least
strength required to obtain the desired object. The arm should not
be extended until after the beat has been made, so as to ensure that
the beat is made with the forte of the blade on the foible of the

opponent's blade. Use of the forearm when making a beat will lead to heavy, wide movements, which the opponent will easily deceive and which will proportionately increase the chances of his making a successful counter-attack.

The strength of the beat is varied according to the object in view. A strong beat is designed to knock the opponent's blade aside and make an opening for a direct attack before he can close the line. A light beat seeks to draw the natural reaction of answering the beat by returning the blade to its original position, when this movement can be deceived with an indirect or compound attack.

(b) **The Pressure.** The pressure displaces the opponent's blade by pressing it aside without detaching the blades. By a pressure, the opponent's blade may be deflected sufficiently to create an opening for a direct attack, or the opponent may be induced to react by returning the pressure, or closing the line, which gives the opportunity to make an indirect or compound attack.

Pressure is applied, preferably at about the centre of the opponent's blade, by closing the last three fingers of the sword-hand and slightly flexing the wrist in the direction of the opponent's blade. It should be applied as a smooth, insinuating movement to give the opponent the impression that possession is being taken of his blade. The degree of pressure will obviously depend on the reaction which it is hoped to produce.

A pressure may be made during or immediately after a change of engagement, but in either case it is a more subtle form of preparation than the beat and has the advantage of enabling the fencer who applies it to feel the reactions of his opponent on the blade.

(c) **The Graze.** The graze or *froissement* displaces the opponent's blade by grazing it with a strong sharp movement, which applies the forte of the attacker's blade diagonally from the foible to about the middle of the defender's blade.

The graze is made by slightly extending the arm, closing the last three fingers of the sword-hand, while flexing the wrist and turning the hand into pronation, so as to apply a sharp, strong graze along the opponent's blade from near the point to about half-way down towards the hilt. The arm should not be fully extended until after the graze is completed.

This stroke must be applied with considerable authority to force the opponent's blade aside, so as to make an opening for a direct thrust before he has the opportunity to cover or deceive the attack.

Considerable practice is required to control and co-ordinate the hand and arm movements when making a graze, and prevent it becoming a slow or wide movement which the opponent can easily deceive.

The graze may be used effectively against an opponent who has momentarily relaxed his guard, or against a heavy-handed fencer who has a stiff arm and blade and does not react to a beat or pressure.

PRISES DE FER (TAKING THE BLADE)

A *prise de fer* is the action used to deflect an opponent's blade which is threatening the target and, while maintaining contact with and authority over it, to launch an attack.

A *prise de fer* cannot be made unless the blades are engaged; indeed, the engagement or the change of engagement are in themselves in some measure *prises de fer*. However, it is best made against an opponent who has, and maintains, a straight arm.

Under the rules governing foil fencing, a fencer who has his arm straight with the point of his weapon threatening his opponent's target has established the right of attack, whether he moves forward or maintains the normal stance on guard. His opponent cannot obtain the right of way for his attack so long as his opponent maintains this position, unless he first removes the threatening blade by an attack on the blade or by a *prise de fer*. The *prise de fer* is the surest way to do this because it maintains contact and authority over the opponent's blade and is less easily deceived than a beat or a pressure or a graze. The *prise de fer* is, however, unlikely to be successful unless the opponent maintains his straight-arm position while the blade is taken.

All *prises de fer* require surprise, exact timing and control of sword-hand and blade if they are to succeed. The type of *prise de fer* used should be varied as much as possible, to make it as difficult as possible for the opponent to counter it.

These strokes may, of course, equally well be used as preparations for a riposte against an opponent who maintains a straight arm after his attack has been parried.

(a) **The Envelopment.** The envelopment is the action of engaging the opponent's threatening blade and, by causing the blades to describe a circular movement while remaining in contact, returning to the original line of engagement.

To obtain the necessary authority over the opponent's blade, it is necessary when making the engagement to apply the forte of the attacker's blade to the foible of the defender's blade, maintaining contact throughout the movement by using the fingers of the sword-hand and causing the blades to describe a circle by rotating the wrist. This circle must be kept small by using the wrist and not the forearm, to minimize the chances of the opponent deceiving the movement. The circle will be away from the target, that is to say, clockwise when in sixte and anti-clockwise when in quarte.

The sword-arm is extended as the circle is completed, to obtain the position of authority on top of the opponent's blade, and the movement is usually finished by a straight thrust made with a lunge or *flèche*.

Indeed, the object of the envelopment is not only to deflect the opponent's threatening blade, but to obtain the position on the top of his blade. As in most movements, the fencer whose blade is on

Fig. 37 The Envelopment

A. Attacker (on left) is parried in sixte and maintains an extended arm
B. Defender, maintaining contact with the attacker's blade, describes a clockwise circle carrying the attacker's blade in the same circle
C. Having thus taken control of the attacker's blade and dominating and deflecting it, the defender completes his riposte over the 'top' of the blade

top is in the stronger position, because he can then best control and exercise authority over his opponent's blade and more easily penetrate his defence.

Although the envelopment can, in theory, be made in any line, in practice it is generally made in sixte because, when attempted in any other line, difficulty is found in maintaining contact with the opponent's blade.

The envelopment should be made as a continuous, smooth, authoritative movement and, when it is correctly timed, it rarely provokes any resistance.

(b) **The Bind.** The bind is the action of engaging the opponent's threatening blade and, by making a half-circular movement with the blades continually in contact, carrying the opponent's blade diagonally from a high to a low line on the opposite side of the target or vice versa. The attack is then made by extending the arm and lunging, while holding the opponent's blade. Thus during a bind the opponent's blade will be carried from, say, sixte to septime or from octave to quarte.

To make a bind from a high line, the foil is pivoted over the opponent's extended blade, so that the forte of the blade is in contact with the foible of the opponent's blade with the point about level with his hips. By a movement of the forearm and wrist, the opponent's blade is then carried into the diagonally opposite line which is then covered. Only then is the arm extended to make the attack with a lunge, while the opponent's blade is firmly held. Accuracy of point is obtained by turning the sword-hand into full supination for the final thrust, which will cause the blade to angulate correctly towards the target.

From an engagement in the low line, the forearm and blade is raised with the point slightly out of line. This is in order to gather and raise the opponent's blade, which is carried across to the opposite high line which is then covered, and the attack completed with an extension of the arm and a lunge.

The bind must, of course, be co-ordinated with the lunge which accompanies the final thrust, to reduce the chance of the opponent freeing his blade to make a stop hit.

The bind has the advantage of being swifter to perform than the envelopment, because only half a circle has to be described by the blade. There is, of course, the danger of the point of the opponent's weapon coming in contact with the body or legs while it is travelling diagonally across the target, particularly when it is moving from a low to a high line. This danger can be largely obviated if care is taken not to extend the sword-arm too soon while this movement is being carried out.

(c) **The Croisé.** The croisé is the action of engaging the opponent's threatening blade in the high line and carrying it to the low line on the same side of the target as the engagement and not diagonally

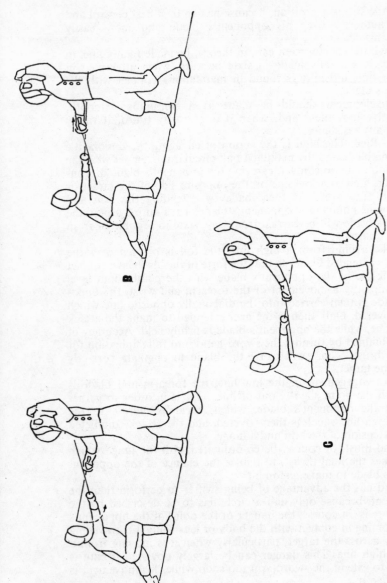

Fig. 38 The Bind

A. The attack (from left) is parried by quarte
B. Defender pivots over the attacker's blade and carries it diagonally across into octave
C. Defender ripostes in the low line, with his legs well bent and his hand in full supination, while maintaining contact with his opponent's blade

across the target as in the bind. It can only be executed from a high to a low line and not vice versa.

Three distinct actions are required to make a *croisé* correctly. First, the foil is pivoted across the opponent's threatening blade, with the forte of the attacker's blade engaging the foible of the defender's blade; second, the attacker bears down on the opponent's blade by lowering the wrist and forearm; finally, the sword-hand is turned into complete supination and the foil is angulated to direct the point towards the opponent's flank, this movement being assisted by slightly bending the legs. The attack is then completed by lunging while holding the opponent's blade.

When correctly timed and welded into a smooth, continuous movement completed by the lunge, the *croisé* should prevent any diagonal movement of the opponent's blade across the target. This is ensured by the bearing down on the opponent's blade in the second stage with the wrist and forearm, and by the correct angulation of the blade prior to the lunge.

(*d*) **Defence Against a *Prise de Fer*.** Defence against a *prise de fer* can be effected by making a parry with opposition against the final movement of the attack, or by using the ceding parry.

The successful defence depends mostly on timing. It is essential to keep the arm straight until the attacker's final movement is made, so as to induce him to complete his *prise de fer* and launch his attack beyond recall. Any premature lack of opposition with the blade by the defender, for example a premature bending of the arm, will be a warning to the attacker and he will be unlikely to complete his attack, or the defender may miss the blade altogether. Once the attacker's movement is in its final stage, that is when the final thrust is made with the lunge or *flèche*, a parry by opposition in the final line will be sufficient to deflect the blade. For example, an envelopment in sixte, followed by a direct thrust, can be parried by returning to guard in sixte covered, with opposition to the straight thrust. A bind from quarte to octave can be parried by opposition in octave, and so on. It is again stressed that the bending of the arm to return to the position to parry must be made at the last possible moment as the attack develops.

The ceding parry, as its name implies, consists in allowing the attacker to take possession of the defender's blade for his *prise de fer*, without offering any opposition while the *prise de fer* is executed. As it is completed, the defender merely bends his arm to form a parry in the appropriate line to which the *prise de fer* has brought his blade. By this action the point of the attacker's foil, as the thrust develops, falls into the forte of the defender's blade and is carried clear of the target.

The ceding parry to quarte is effective against a bind into octave and the ceding parry of tierce, with the hand in pronation and the point high, will deal with a bind into septime.

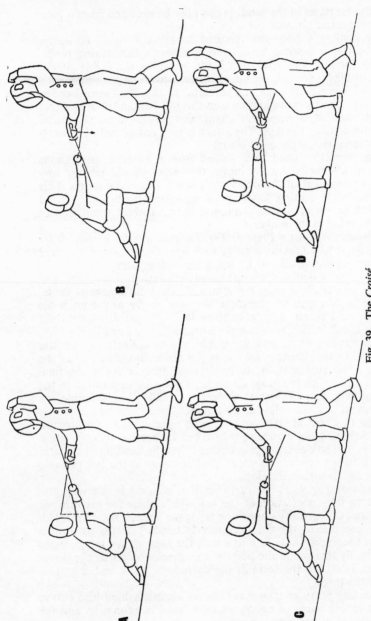

Fig. 39   The *Croisé*

A. The attack (from left) has been parried by quarte
B. Defender (on right) pivots over his opponent's blade
C. Defender bears down on his opponent's blade while angulating his blade towards the target
D. Defender ripostes to flank, bending his legs and turning his hand into supina-

THE STEP FORWARD OR THE STEP BACK

Gaining and breaking ground may be used as a preparation of attack. The step forward is obviously used to obtain the correct distance for attacking and the step back can be used to draw the opponent within distance.

The step forward may precede an attack or may be combined with a feint or a preparation for the attack. To combine it with a blade movement such as a preparation or a feint will add speed to the attack, but the attacker is vulnerable to a stop hit which deceives the blade movement. If, therefore, it is anticipated that the defender may make a stop hit, it is better to step forward prior to making the attacking movements, because the attacker is then in a better position to parry a stop hit than if his blade is already engaged in an offensive action.

Any attack which includes a step forward must be made in more than one period of fencing time and must, therefore, at any rate in theory, be vulnerable to a counter-attack. If the step forward is made with the line of engagement covered, the attacker will be in the best position to deal with a stop hit launched during this movement. In order to shorten the period of vulnerability as much as possible, the blade movements which constitute the attack should be made as the step forward is completed, that is to say as the rear foot reaches the ground, which is the first moment when the attacker is ready to make his lunge.

The *balestra* or jump forward, which is much favoured by the Italian school, is a useful alternative to the step forward and adds speed and surprise to the attack. The *balestra* is often combined with a preparation on the blade and, when made at the correct distance and with perfect balance, can ensure a very fast and penetrating attack.

The step back can be used tactically against an opponent who has formed the habit of retiring whenever any feint or other offensive movement is made, and is therefore very difficult to reach, especially if he is superior in height or length. One or more steps back, varying the length of the step, will often be successful in drawing such an opponent within distance for an attack.

Constant steps forward and back, with a carefully regulated length of step, can conceal a fencer's intentions, and enable him to lodge himself at the ideal distance for an attack, often as the opponent is momentarily off balance.

ATTACKS ON PREPARATION

When a fencer makes a preparation for an attack he is, for a fraction of time, concentrated on attack rather than defence. This is a propitious moment for his opponent to launch an attack.

An attack on preparation is often effective against a fencer who

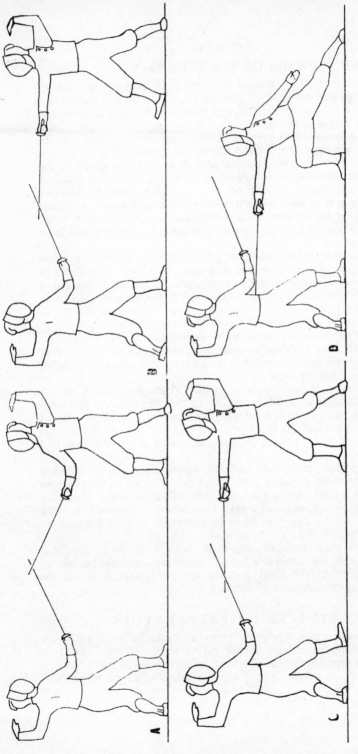

Fig. 40   An Attack Combined with a Step Forward

A. The fencers engaged in sixte
B. Fencer on right makes a feint while stepping forward. His opponent retreats
C. The step forward is completed
D. Fencer on right, having maintained his distance, completes his attack in the low line

maintains a particularly accurate fencing measure and who is difficult to reach because he keeps just out of lunging distance whatever offensive movement is made. The attack can often be made after the opponent has been drawn within distance and induced to prepare an attack by a short step back.

An attack on preparation must not be confused with an attack into an attack. The former is made during the preparation and before the opponent's attack begins, and secures the right of way under the rules governing foil fencing. The attack into the attack will not have this priority, because it is in fact a counter-offensive movement and is subject to the rules governing the stop hit which have already been mentioned.

A very exact choice of distance and careful timing is required if the attack on preparation is not only to obtain priority in time over the opponent's attack, but so to appear to the judges.

DECEPTION AND EVASION

(*Trompement and Dérobement*)

(*a*) **Deception** (*Trompement*). A deception or *trompement* is the action of avoiding the opponent's attempts to parry an offensive movement. Therefore a *trompement* is a deception of the opponent's parry.

All attacks which depend for their scoring on a feint to draw a premature parry that is deceived, are attacks by deception. Deception is similarly used in composed ripostes.

(*b*) **Evasion** (*Dérobement*). An evasion or *dérobement* is the action of evading an opponent's attempt to take the blade, or to make an attack on the blade. It is always made with the arm straight and the point threatening the opponent's target.

When a fencer is on guard with his arm straight and the point of his foil threatening the target he has, by the rules of foil fencing, established the right of attack. His opponent can only gain priority for his attack by deflecting this threatening blade from his target, by means of a beat or other attack on the blade. If the fencer who had his point in line evades his opponent's beat or other attempt to deflect his blade by, say, a disengagement, he has executed a *dérobement* or evasion and has retained his right of attack or priority over any subsequent attacking movement his opponent may make.

The *dérobement* must be made entirely by finger play and without bending the arm, otherwise the right of attack first established will be lost. The essence of the rule mentioned above is that the sword-arm must be straight and the point directed towards the target *before* the opponent attempts to deflect the blade. Many fencers, who imagine that they have executed a perfect *dérobement*, feel much aggrieved when the President gives priority to their opponent's attack. They do not realize that they did not have their arm straight before the opponent started his offensive movement, but merely straightened the arm as they were executing the *dérobement* and therefore *after* the opponent started his attack. They have, in fact, although quite unwittingly, made a stop hit by disengagement which is out of time.

Tactically a *dérobement* may be used against an opponent who makes a habit of attacking with a preparation on the blade. By offering such an opponent a straight and threatening blade, he can be incited to attempt his favourite attack on the blade, which can then be evaded as described above.

The deception and the evasion have one thing in common—there must be no contact with the opponent's blade while they are being executed, if they are to be successful.

THE ELECTRICAL FOIL

Judging is one of the most difficult, and often one of the most unsatisfactory features of competition fencing.

Anyone who has watched, or taken part in, first-class foil fencing will appreciate that the task of the judges is no easy one. Not only is the restricted target often momentarily obscured by the movements of the fencers, but a judge has to see the arrival of any hit on or off the target and recognize at what stage of the phrase it has occurred.

Fencers have long sought for some device which will register hits independently of the human eye. As long ago as 1896 an 'automatic electrical recorder' was demonstrated at Monsieur Bertrand's Academy in London. Various colouring devices were used from time to time, especially at épée, but none proved entirely satisfactory.

In the 1920s a judging apparatus for épée was developed by a French engineer named Laurent, which was improved in Geneva by Monsieur Pagan of the Société d'Escrime de Genève.

The Laurent-Pagan apparatus was demonstrated at the congress of the Fédération Internationale d'Escrime at Geneva in 1931 when two competitions were held, one of which was won by the writer.

This apparatus was adopted by the FIE for official épée competitions in 1933 and was first used in the Championships of Europe at Budapest that year. It was soon universally adopted for all épée competitions.

In 1937 the International Federation embarked on an official scheme for perfecting a judging apparatus for foil and earmarked funds for this purpose. Inventors in many countries interested themselves in this research and a number of machines, some of great complexity, were produced before the Second World War. I remember in 1938 attending a demonstration of a machine which attempted to differentiate between the various movements of a phrase—attack, riposte, counter-riposte, and so on—by a series of coloured lights.

Another rather simpler device caused a coloured light to shine through a plastic *coquille* when a hit was made.

After the war an Italian engineer, Signor Carmina of Milan, perfected an apparatus which merely sought to register the materiality of hits on or off the target. Various invitation tournaments were held to test this machine, including a pool during the 1950 World Championships at Monte Carlo, which was won by René Paul of Great Britain.

In 1954 the International Federation decided, as an experiment, to have all the foil events at the 1955 World Championships and 1956 Olympic Games judged with this apparatus. It was used in England for the first time in a major event at the Ladies' World Team Championships in London in September 1956, when the apparatus was designed by Dr R. Parfitt.

After very considerable and heated argument, the 1957 congress of the International Federation finally adopted this apparatus for all official foil competitions.

The electrical apparatus used for judging foil works on a different principle to the one used at épée. At épée a hit which lands anywhere on the fencer or his equipment is valid; when the spring-loaded point of the weapon is depressed, the electrical circuit is closed and the apparatus registers a hit, on the same principle as is used for an ordinary domestic electric bell. At foil, it is necessary that the apparatus should register a different signal for a hit made on the restricted target than for one made off the target. When a hit is made with the point of the electrical foil, the electrical circuit is interrupted.

The foil target is covered by a metallic over-jacket and hits on this target area are registered by the apparatus by a coloured light. Hits off the target, that is hits which do not arrive on the metallic over-jacket, are registered by a white light. It is not practicable to have the bib of the mask in electrical circuit with the jacket and it has therefore been agreed that hits on the bib are not counted as valid when the electric foil is used, and this has been extended to ordinary foil. The length of the bib is controlled.

Should a hit made off the target be followed by a hit on the target, both a coloured and a white light are shown on the apparatus. A coloured light alone is shown when a hit on the target precedes a hit off the target. The President can therefore know that if both a coloured and a white light show on the apparatus, a non-valid hit has preceded a valid hit. This is the only priority registered by the apparatus, which does not otherwise differentiate between the time of the arrival of hits on either competitor.

The electrical foil apparatus is therefore merely a device for registering the arrival of hits and, whenever both fencers are hit, the President still has to analyse the phrase and award the hit which he considers valid, according to the rules and conventions governing

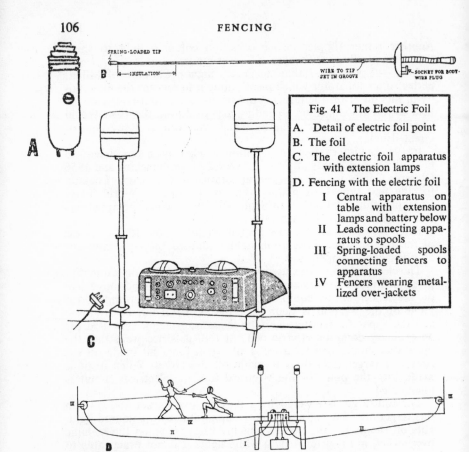

Fig. 41   The Electric Foil

A. Detail of electric foil point
B. The foil
C. The electric foil apparatus with extension lamps
D. Fencing with the electric foil

    I   Central apparatus on table with extension lamps and battery below

    II Leads connecting apparatus to spools

    III Spring-loaded spools connecting fencers to apparatus

    IV Fencers wearing metallized over-jackets

foil fencing. The complexity of these rules makes it unlikely that any apparatus will be able to give a complete judgment of both materiality and validity at foil, as is possible at épée.

Human error of appreciation is still possible, because the President is often called upon to read the fencing phrase—for example, he alone can decide whether a hit registered as valid was the result of an attack or a remise; but the electrical foil apparatus has, at any rate, eliminated the errors of the judges. It replaces completely the human eye as regards the materiality of hits and this alone has brought about a marked improvement in the serenity of international competitions and the justice of their results.

When this apparatus was first used at the 1955 World Championships at Rome, many experienced fencers had severe misgivings about the effect it might have on classic foil play. It was feared that the lack of balance of the electrified weapon would make it impossible for the finer and more complex blade movements to be made, and that the standard of foil fencing would rapidly degenerate, as advantage was given to speed and strength rather than finesse.

Now that the leading foil fencers have accustomed themselves to the use of the electrical weapon, and the foil itself has been improved in weight and balance, these fears have largely disappeared and the electrical foil has been, almost universally, accepted as of great benefit to fencing.

No special alteration in technique is required when using the electrical foil, but considerable practice is advisable before a competition with it, or with a dummy foil weighted in the same way. This is because the electrification of the weapon and the spring-loaded point make the foil rather heavier and alter the balance as compared with a non-electrical foil. A stiffer and less flexible blade should be used with the electrical weapon, to prevent whippiness and ensure penetration of the point.

Accuracy in placing the point is essential with the electric foil. It is often difficult for the human judge to be sure whether a hit has arrived directly with the point or flat, or whether it had sufficient penetration to be counted as good. The electrical apparatus makes no mistakes on this score.

The electrical apparatus registers every hit which arrives. Anyone who watches it in use for the first time is struck by the number of hits that are registered as arriving off the target during a bout, many of which would have been missed or disregarded by human judges. With this apparatus it is therefore necessary to take particular care to cover the line, parry by opposition and lift the hand in the riposte to cover, if the hit achieved is not to be annulled by some chance hit on the arm, head or legs. But this is the fundamental rule of fencing technique—to hit without being hit—which has been too long neglected with the ordinary foil.

With the electrical foil, movements ending in the low lines are

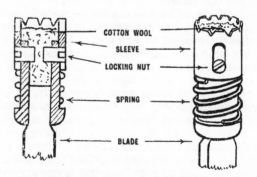

Fig. 42 The Russian Marker-point

particularly effective, because the angle at which the point reaches the target helps to achieve the degree of penetration required for the apparatus to register the hit.

The high cost of the electrical foil, apparatus and equipment is the worst feature of this device. No doubt in time this cost will be considerably reduced; but the extra cost of the metallic over-jacket and other equipment makes it unlikely that, for some time to come, this device will be universally adopted for all foil competitions and matches, as is the case for the electrical épée.

THE RUSSIAN MARKER-POINT

At the 1957 World Championships at Paris the USSR Fencing Federation aroused much interest by demonstrating a new marker-point, invented by the Russian fencer Tchakirzianoff.

This device consists of a hollow, cylindrical, spring-loaded point, which is affixed to the end of an ordinary foil blade. The cylindrical head of this point, which has a serrated front edge and moves like a sleeve over the base of the point, contains a tightly packed wad of cotton wool. This wad can only come in contact with the opponent's clothing when a hit is made which depresses the head fully. It requires a pressure of 500 grammes (as for the electrical foil point) which ensures that flat or too light hits are not registered as good.

Before coming on guard, the fencer impregnates the cotton-wool wad in his point with a mixture consisting of ninety-seven grammes of distilled water, 0·15 grammes of phenolpthalein ($C_{20}H_{14}O_4$) and three grammes of commercial ammonia (NH_4OH).

When a hit is made, a bright red stain appears on the clothing of the fencer who has received it, but this stain completely disappears in about thirty seconds—the time can be varied according to the amount of ammonia added to the mixture. This enables the jury to determine exactly when a hit has arrived. The device does not register on a metallic surface.

With this point the balance of the foil is scarcely disturbed and there is, of course, no particular expense as with the electrical foil. Only one judge is required to watch each fencer and to spot the hits which are visible to competitors, jury and spectators alike. These judges are available to help the President decide at what stage in the phrase a hit arrives, so that validity has not always to be decided by the President alone, as with the electrical foil.

Experiments are continuing to perfect this device. Its disadvantages are that hits on the metallic parts of the mask are not registered, hits do not always mark clearly on very wet clothing and sometimes the liquid impregnating the point evaporates before a hit is made, if the competitors remain overlong inactive during a bout.

If these difficulties can be overcome, this device may well become an important contribution to judging at foil.

III

The Épée

FOIL fencing developed throughout the seventeenth and eighteenth centuries into a complex and conventional art. The limited target and traditional conventions encouraged complicated phrases and a conversation with the blades. It provided a fascinating exercise of subtlety and finesse, which developed co-ordination of mind and body for the delight of its devotees, under the ideal conditions of the *salle d'armes*.

Duelling, however, continued to be prevalent among the *beau monde* which frequented the fencing schools. The courteous exchanges with the foils practised in these schools were of little use as a preparation for more serious encounters with heavier weapons, on greensward or gravel path, at first light, often under dripping trees, and against an opponent whose sole object was to inflict a mortal wound—regardless of the conventions of right of attack.

During the latter half of the nineteenth century, the *épée de combat* was introduced in the schools for those who required preparation for a duel. The weapon used was a regulation duelling sword with a blunted blade, and the comprehensive target and absence of conventions in épée fencing were intended to approximate to the conditions of the *jeu de terrain*. At the end of the century, matches and competitions with the épée initiated competitive fencing as a sport.

The épée was introduced to English fencing in 1900 by Mr Charles Newton Robinson, and the first English team to fence in an international meeting was the épée team which competed for the International Cup at the Palais Royale in Paris on 5 May 1903. Since that time, British fencers have obtained more successes in international competitions with the épée than with either of the other two weapons.

Épée fencing was therefore based on the idea of practice for a duel. In competitions, bouts were usually fought for one hit out of doors and caution and technique were respected, because simultaneous hits counted as a defeat against each competitor. An épée bout cannot, however, be made exactly to resemble a duel, because the wearing of protective clothing and a mask destroys most of the psychological effect of naked steel.

When the writer was a member of the Salle Mangiarotti in the

1920s, training someone for a duel was a common occurrence. The method used was to fence stripped to the waist, without masks and with especially long *pointes d'arrêt*. No one who has had this experience will retain the illusion that normal épée fencing with masks and jackets can be made to resemble a duel.

As competitive fencing developed, the basic conception of approximating épée bouts to the conditions of a duel was progressively abandoned. Bouts were fought for two, three and eventually for five effective hits. The double hit remains some deterrent to rashness, but the double defeat has now disappeared.

The most profound change in the character of épée fencing came about with the general introduction of the electrical judging apparatus in the 1930s. This apparatus was designed to overcome the difficulty of seeing and timing hits with the human eye. No one could foresee that within a few years of its introduction it would radically alter the whole method of épée fencing.

The great advantage of the apparatus was the certainty that all hits, wherever they landed, would be registered. This enabled fencers to practise hits, for example under the hand, which the human judge could not be relied on to see. This soon brought an admirable (and novel) serenity and justice to épée competitions—which had long been sorely needed.

At the same time, the arrival of hits was timed electrically to an agreed fraction of a second for the double hit. With human judges, attacks had to be made with caution to prevent simultaneous hits which, if there was no distinct difference in the time of their arrival, would probably be given as double hits. The apparatus encouraged fencers to endeavour by speed or forceful play to hit *before* they were hit, thus departing from the basic ideal which is to hit *without* being hit, and to take risks which no one would dream of taking in a duel.

There can, unfortunately, be no question that the quality of épée fencing has deteriorated during the last twenty years, and experiments in altering the timing of the apparatus have signally failed to reverse this trend. The fault does not lie entirely with the apparatus, although it has undoubtedly encouraged fencers to try to 'beat the bell' as described above. The desire to make épée fencing less chancy has led to an increase in the number of hits, the abandonment of the double defeat and even to the abandonment of the double hit being tried as an experiment[1]. All this has contributed to modern épée losing its character as a game of caution, courage, tactics and subtlety and has accentuated the tendency for it to become increasingly like foil play, the finer movements of which are not designed to be applied with the heavier weapon and the wider target.

In the writer's opinion it is the approximating of épée rules to those used for foil which has been the main factor in the debasement

---

[1] The double hit and the double defeat have now been restored to the Rules for 'épée'.

of true épée fencing. These changes tend to remove the need for caution (through fear of the stop hit, fear of the surprise attack, fear of the double defeat) on which are based the tactics which made épée the purest form of the art of fence, with the cardinal virtue of 'hitting without being hit'.

Nevertheless, the advantages of electrical judging over the human jury are so marked at épée that it is universally used in all competitive events. It is to be hoped that more attention by masters to the special technique required for true épée will, in time, overcome the mediocrity of modern épée fencing and revive the glories of this weapon.

The fascination of épée fencing lies, for many people, in the fact that it approximates more nearly to a real fight than do the other two more conventional weapons. It gives scope for speed, opportunism and the psychological study of the opponent, to a high degree. Subtlety, bluff and courage are salient features of this game.

THE TARGET AND CONVENTIONS

At épée the target consists of every part of the competitor's body (head, trunk and limbs), his clothing and equipment.

There are no conventions, like priority for the attack, such as are applicable at foil and sabre. If both fencers are hit, the question of priority is only considered when there is an appreciable difference of time between the arrival of the hits. This interval has been fixed at one twenty-fifth of a second. If no such difference of time exists, a hit is scored against each competitor, called a double hit, on the grounds that in a duel both contestants would in such circumstances be wounded or dead!

Since true épée fencing differs greatly from foil play, the question is often debated whether a beginner should learn his fencing with the épée or with the foil, assuming that his build or temperament inclines him to become an épéeist.

Excellent results have been obtained by masters, notably in Italy and France, who teach their pupils from the outset with the épée without reference to the foil. The writer, however, believes that for the average person the best results are obtained if the basic technique of fencing is learned with the foil and this technique adapted to épée or sabre thereafter.

The basic techniques of fencing, such as the stance, footwork, lunge, manipulation of the weapon in attack and defence, sense of time and fencing measure, appreciation of the opponent's intentions and reactions through observation and experiment, and the feeling through contact of the blades (*sentiment du fer*), are common to all three weapons. They must be acquired by every beginner, whichever weapon he eventually chooses.

All basic blade movements can be made with the foil, some of which are not practicable with the épée, while its lightness gives ease of manipulation and helps the beginner to develop finger play, the feel of the blade and blade control.

The rules and conventions applicable to foil teach appreciation of fencing time and phrasing and the closer fencing measure necessitated by the limited target develops reflex actions.

These are the chief reasons why the foil is the best weapon with which to lay the foundation of a sound, basic fencing technique. Once acquired it will stand the fencer in good stead in any branch of fencing art.

Nevertheless, épée requires a highly specialized adaptation of the basic technique. At foil or sabre the conventions enable the fencer to accept a remise, sure in the knowledge that his direct riposte will be awarded priority, even if both hits arrive together. The whole art of épée fencing is based on the principle: 'Hit without being hit'. The épée fencer must develop an exact sense of timing and distance, speed of hand and foot, opportunism and especially accuracy and precision in placing hits on any momentarily exposed part of the wrist or sword-arm, from varying distance and from any angle.

The basic technique of fencing having been described in the previous chapter dealing with the foil, it is not proposed to repeat it in detail in the present chapter. Its adaptation to épée, necessitated by the wider target and absence of conventions, will alone be described below.

HOW TO HOLD THE ÉPÉE

The épée is held and manipulated by the fingers in exactly the same manner as the foil. It is a heavier weapon than the foil and it is particularly important that the hand should be relaxed, by forming the habit of 'carrying' the weapon in the hand, even though it is necessary to grip the handle more strongly with the index finger and thumb than is required with the foil in order to direct the point.

If the hand is not relaxed, the arm and shoulder muscles will also be contracted and wide movements which expose the forearm will result. It is advisable to build up the strength of the fingers and wrist of the sword-hand, particularly if the ordinary French épée is used.

An excellent exercise to strengthen the fingers is to extend the arm fully and open the hand flat, straining the fingers and thumb as far back as possible; hold this position for a few seconds, then relax the hand. Repeat this exercise a number of times, but keep the arm extended all the while. To strengthen the wrist, again extend the arm fully (level with the shoulder), lightly clench the fist with the knuckles upwards and strain the wrist downwards as far as possible; hold this position for two seconds, then strain the wrist upwards as far as possible, again for two seconds. Repeat these movements, keeping

I and II

THE ON-GUARD
POSITION AT FOIL
(illustrated by
Professor R. J. G.
Anderson.
National Fencing Coach
for Great Britain)

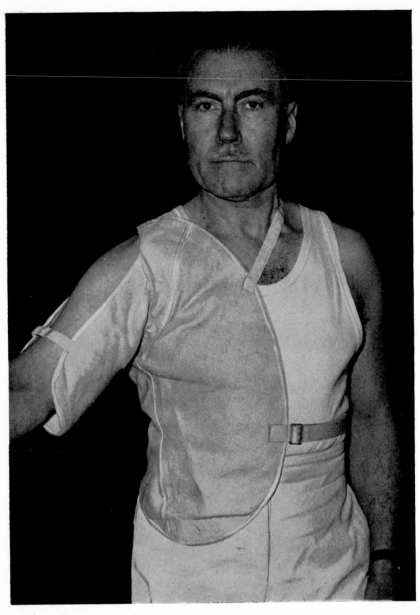

III THE ÉPÉE PLASTRON

IV and V

THE ON-GUARD
POSITION
AT ÉPÉE

VI STOP HIT WITH
RASSEMBLEMENT
(ÉPÉE)

VII USING THE
GUARD TO PARRY
(ÉPÉE)

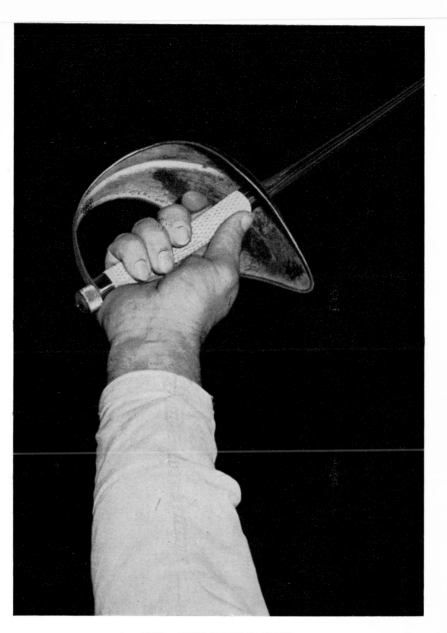

VIII   THE SABRE GRIP

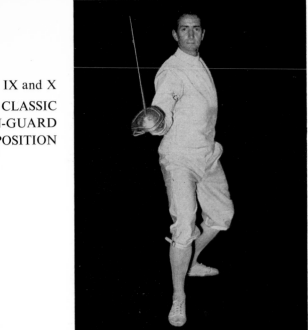

IX and X

SABRE: THE CLASSIC
ITALIAN ON-GUARD
POSITION

XI and XII
SABRE: THE MODERN
HUNGARIAN ON-
GUARD POSITION
(illustrated by
Professor Bela Imregy)

XIII
THE DEFENCE
AT SABRE:
FIRST
TRIANGLE
(front view)

The Fifth
Parry

The Second Parry

The First Parry

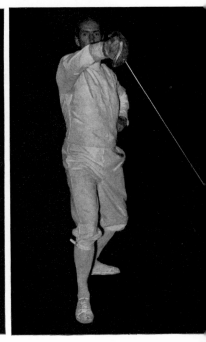

XIV
THE DEFENCE
AT SABRE
SECOND
TRIANGLE
(front view)

The Fifth
Parry

The Third Parry

The Fourth Parry

The Fifth
Parry

The Second Parry   The First Parry

XV

THE DEFENCE AT SABRE:

FIRST TRIANGLE (side view)

The Fifth
Parry

The Third Parry   The Fourth Parry

XVI

THE DEFENCE AT SABRE:
SECOND TRIANGLE (side view)

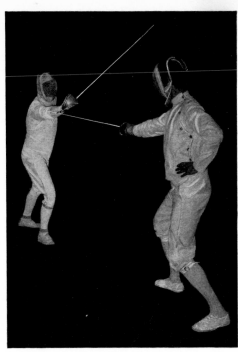

XVII and XVIII
STOP CUT INSIDE
AND OUTSIDE
THE ARM

the arm straight throughout. During both these exercises try consciously to relax the shoulder muscles, and rest as soon as the shoulder and upper-arm muscles begin to contract. Many people who have weak fingers or wrists find that they can control the épée better by using one of the moulded or orthopaedic handles.

With a normal French épée a fencer is permitted by the rules to hold the handle at any point he wishes, provided he does not have a strap, a shaped handle or other device to help him to hold it otherwise than in the orthodox position. This position is with the hand close to the inner surface of the guard, so that the thumb, when fully extended, is less than about three-quarters of an inch from the guard. While with the normal handle the position of the hand can be altered during a bout, in no circumstances may the weapon be 'thrown', that is to say, slipped through the hand during a thrust.

The normal or orthodox position of the hand on the handle is undoubtedly the best, and enables the fencer to exercise maximum control and direction of the weapon in all fencing movements. It is, however, useful to develop strength of the fingers so that it is possible to alter the position of the hand and grip the handle further back, or even by the pommel; this helps to gain length without losing control, so as, for example, to hit the opponent under the hand or on the knee or toe.

Many épéeists achieve considerable success while habitually holding the handle in a variety of unorthodox ways, which suit their particular game. One of the most common is the grip with the forefinger lying flat along the side of the handle, the épée being directed by this finger and manipulated by the thumb and the remaining fingers. The writer practised this method for some years but abandoned it because, while great accuracy is obtained for hits at the wrist, this is no compensation for the limitations imposed on finger play and speed of manipulation in defence.

THE ON-GUARD POSITION

The position on guard at épée is basically the same as at foil, with the following variations (see plates IV and V).

The stance is rather shorter and the body is held more upright and is more effaced; that is, it is placed facing more sideways, so as to present less target to the opponent. The effacing of the target is achieved by holding the rear shoulder further back, but one must be careful not to swing the hips back, or the leading knee and foot will be taken out of line; the knees will be more at right angles, but the effacing of the target must not be exaggerated or it will result in a cramped position. The more upright stance keeps the head, the knee and the leading foot out of range for sudden attacks.

The sword-arm is the most vulnerable part of the épéeist's target, and its position when on guard is therefore of particular importance,

E

so that maximum protection can be obtained from the guard of the épée.

At épée the sword-arm is generally less flexed, when in the on-guard position, than at foil, being half extended with the forearm parallel to the ground. The épée follows the line of the forearm with the point slightly lower than the hilt and directed towards, or just below the opponent's guard.

Normally the épéeist comes on guard in sixte, when the hand is in a half-supinated position, but with the finger-nails turned slightly more upwards than at foil. To cover the arm by the guard, it is essential that the elbow should be tucked well in; this can only be done by *slightly* flexing the wrist outwards.

Some practice is needed before this position, with the point inwards, the wrist outwards and the elbow inwards, becomes a natural, comfortable one. When the épée is held correctly in this way, the opponent should only be able to see the *coquille* and the upper arm, the hand, wrist and forearm being completely hidden from his view behind the guard.

The normal on-guard position at épée is either sixte or octave, or a blade position half-way between these two lines. With the hand in any other line the sword-arm will be more or less exposed. Such positions are therefore rarely adopted except as invitations.

At épée there is little difference of stance or on-guard position between the French and the Italian schools, except that in the latter there is usually a tendency to efface the body in a rather more exaggerated way.

Fig. 43   The Fencing Measure at Épée

THE FENCING MEASURE

The normal fencing measure at épée must be longer than at foil because, the sword-arm being the nearest and therefore the most vulnerable part of the target, the épéeist takes his distance from his opponent's hand instead of from his body. Too close a measure will obviously enable the opponent to lodge his point for a rapid attack at the hand. The épéeist therefore sees that his opponent's point is maintained some way from the guard of his own weapon.

Normally the length of the fencing measure maintained at épée precludes the possibility of the blades being engaged, so that the usual on-guard position is with absence of blade.

The épéeist has a wide target to defend, and his chances of success are much reduced if he allows his opponent to get to close quarters where, at best, there is always the possibility of a double hit if a *mêlée* occurs. Great attention to maintaining a correct fencing measure, which involves an exact judgment of distance, is essential at épée. Variations of the measure by lengthening or shortening the steps forward or backwards are much used as a tactic, to achieve the ideal measure for an attack or to lure a wary opponent into a vulnerable position.

FOOTWORK

Mobility and lightness of footwork are essential for the épéeist. The longer fencing measure normally maintained means that the fencer generally has to advance to get within distance to lodge his attack, while the wide target to be protected requires that he should be able to retire with equal rapidity.

Accuracy in placing the point on the small and usually moving target provided by the forearm necessitates perfect balance during all fencing movements. This can only be achieved by sound footwork.

When lunging, the épéeist usually keeps his body and head more upright than the foilist to avoid hits on the mask. Owing to the possibility of double hits at close quarters, the épéeist rarely risks making parries and ripostes and counter-ripostes while remaining on the lunge. He must be able to recover rapidly from the lunge and, when necessary, to make the spring backwards from that position without loss of balance.

Exercises for developing strength, elasticity and suppleness of the legs and back should be practised. For example, advancing two steps, retiring one step, lunging fully, reprise forward with full lunge, return to guard, retire one step, full lunge and reprise forward three times, ending with a spring backwards from the full-lunge position; these movements are made in rapid succession, with careful attention to balance and correct position of body, legs and feet. Another exercise is to make a full lunge and rock back on the rear foot from the front heel, which remains where it was, return to full lunge and repeat. Standing exercises to develop the thighs and ankles include the following: from the upright position, raise the heels, bend the legs as slowly as possible until fully down on the heels, spring to the upright position as rapidly as possible and repeat a number of times, keeping the heels raised throughout.

Alternate with rapid knee-bends and slow return to the upright position.

The *balestra* is often used in preference to the step forward when attacking to get within distance for the lunge. This has the element of speed and surprise and reduces the period of time during which the attacker is particularly vulnerable to a counter-attack.

The *flèche* is much used at épée to overcome the increased distance usually maintained by the opponent. Timing is, of course, the essence of a successful *flèche* because, if badly executed or made from too great a distance, this movement is easily parried or the attacker is open to a stop hit. The speed and penetration of the *flèche* depends mainly on the length of the initial step, that is on the speed with which the rear leg is swung past the front foot and the distance it lands on the ground in front of this foot. When it is intended to make a *flèche*, the weight of the body should be shifted appreciably

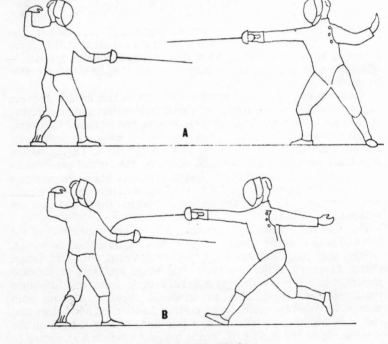

Fig. 44   The *Flèche*

A. The fencers are out of distance to hit with a lunge. Fencer on right extends his arm and commences his *flèche* by a loss of balance forwards
B. The loss of balance causes the rear leg to swing forwards. Note that the hit arrives as the rear leg reaches the ground

on to the front foot just before the movement is commenced. A well timed *flèche* is a most effective movement, but it depends for its success on surprise. It must not, therefore, become an obvious habit, or the opponent will have little difficulty in dealing with it.

The *rassemblement* is a movement of footwork which is peculiar to the épéeist and is especially effective for the tall man. It is made by bringing the front foot back to the rear foot, while straightening the legs and rising to the full height, drawing back the body and leaning as far forward as is possible without losing balance. The *rassemblement* is mostly used when making a riposte or a stop hit and may be made from the lunge or the on-guard position. It ensures maximum length, while removing the legs and body out of reach of the opponent's attack (see plate VI).

Litheness, agility and speed, which are essentials for the successful épéeist, are largely based on his footwork.

THE HIT

At épée the point is fixed on the target by the fingers and penetration is achieved by a smooth extension of the arm, exactly as at foil.

Accuracy and precision in placing the point are more important for the épéeist than for the foilist, because the former often has to hit a moving target, for example the wrist, which may only be exposed for a fraction of a second. The foilist generally scores his hits by extending his sword-arm and weapon in a straight line, because his target is restricted to the body. The primary target for the épéeist is the wrist and forearm of his opponent, because these are the parts of the target nearest to him; also, if he directs his attack or riposte to the body, he must obviously be more vulnerable to his opponent's remise or counter-attack, which may force a double hit. The épéeist must therefore be trained to land a hit on the small target presented by the wrist and forearm and, since his opponent is well aware that these are the most vulnerable parts of his target and is likely to keep them covered, he must be able to land a hit from any angle.

An experienced épéeist, trained to a fine judgment of time and distance, should be able to hit an opponent's wrist, even when the latter is correctly on guard covered, by angulating his wrist and blade at the last possible moment from lunging distance. It is similarly an advantage to angulate the hit when making a riposte.

Considerable practice is necessary to attain accuracy of point when angulating a hit. For example, an opponent who is covered in sixte can be hit under the hand by lunging directly, with the arm straight, towards the lower edge of the *coquille*, turning the sword-hand into full pronation at the moment the attacker's point is passing the edge of the *coquille* and slightly angulating the wrist.

Angulated hits are, of course, always vulnerable to a stop hit if

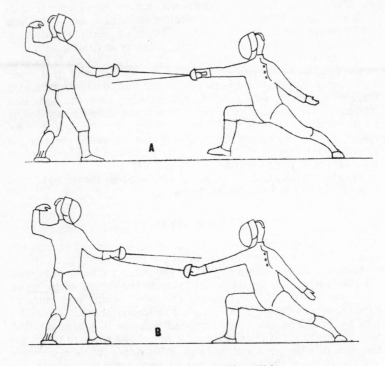

Fig. 45   The Angulated Hit at Wrist

A. Fencer on right thrusts towards the under side of wrist. His opponent knows
     that he is covered by his *coquille*
B. As his point passes the rim of his opponent's *coquille*, the fencer on right
     angulates his hit at wrist merely by turning his hand into full pronation,
     which raises his point

the opponent merely leaves his point in line. For this reason it is
generally necessary to induce the opponent to move his point, by
making the angulated hit at the wrist at the last possible moment in
an indirect or compound attack. When using an ordinary French-
type épée, it is often advantageous to shift the position of the sword-
hand towards the pommel before commencing such movements, in
order to gain the few inches necessary to avoid impaling one's wrist
on the opponent's point.

Useful practice can be obtained for developing accuracy of point
by hanging a tennis ball by a string or piece of elastic, so that it is
about four feet from the ground; hits are made on the ball, while it
is in motion, from various distances and angles.

ATTACKS

The unlimited épée target would seem to afford a wider scope for attacks than that offered by the limited target at foil. This is largely discounted by the constant danger of a counter-attack or stop hit.

The absence of conventions at épée imposes no obligation on the defender, as at foil, to parry; he can take every opportunity to make a stop or time hit even on a simple attack or a direct riposte. The classic on-guard position at épée is with the point always threatening the opponent's forearm, and those fencers who habitually adopt some less orthodox position are always liable to place the point in line at any offensive attacking movement made by their opponents. If, therefore, attacks are launched without preparation, from too great a distance, uncovered or preceded by a number of feints, they will probably be stopped even unintentionally when, at best, they will result in a double hit.

It is generally unwise to employ any wide movement such as the cut-over or a number of feints during an attack, because of the exposure of the forearm which results. The more complicated an attack becomes, the greater the risk of impaling oneself on the opponent's point which may have been extended, quite unintentionally, in the natural desire to ward off the attacker's blade.

Against the complete and orthodox fencer it is necessary, as at all weapons, for the épéeist to study the form of defence his opponent is likely to adopt. Against the unorthodox épéeist other tactics must be added to this anticipation of the defence, some of which are dealt with later on. In all cases the cardinal rule is to keep the form of the attack as simple as possible and employ the least number of feints in any compound attack to achieve one's aim.

At épée attacks and ripostes tend to be concentrated at the nearest part of the opponent's target—the wrist and forearm. Indeed, the épéeist should train himself to regard the target as not going further than the opponent's elbow, the upper arm as an extension of this target and the opponent's body as something to be hit in exceptional cases, when at close quarters. This does not, of course, preclude hits at the mask, knee or foot, but these are rarely performed safely unless made with a preparation on the blade.

Every feint, indeed, every movement which takes the épée out of line, involves the risk of a momentary exposure of the hand or forearm to a stop hit. All attacking movements must therefore be made as small as possible, that is with the least deviation of the blade necessary to induce the opponent to react. Caution demands that attacks should, whenever possible, be completed covered.

Épée fencing is *par excellence* a game of timing, tactics and bluff. Two of the most effective means to this end are:

(a) The attack from immobility.
(b) The variation of cadence.

(*a*) **The Simple Attack from Immobility.** This will often surprise the opponent, especially after a series of false attacks and feints have been executed, so that the defender is subconsciously expecting a preparation or more complex movement and fails to react in time to the swift and unannounced simple movement.

(*b*) **The Variation of Rhythm or Cadence.** Made prior to, or during an attack, this may achieve the same element of surprise. For example, a series of judiciously slowed-down feints to the arm and slow gaining and breaking ground may be used, as the French say, to 'put the opponent to sleep'. A final simple movement which suddenly erupts at highest speed will often take him unawares. Again, some rapid feints followed by a deliberately slowed-down or broken-time final movement will often disconcert a vigilant opponent.

By deliberate feints in a certain line, it is often possible to induce the opponent gradually to raise or lower his sword-arm or displace his on-guard position, to create an opening for the real attack. Similarly, a number of feints in the high lines can pave the way for a sudden disengagement to the knee.

Many épéeists are very successful with simple, unprepared shots at the hand, the foot or the mask and, when these shots are brought off successfully, they are certainly very disconcerting to even the most experienced opponent. For success they depend not merely on accuracy of point, but more particularly on a perfect choice of time and distance. Unless used very sparingly they are bound to encounter the intentional or unintentional stop hit.

Some fencers, especially foilists, form the habit of withdrawing the sword-hand when a hit is directed towards it. Such fencers are particularly vulnerable to an immediate renewal of the attack by *flèche*.

Attacks which are suddenly switched to the low lines can often catch the opponent unawares. They must, however, be used sparingly, because if they lose the element of surprise they will be very likely to be met with a stop hit.

For safety reasons épéeists mostly confine their defensive movements to variations on the parries of sixte and octave. While this often simplifies the task of anticipating their reactions, the possibility of their introducing a stop hit at any stage must constantly be borne in mind. A feint under the arm followed by a hit at the upper arm and vice versa are paying strokes, varied by a feint under the arm followed by a hit inside the wrist.

The wide measure usually maintained at épée generally requires attacks to be combined with a step forward, *balestra* or *flèche*. Indeed, the épéeist is constantly trying to impose his measure on his opponent, either to lodge himself at the ideal distance for an attack, or to prevent his opponent doing so.

Preparations on the blade and *prises de fer* are much used to reduce the fencing-time factor, which favours the stop hit when getting within distance for an attack. Conversely, attacks on preparation are particularly effective at épée. These will be studied later.

The invitations are widely practised at épée especially for counter-time movements. They are unlikely to draw the desired reaction unless they are so made as to appear unintentional to the opponent.

Whether an attack is made fast or slowly, with strength or subtlety, it is particularly important at épée to keep the arm straight and on no account to bend or withdraw it during the movements which constitute the attack, or the renewal of the attack, counter-riposte or stop hit on the riposte which so often follow the attack at this weapon.

COUNTER-ATTACKS

The stop hit or time hit and the counter-time or second-intention attack are among the most prevalent and useful strokes in the épéeist's repertoire.

STOP AND TIME HITS

Almost any offensive blade movement must expose some part of the fencer's wrist or sword-arm. Indeed, in the old days of one-hit épée, it was said that the best tactical approach was 'to remain on guard well covered in sixte with the point in line and wait for the other fool to make a mistake'. The author would certainly not subscribe to this negative approach, especially under modern conditions, but it remains true that the épéeist must train himself to be constantly prepared to make a stop hit during the course of any movement of a phrase. The successful introduction of a stop hit not only enables many valuable hits to be scored, but has a devastating moral effect on a forceful and confident opponent.

The chance to place a stop hit at the wrist, forearm or shoulder where, as a general rule, such counter-attacks must be concentrated for safety, is likely to be momentary. It is therefore essential that the épéeist should develop opportunism and train himself to place his stop hits with speed and accuracy and from a variety of angles.

Even when a stop hit is correctly placed in time, there is often the danger of a forceful opponent forcing his attack home through the bend of his opponent's blade, within the twenty-fifth of a second allowed by the electrical apparatus, to make a double hit. The placing of the stop hit must be done entirely with the fingers, displacing the hand as little as possible, so as to cover the line with the *coquille*, or it must be made with pronounced angulation of the wrist. Accuracy, timing and judgment of distance are obviously of primary importance, especially in the latter case, and can only be achieved by constant practice.

The *rassemblement* is particularly useful when stop-hitting, especially when it is used against an opponent who attacks in the low line or who drops his hand or falls forward during his lunge.

A superior sense of distance will often enable an experienced épéeist to score premeditated stop hits against a less well trained opponent. By variation of the length of steps forward and backwards on the *piste* the opponent can be induced to launch an attack slightly out of distance; the stop hit is placed at the last possible moment, when the attacker is fully extended at the completion of his movement, which becomes short by reason of the defender's well judged step back or *rassemblement*.

Obviously the ideal to be aimed at when making a stop hit is either to stop or definitely halt the attack, or cause the attack to miss. The safest form of counter-attack is therefore a time hit, which is in fact a stop hit made while covering the line in which the attack is being made, usually by deflecting the opponent's blade with the *coquille* as the stop hit lands.

A very effective time hit is one made with a *croisé*, which gives complete control of the attacker's blade until the movement is finished. The most common is perhaps the *croisé* of octave against an attack ending in quarte.

Both the stop hit and the time hit are often made as opportunist strokes. Since, as already mentioned, they depend so much on accuracy of timing and measure, they are most likely to be effective and avoid the double hit if they are premeditated movements, based on observation of the opponent's weaknesses and habits.

One of the greatest artists with the stop hit was the Italian champion, Gian-Carlo Cornaggia-Medici, who won the Olympic épée title in 1932. He had a natural judgment of distance which was uncanny, and he used to allow his opponent's point to come within a few inches of his chest, even in the course of a full-speed *flèche* attack, before placing his renowned angulated stop hit inside the wrist.

So accurately did he time this movement that when, during the final of the épée individual title match at the 1936 Olympic Games, he was hit twice in succession in a bout while carrying out this manoeuvre, he stopped, removed his mask and asked the President to have his opponent's épée measured—it was in fact found to exceed the regulation length by a few centimetres.

COUNTER-TIME

The counter-time or second-intention attack is the natural answer to the épéeist's predilection for the stop hit. It is the penalty awaiting the fencer who forms the habit of making stop hits on his opponent's every move, generally as an opportunist rather than a premeditated stroke.

The second-intention attack depends on drawing the opponent's stop hit so that it can be parried and the movement completed either by a riposte or by some form of attack. The invitation used to draw

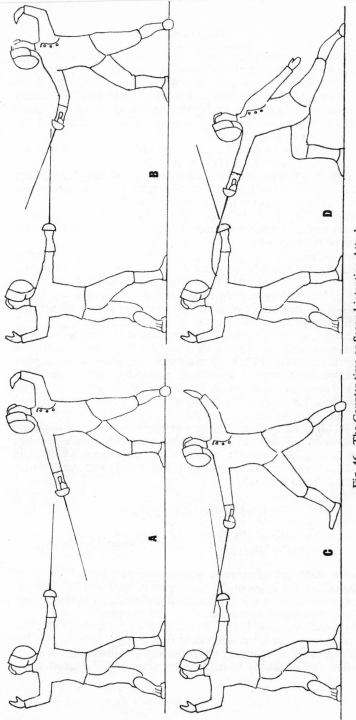

Fig. 46   The Counter-time or Second-intention Attack

A. Fencer on right feints low to draw a stop hit
B. Fencer on right parries the stop hit by sixte
C. Fencer on right begins his straight thrust
D. Fencer on right completes his second-intention attack at arm covered

the opponent's counter-attack must, of course, be made convincingly; that means it must give sufficient opening to induce the opponent to attempt a stop hit, but not be so obvious as to warn him of the intended sequel. After the stop hit has been drawn and successfully parried, it is important to make the riposte or other movement covered or with a *prise de fer*, in order to avoid a double hit if the opponent stays in line.

The wide target at épée increases the variety of the invitations which may be made to draw the stop hit. For example, an invitation may be made when engaged in sixte by merely relaxing the covered position to expose the forearm, or by a pressure in quarte which invites a disengagement, or by a feint at the foot followed by an immediate *flèche*, taking the opponent's blade in sixte as he attempts a stop hit in the exposed high lines. Invitations can include the step forward or the step back.

Counter-time is of the essence of the tactical art of épée fencing. Épéeists usually maintain a greater distance from each other during a bout than foilists and often fence with absence of blade. Counter-time is the surest way to draw the opponent's blade into a position in which it can be dominated, in such a way as to score a hit without oneself being hit.

Épée is a game of wits and, if counter-time is the best way to deal with an opponent who habitually stop-hits, this may be carried a step further by tactical bluff. Thus a number of attempts to stop-hit on an opponent's feints or invitations may induce him to decide to make a second-intention attack. On his invitation, a feint of a stop hit will draw his parry and riposte, when the tables can be turned by making a counter-riposte after parrying his riposte by opposition, or by a ceding parry if his riposte was made with a *prise de fer*.

Needless to say, a series of movements of this nature requires perfect timing and forms a carefully devised phrase which it is difficult to conclude satisfactorily—but it brings one tremendous satisfaction when successful.

RENEWED ATTACKS

The renewal of attacks by remise, redoublement or reprise is as characteristic of épée fencing as is the use of the stop hit and counter-time.

The constant use of renewed attacks provides one of the most striking differences between the techniques of épée and foil fencing. It illustrates, of course, a fundamental difference in that the conventions which apply to the foil are absent at épée.

The immediate renewal of the attack at épée by remise or redoublement is, in some measure, equivalent to making a stop or time hit on the riposte. For example, when fencing a foilist with the épée, one often finds that he is inclined to withdraw the hand when attacked forcefully or to bend the arm before riposting, rather than keep the arm extended and retire if more room is required for the parry or riposte. Against such an opponent the obvious tactic is to make a false attack, followed by an immediate remise or redoublement at the hand or shoulder.

Against an opponent who keeps his hand high when taking a parry, an immediate redoublement by disengagement to the under side or inside of the hand, with strong angulation of the blade, is often very successful. The reprise forward is often the only way to reach an opponent who has the habit of retiring whenever any offensive movement is made.

At épée the remise or redoublement can equally be used following a riposte. Indeed, the épéeist should be prepared to make a remise or redoublement if the opportunity presents itself during any of his offensive or counter-offensive actions.

During any renewed attack, the fencer concerned is always vulnerable to a double hit. Renewed attacks should therefore be made covered whenever possible; this can be effected by slight flexing of the wrist of the sword-arm, in order to oppose the guard to the opponent's blade. Indeed, at épée, covering the line should normally be done by using the *coquille*, rather than the blade as is usual with the foil.

An épéeist, ever mindful of the stop hit or double hit, is trained to make his ripostes covered or with a *prise de fer*. If his opponent makes a redoublement by disengagement whenever he feels a contact of blades, he will be disconcerted and the riposte is likely to be slowed up, since the fencer finds himself presented with an evasive and threatening point which he will have considerable difficulty in controlling.

The remise or redoublement will naturally be most effective when it is applied as a premeditated stroke. Considerable practice is required to obtain the necessary accuracy and timing, especially when making the renewed attack by angulation to the wrist, or from a high line to the knee when it is not possible to ensure the avoidance of the double hit by covering the line.

The remise and redoublement should be practised on the lunge, while recovering from the lunge, or with a *rassemblement*. They should be concentrated, as far as possible, at the wrist or forearm and should be made from all angles. Against an opponent who maintains a wide measure by retiring judiciously when attacked, the remise or redoublement with a *flèche* can be an effective alternative to the reprise forward. In this case the weight of the body should be shifted on to the leading leg as the original attack or feint is made, so that the renewed attack can be launched immediately with the *flèche* and, of course, without withdrawing the arm.

The épéeist, while using the renewed attack whenever possible, must guard against this becoming an automatic or habitual stroke.

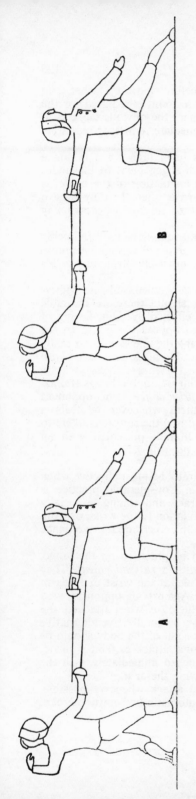
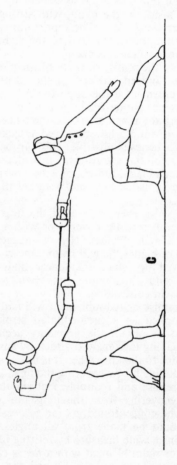

Fig. 47 The Remise

A. Fencer on right attacks at top of wrist and his opponent parries with his *coquille*. As the attacker has premeditated his remise he has lunged short
B. Fencer on left lowers his hand to riposte under his opponent's hand
C. Attacker makes his remise to forearm with full lunge, covering with his *coquille*

The essential tactical approach against such a fencer is to prevent him imposing his strokes. This can be achieved by parrying several times until one feels, through contact of the blades, that he has completed his movements (when he will probably be vulnerable to the riposte) or he can be harassed by constant changing of the line or by a *prise de fer* after the parry, until possession of his blade can be obtained. In this way the precision and accuracy of the renewed attacks can be impaired.

DEFENCE

All the parries described for the foil can be used at épée. In practice, however, those parries which expose the forearm to a remise or stop hit, that is those which take the weapon out of line, are rarely safe except at close quarters.

Sixte and octave, since they deflect the attacking blade outside the sword-arm, are the safest and most commonly used, either as simple, counter- or semicircular parries.

In lessons, parries other than sixte and octave should, of course, be practised. There will be occasions when they will be required. For example, against a forceful or a *flèche* attack, quarte and seconde are often the most appropriate parries to use, and we have already seen that the ceding parry to quarte is often the best answer to a *prise de fer* in the low line.

At épée, cardinal virtues are keeping the point in line and making movements covered whenever possible. Parries with the épée are therefore made with the blade much more in line than at foil, so as to avoid exposing the sword-arm to the renewed attack and cut to a minimum the time factor between the parry and the riposte.

Against an opponent who makes wide movements, it may be necessary to raise the point when forming a parry, in order to gather the blade; but as a general rule, parries at épée are made much 'flatter' than at foil, that is with the blade as much in line as possible and using the *coquille* to assist the blade in deflecting the attacker's point.

For the same reason, parries at épée should normally be made with opposition. Parries by detachment incur the risk of a remise turning the riposte into a double hit.

The épéeist should use his *coquille* with opposition to parry thrusts made at his wrist or forearm. This is done by flexing the wrist or slightly displacing the forearm in the required direction the least possible amount needed to deflect the opponent's point. The guard of the épée of an experienced fencer is usually closely pock-marked, where he has caught the *pointe d'arrêt* as he 'blocked' hits directed at his sword-hand with his *coquille*. The épéeist may be as proud of these marks as of the lack of tears on the gauntlet of the glove he is constantly using (see Plate VII).

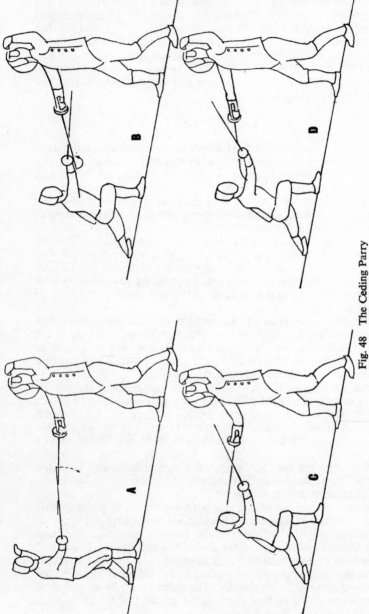

Fig. 48   The Ceding Parry

A. Fencer on left begins a *prise de fer*
B. Fencer on right offers no resistance as his opponent takes his blade, but allows his blade to be rotated
C. Merely by bending his arm and raising his point as the rotation of his blade is completed, the fencer on right has formed a parry in quarte
D. Fencer on right ripostes with opposition in quarte

At épée the arm should be withdrawn as rarely as possible when parrying; parries should be taken with the arm half extended. To lift or bend the arm, as at foil, will expose the forearm and encourage the opponent to make a premeditated remise or a *flèche*. It is often necessary to step back when parrying, in order to maintain the safe distance so essential at épée and have room to parry effectively against a forceful attack.

The ceding parry is the épéeist's most effective answer to a *prise de fer*, but it requires considerable practice to achieve the correct timing without which it is useless. The difficulty arises from the necessity of allowing the attacker to take possession of the blade to launch his attack, without the defender offering opposition or withdrawing his arm until the attack is in full flight. At that moment only the defender comes back to the on-guard position, in the appropriate line covered. When making the ceding parry, it is necessary to bend the arm and raise the point higher than is usual in an épée parry, so that the attacker's blade falls into the forte of the defender's weapon as it is deflected off the target. When correctly executed, the ceding parry requires no opposition by the defender until the covered position is reached; indeed, he has the feeling that it is the attacker who is carrying his blade into the position of the parry, and that he is merely bending his arm to assist in this movement.

Since, for the reasons already given, the épéeist restricts his parries mostly to sixte and octave, the use of successive parries is more limited at épée than at foil. The épéeist must, however, be careful not to form the habit of always taking the same parry, as this will obviously soon be noted and turned to advantage by his opponents in choosing their form of attack. One sees, for example, fencers who continually take counter of sixte even when they are on guard out of distance, or others who take counter of sixte-octave with monotonous regularity.

Even when relying on sixte and octave as the main parries, a fencer should alternate these as simple or counter-parries to make the anticipation of his reactions as difficult as possible for his opponent. For example, by taking counter of sixte-octave the defender is reversing the circle in which his blade is moving and it will require much better blade control by the attacker to deceive these movements than to deceive, say, two counter-sixte parries, as in the latter case the defender's blade is always moving in the same direction.

Finger play is the essence of making alternate parries. The fingers alone should control the blade. The blade movements should be as small as is compatible with gathering the opponent's blade successfully, and the point should be taken out of line as little as possible, while using the *coquille* to cover the line in conjunction with the blade.

THE RIPOSTE

Just as it is essential at épée to use the parry by opposition to prevent the opponent scoring a double hit with a remise, so it is of equal importance to make ripostes covered. The opponent at épée is under no obligation to parry a riposte, as at foil, and, if his blade is quitted after a parry, he will instinctively renew his attack.

The parry at épée being formed in such a way as to take the sword-point as little out of line as possible (relying on the *coquille* and the greater strength of the triangular épée blade to deflect the attacker's blade), the defender finds his blade, after a successful parry, in the best position for an immediate riposte to the forearm or shoulder.

The ideal to be aimed at in épée is to weld parry and riposte as closely as possible together. At best it becomes, of course, a time hit.

Maintaining contact with the opponent's blade, that is riposting along the blade, is particularly important when riposting from quarte or septime. If his blade is released when in these lines, the opponent will most probably, and even unintentionally, score with a remise or a stop hit and a double hit is the likely result.

From the parry of quarte, the riposte by *croisé* is probably the safest, because it enables the defender to maintain complete domination of the attacker's blade until the riposte has landed. It is particularly effective against a left-hander.

The parry of septime with angulation of the point to the opponent's flank, while maintaining strong opposition to his blade with the *coquille*, is effective against a *flèche* attack in quarte, especially when combined with the *rassemblement* or the *in quartata*.

While the riposte covered should be cultivated as a habit by the épéeist, he must not neglect the riposte to the under side or the inside of the wrist. These ripostes cannot be made covered but should be made with marked angulation. While particularly effective against an opponent who bends or withdraws his arm after his attack has failed, or raises his hand or takes it out of line while keeping his arm straight, these ripostes must obviously be perfectly timed if they are not to result in a double hit.

Counter-ripostes at épée rarely continue beyond the first or occasionally the second, because of the difficulty of maintaining opposition to the opponent's blade during a series of such movements.

The riposte can with advantage often be combined with a *prise de fer*. The riposte by *croisé* from quarte has already been mentioned. Another example is the lifted riposte from septime. After the parry of septime, the attacker's blade is lifted strongly by a circular motion of the defender's wrist, the riposte being made over, and while maintaining continual contact with the blade. This preparation is most effective when combined with a step forward, so that the opponent's point is cleared past the body before the riposte is made.

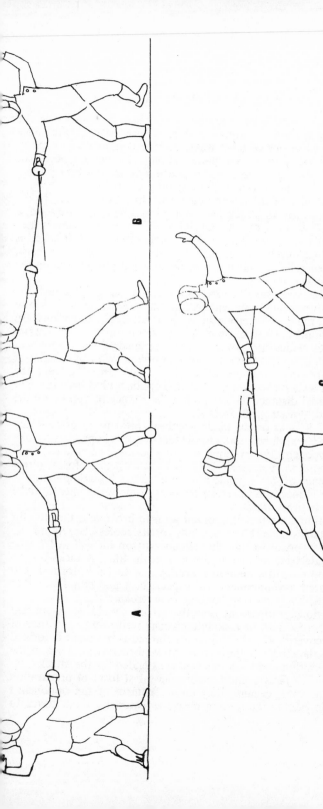

Fig. 49 *In Quartata* with a *Croisé*

A. The fencers on guard with absence of blade
B. Fencer on left begins his attack. Fencer on right begins to take his body out
    of line by pivoting in an anti-clockwise direction, while making a time hit
    with a *croisé*
C. The movement completed

PREPARATIONS OF ATTACK

Preparations of attack by variation of distance, by attacks on the blade and by *prises de fer* are much used at épée. Attacks often have to be prepared in one of these ways, or by a combination of them, because of the wide measure usually maintained between fencers, the large target area and the need to guard against the ever-present danger of a stop hit in response to any form of attack.

The shortening of the fencing measure which is necessary to get within distance for an attack may be achieved by a step forward, a *balestra*, a *flèche* or a reprise. During such movements, unless they are combined with another form of preparation, the attacker is vulnerable to a stop hit before or as his attack develops. The épéeist, therefore, generally combines his advance with a preparation on the blade or a *prise de fer*.

The step back can also be used as a preparation for an attack. Its object is to draw the opponent within distance for the attack and by a tactical move to deceive him as to the attacker's intentions. An aggressive opponent can often be drawn within distance by a series of steps back which are progressively shortened; a wary opponent can sometimes be manoeuvred into the same position by a series of steps forward and backward of varying length. In either case the attack must be launched immediately the opponent has been brought to the required distance, before he has the chance to appreciate the position and himself profit from it.

As at foil, attacks on the blade—by beat, pressure or graze—may be varied in strength according to the reaction it is hoped to provoke from the opponent. For example, a strong beat will be used to knock the defender's weapon aside and make an opening for a direct thrust by lunge or *flèche*, while a more insidious beat or pressure is designed to induce him to return the beat or close the line, to make way for an indirect attack.

The reaction the attacker does *not* want to provoke is the stop hit and the attack on the blade depends for its success largely on the element of surprise, so that the defender's stop hit will at least be sufficiently delayed for the attack to land in time. Attacks on the blade should therefore be used sparingly and varied in form. If too often repeated, the opponent will expect them and stop-hit, rather than react with a parry or other defensive stroke.

It is obviously important that the attack should be completed with the line covered, or a double hit may well result. Accuracy of point and covering the line will be facilitated if the habit is formed of keeping the elbow of the sword-arm well tucked in, when in the on-guard position and while the arm is extended for the attack.

The *prises de fer* are undoubtedly the safest form of preparation of attack at épée, because they ensure control of the opponent's blade while gaining the fencing measure required for the attack to land. When correctly executed, they greatly reduce the possibility of a successful counter-attack.

A *prise de fer* can profitably be combined with the step forward, the *flèche* or other means of shortening the measure. They must be made with authority and accurately timed, in order to dominate the opponent's blade throughout the attack and disconcert him. Care must, of course, be taken to avoid drawing the opponent's point on to the target during a *prise de fer*, thus causing a double hit.

The envelopment and the bind are the *prises de fer* most commonly used as preparations for attacks at the upper arm or body; the *croisé* is generally used as a preparation for a riposte.

An épéeist who has a good sense of distance can often deceive attempts to take his blade by a series of *dérobements* when, if the point has been kept in line, a stop hit can be scored if the attacker continues his attack without having found the blade.

Against an opponent who evades attempts to take his blade in this way, two or more *prises de fer* in rapid succession and, when possible, in opposite directions will often enable the opponent's blade to be found and controlled before the final movement of the attack is launched.

Attacks on the blade can often be resisted by strong opposition which 'blocks' the beat or pressure; if the point is kept in line, a stop hit can be registered on the opponent's forearm or shoulder.

As already mentioned, a most effective counter to the *prise de fer* is the ceding parry. A *prise de fer* cannot be made effectively unless the opponent maintains an extended arm; therefore such an extension can be used as an invitation to draw a *prise de fer*, which is then resisted by a parry by opposition, or by returning to guard covered with the ceding parry.

Finally, a valuable tactical movement, which is facilitated at épée by the wide measure, is to attack the opponent on his preparation of attack. Such an attack should be launched on the inception of the preparation, when the opponent is particularly vulnerable; the point should be kept in line and care taken to cover to avoid a double hit or, if distance allows, to angulate hits made at the wrist.

THE ELECTRICAL ÉPÉE

All épée competitions and matches are judged with the electrical judging apparatus. This device entirely replaces human judges, because it records not only the materiality of hits but their validity, that is to say the priority between hits on both competitors.

The apparatus is so constructed that if each competitor makes a hit on his opponent and these hits arrive within one twenty-fifth of a second of each other, a double hit is scored and a signal light appears on both sides of the apparatus. If, however, one hit arrives one twenty-fifth of a second or more before the other, only the first hit is signalled and the later hit is nullified by a relay in the apparatus. Hits which arrive on the *coquille* or on the insulated *piste* do not cause the apparatus to function.

Épée is fenced on a *piste* fourteen metres long, but when a competitor has retired with both feet over the rear limit of the *piste*, he is replaced on guard again with his rear foot on the warning line which is two metres from the rear limit. A hit is scored against him if he again retires over the rear limit with both feet. In practice, therefore, an épée bout is fenced on a *piste* of total length of eighteen metres (59ft 11ins). It would be impracticable to use one *piste* eighteen metres long because the spring loaded spools, which are placed at the ends of the *piste* to pay out and take up the wire attaching each competitor to the apparatus, cannot carry such a length of wire. For convenience, the standard *piste* is always fourteen metres long and about two metres wide. At épée and sabre it is used as stated above while at foil it is only used once. It will be noted that the warning line for épée and sabre is two metres from the rear limit of the *piste* while at foil this line is one metre from that limit.

In a bout judged with the electrical épée, the President merely starts and stops the bout and sees that certain rules are observed, for example, those governing crossing the limits of the *piste, corps à corps*, and testing the apparatus and equipment. He is not concerned with judging either materiality or validity of hits. He can never award a hit which is not registered by the apparatus (except as a penalty for infringement of the rules) but, under certain circumstances, he can annul a hit which has been registered.

It should not, however, be thought that the rôle of President in an electrical épée bout is a sinecure. An inattentive President or one who is not conversant with the rules can do much to spoil the correct running of a bout and even falsify the result.

For electrical épées it is as well to choose somewhat rigid blades, with sufficient spring to maintain their direction after being bent. Soft blades which remain in any position into which they are bent, or too whippy blades, detract from accuracy when placing the point.

A rigid blade will enable a stop hit in fact to stop the opponent's attack from landing. With a soft blade there is the danger that a forceful attacker, correctly stopped on the hand, may yet force his point on to his opponent through the bend of the latter's blade, thus turning a legitimate stop hit into a double hit.

In order to get sufficient rigidity and the balance necessary to compensate for the extra weight of the electrical point, rather heavier blades must be used at electrical than at ordinary épée. Excessively heavy blades must, however, be avoided or wide, slow

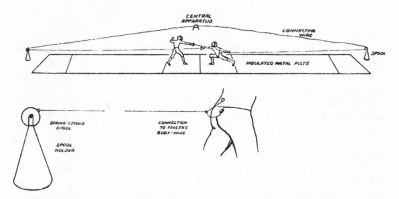

Fig. 50   The Épée Piste and Electrical Judging Apparatus

blade movements and a tired hand will result.

Before a competition it is desirable for a competitor to have some practice with the electrical apparatus. It is wise always to have the ordinary épées one uses for lessons and loose play in the *salle* weighted and balanced approximately the same amount as one's electrical épées.

The personal equipment of a fencer consists of his electrical épée and his body-wire. He is responsible for the correct plugging of his body-wire not only to his épée, but to the wire at his back which connects him, through the spool at the end of the *piste*, to the apparatus. If, during a bout, a fencer is placed at a disadvantage owing to the unplugging of his body-wire at either end, he cannot claim the annulment of a hit scored against him because his body-wire has become unplugged from his épée. He can only claim such annulment for the unplugging of his body-wire at his back if the plug situated there is not fitted with a safety device. Normally, before a bout begins, a fencer is plugged on to the apparatus at his back by an official appointed for the purpose; but this does not absolve him, under the rules, from the obligation to ensure that the plugging is properly done.

Fencing with the electrical apparatus is governed by special rules, with which the épéeist will be well advised to acquaint himself. The following are particularly important:

(*a*) A fencer should form the habit of testing his weapon each time he comes on guard during a bout, to make sure that it is working correctly. Such a test should be made, after asking permission of the President, when a hard hit has been made on the opponent's *coquille*.

This is in addition to the test normally made at the beginning of a bout to ensure that a hit is not registered on the opponent's *coquille*. It is wise, also, to test the weapon immediately after a hit has been scored against one. If the weapon is found to be faulty, even if there is no question of having hit one's opponent, this may justify the annulment of the opponent's hit.

(*b*) If a fencer finds that his weapon does not work after he has been hit, he should *immediately* ask the President to test it. He must be careful not to unplug or alter his weapon in any way until such tests have been carried out, or he will lose the benefit of a possible annulment of his opponent's hit.

(*c*) It is a wise precaution to ask the President to have one's opponent's weapon tested if there is reason to suppose that it may not be working—for example, if one thinks one has been hit, without the hit being registered by the apparatus, or if the opponent has made a hard hit on one's *coquille*. Nothing is more infuriating than to score a clear hit without the opponent scoring at all, only to find that this hit is annulled because the opponent's weapon is not working.

(*d*) A fencer is responsible for ensuring that his blade and guard (*coquille*) are clean. Dirt, rust or oxidization on the guard or blade may cause a hit on the *coquille* or blade to register. Such a hit will not be annulled. A fencer should therefore keep these parts of his weapon clean, by rubbing them lightly at regular intervals with fine sandpaper.

(*e*) A fencer should ensure that the plugs at each end of his body-wire fit tightly into the sockets of the plugs at his hand and back, and should discard his body-wire when the plugs cease to do so. A momentary failure of electrical contact caused by a badly fitting plug may enable a hit made by the opponent on the *coquille* to be registered by the apparatus as a valid hit. It may not be possible to make the fault manifest itself again during the tests made by the President or the experts to see whether a hit on the *coquille* registers, because the badly fitting plug only causes failure of contact inter-mittently, in which case the opponent's hit will not be annulled.

NOTES ON COMPETITIVE PLAY

Épée fencing requires a special technique, courage, opportunism and concentration of effort in the highest degree. It is the highest expression of the art of fencing, because it alone is based on the conception of hitting the opponent without oneself being hit.

At foil and sabre the conventions allow a fencer to accept a remise or a stop hit, knowing that his direct riposte or attack will have priority. At épée such a departure from the fundamental conception of swordsmanship is penalized by the double hit.

The absence of conventions leads many beginners to think that fencing with the épée must be easier than with the foil or sabre. The universal target and sense of having a fight attracts those with a special advantage of height or reach. Others who enjoy speed and combat think that at épée they can exploit these qualities without painfully acquired technique.

At épée, in consequence, one meets more unorthodox fencers than at the other two weapons, and many who exploit special shots with devastating effect—at times. Such fencers often enjoy considerable success in competition, because at épée there are no restrictive targets or conventions to help the orthodox fencer to deal with them, as is the case at foil or sabre.

There are fencers who regard épée as an inferior form of foil fencing, or as a game where easy success can be obtained with a few favourite shots—such persons never know the interest which derives from true épée play.

In fact, of course, true épée fencing is as skilled, complete and distinctive in its own way as foil or sabre. The technique required for épée is more limited in scope than that used at foil, in the sense that a number of fencing movements used at foil are not applicable at épée. But this is compensated for by the greater accuracy of point which the épéeist must develop, the psychological and tactical approach required by a wider measure and the vigilance and caution enforced by the ever-present danger of stop hit or double hit.

While, for the reasons already elaborated elsewhere, the foil is the weapon with which the basic technique of fencing should be learned, the aspiring épéeist should approach épée fencing as a distinct art. He must realize that the movements which he has acquired with the foil must be adapted and often differently applied at épée. It is just as necessary to have regular lessons at épée as at the other two weapons. Naturally such lessons must be taken from a master well grounded in épée technique and not, as regrettably often happens, from one who follows a mainly foil technique with an épée in his hand.

The first essential for the épéeist is to acquire accuracy of point and an exact judgment of time and distance. Accuracy of point means the ability to land a hit on the opponent's moving wrist or forearm either direct or from any angle, at varying distance and so timed as to avoid a stop hit.

The épéeist is trained to make most of his offensive or counter-offensive movements covered. This means that the wrist or forearm of one's opponent is likely to be exposed for only a fraction of a second. The épéeist must be able to place his point accurately at an exact moment if he is to succeed. Often only an instinctive reflex action, developed through constant practice, can achieve this.

The épée fencer needs, perhaps more than the performer at almost any other game, to be 'on his day' and to 'have his eye in' to win a championship. This explains why épéeists are generally less regular in the results they obtain than foilists or *sabreurs*. For example, in the

annual World or Olympic Championships, only two fencers have
won two consecutive épée individual titles and no one has won three
times running during thirty-eight years. The British Épée Championship has only twice been won by the same fencer in three consecutive
years since 1904.

Most first-class épéeists have experienced wonderful days, during
the course of their careers, when everything seemed to go right for
them—most secretly hope that such a day will occur at the final of
an important event. I remember that very hot night in Monte Carlo,
during the 1950 World Championship, when Morgen Lüchow, a
Danish fencer who up to then had not even won his national
championship, swept all before him to win the épée title. He told me
afterwards that at one point he felt so confident that he took a shot
at the loop of the body-wire just visible below the hand of his
opponent—and scored a hit on it!

Épée fencing is a highly tactical game and many épéeists have
individual styles and favourite strokes which may sometimes be
extremely unorthodox. It is therefore particularly important with
this weapon to study the opponent's game. Much can often be
learned by watching opponents during their bouts with other
competitors in the pool or match in which one is engaged, so that
one is forewarned of at least some of their moves when the time
comes to fence them.

When meeting a good, or an unorthodox, épée fencer for the first
time, one may find oneself baffled by his game. In these circumstances, a good plan is to increase the fencing distance. This will give
more security while studying his style and may induce him to show
his game, or perhaps to make mistakes which can be turned to
profitable account. The boxer's adage can often profitably be
adapted to épée as 'Fence a fighter—fight a fencer'. In other words,
a useful plan is to use the opposite tactics to those favoured by the
opponent.

The economical use of the *piste* is also important. Against a
forceful or aggressive opponent, it may be necessary to give ground
to draw his attack or to obtain room to manoeuvre or defend
oneself. Never, however, waste the *piste* by retiring unnecessarily or,
all too soon, one will find oneself cramped at the last two metres of
the *piste*, where the opponent will be able the more easily to lodge
himself for attack or force one into exposing the target to a stop hit
or counter-time movement. It is therefore wise, during a bout, to
take every opportunity to regain ground lost on the *piste*. The
tactical use of the step back to draw the opponent within reach has
already been studied; it is therefore essential to watch the measure
when following up an opponent who appears to be running away.

Unless one has decided to hustle an opponent in order to prevent
him imposing his cadence, or to get set for some favourite stroke
such as an attack at the hand, it is seldom wise to hurry unduly at

the beginning of a bout. There is much to be said for a cautious approach when meeting an unknown opponent, especially if one believes him to be inferior to oneself in experience, speed or technique. It is necessary to take time to gain knowledge of his cadence and to read how he will apply his game to oneself, which may be very different from the way one has observed him react to other competitors.

On the other hand, time should never be wasted, especially with the reduced time limit now applied to épée bouts. To allow an opponent to obtain a lead on hits as time is running out must put one in an inferior tactical position.

Variations of cadence and distance are excellent tactics at épée. By deliberately slowing down such movements as feints at the hand and by gaining and breaking ground to maintain a desired measure, it is sometimes possible to lull the opponent into a definitely slower cadence, when a sudden attack or counter-attack at highest speed may catch him unawares. Conversely, a deliberate slowing-down of a movement during a composed attack at the hand, thus converting it into a broken-time attack, can be equally effective.

One often meets an épéeist who has developed an accurate shot at the hand or forearm. However much confidence one has in one's stop hit or sense of distance, it is rarely wise to allow such an opponent to exploit a number of shots at the hand. By so doing one risks falling into his cadence and it is likely that he will at least score a double hit. Against this type of opponent it often pays continually to vary the height of one's sword-hand and the measure in order to prevent him lodging his attack.

An opponent who has developed accuracy at the hand or upper arm with a lunge or *flèche* attack can often be disconcerted by shortening the measure, or stepping into his attack, while taking a series of circular or semicircular parries (displacing the sword-hand as little as possible).

The *corps à corps*, provided it is not made with violence, is not penalized at épée. The President is obliged to stop the bout as soon as it occurs. Indeed, the *corps à corps* should be provoked tactically when one finds oneself at close quarters. At épée the temptation to continue fencing at close quarters for any length of time must be resisted. To do so will probably result in a chance hit landing on the legs or in a double hit.

Most épéeists develop favourite strokes which happen to suit their temperament, style or physical make-up. By concentrating on these movements they achieve considerable success. There is no harm in this, but it is as well not to become too limited. Opponents will soon learn to master a limited game and, besides, it is not very interesting to execute the same stroke all the time, even if it seems to be a winner.

This view may seem to be discounted by world-famous fencers

who have attained the highest honours with a very limited repertoire of fencing movements, often applied in a most unorthodox manner. On analysis, however, it will be found that these fencers possessed some special physical or psychological characteristics not enjoyed by most people.

Gian-Carlo Cornaggia-Medici's uncanny sense of time and distance has already been mentioned. Léon Tom of Belgium had a similar ability to conjure stop hits from the most improbable angles, combined with monumental patience. Franco Riccardi relied on fantastic speed in the *flèche* to win the 1936 Olympic title for Italy. Many such phenomena could be cited, but in every case the fencer concerned was endowed with special attributes not given to the ordinary fencer. Unless so endowed by nature, an épéeist will enjoy his fencing more, and achieve greater and more consistent success in competitions, if he acquires as wide a variety of strokes as possible— even though some will become his favourites on which he will rely in an emergency.

Épée fencing, being one of the highest and most satisfying expressions of personal combat, attracts individualists. In most competitions one meets unorthodox opponents. Much can be deduced by observing the stance or the on-guard position adopted by an opponent.

Some fencers take up an exaggeratedly open guard, with the épée held well in sixte or octave and the point far out of line. They generally seek to maintain a wide measure and have a good sense of distance. They hope to draw an attack at the exposed sword-arm when, being out of distance, they make a stop hit, or an attack at the body when they apply a parry and riposte.

It will obviously be unwise to attack such an opponent directly, unless one has a marked superiority in speed. To do so will only play the game he is trying to invite. The object must be, by feints made *en marchant*, to draw the stop hit in order to score in countertime or with a *prise de fer*. The exaggeratedly open guard will entail some uncovering of the sword-arm when the fencer moves to a parry. It may therefore be possible to hit the opponent with a premeditated remise or redoublement, following a feint to the body which draws his parry.

Another unorthodox hand position when on guard which is sometimes encountered is the ultra-wide one, with the point of the épée held high rather like a fishing-rod. Fencers employing it generally have a good sense of distance and limit their game almost exclusively to throwing stop hits from any angle at the wrist or forearm of their opponent, whenever these targets come within range. They can rarely be induced to react with any other stroke and, having concentrated on this simple gambit and an exact judgment of distance, have usually achieved an astounding accuracy of point and timing.

Here again one must, at all costs, resist the temptation to attack directly at the hand or body which appear so invitingly open. One must either draw the stop hit in order to score by counter-time, or by judicious feints draw the opponent's blade within reach for an attack by *prise de fer*. Such fencers are usually extremely patient, and constant variation of steps back and forward will probably be required to impose on them the necessary measure to launch these attacks successfully.

Then there is the épéeist who adopts an exaggerated, cramped crouch-position on guard. He either leans over the front knee, or backwards with his weight on the rear foot. A wide measure is maintained very accurately and the épée is held low or well to sixte, with the point wide. The object is to draw an attack at the apparently exposed high lines, in order to score with a jab thrown at the under side of the hand or the knee, while relying on judgment of distance to make these manoeuvres safely.

Such opponents are usually dangerous because of their accuracy of point, but by constantly varying the measure and the position of one's sword-hand, one can eventually draw their attack or stop hit; the safest parry is then usually octave, made with a resolute step forward and riposte covered to flank or mask.

The fencer, usually a foilist, who has the habit of bending the arm when taking his parries is obviously vulnerable to an immediate remise. Anyone who withdraws the hand when an attack is made at the wrist or forearm can generally be hit by a redoublement with a *flèche*.

The épéeist maintaining a straight arm held high when on guard is usually a patient type who will rarely attack, but who has a predilection for the *dérobement* which he times to perfection. Knowing that a straight arm invites a *prise de fer*, he hopes, by constant *dérobements*, to lure his opponent to impale himself on the point. This type of straight-arm épéeist is met with today less frequently than in the days of one- or two-hit bouts; with the longer bouts the static game is less effective, as the opponent can take more risks and vary his attacks.

A double *prise de fer* in opposite lines may trap the extended blade, but must be made very rapidly and with decision. Again, a feint to take the blade may be followed by a remise under the wrist as the *dérobement* is made; the blade must be well angulated to avoid running on the menacing point.

Some épéeists make a habit of continually beating their opponent's blade. This is designed to disconcert him and unsettle his attack, and to tire his sword-hand and destroy his accuracy of point. It is obviously unwise to submit to such tactics; the answer is to fence with absence of blade. Alternately, if the opponent has the habit of following his beats with a feint or jab at the hand, by holding the weapon strongly and locking the wrist it is often possible to block the beat so that it scarcely displaces one's épée and, keeping the point in line, score a stop hit at arm or wrist.

Other fencers, with good footwork and supple legs, rely on false attacks immediately followed by a reprise forward or a redoublement by *flèche*. Such fencers require room to manoeuvre so that they can land their hit at the end of their movement. One must therefore not be tempted to retire on their false attack, which will merely help them to attain the desired distance. Rather step into the attack, taking counter-parries and holding the blade long enough for the point to pass the body safely before riposting.

Left-handed fencers are often especially troublesome to the less experienced right-handed épéeist. Remaining usually on the outside of the right-hander's sixte, they can angulate their attacks over the guard. A favourite stroke is a crisp beat followed by an attack at wrist, or a similar riposte with a *flèche*. A right-hander can, therefore, with advantage adopt a rather wide position in sixte when on guard, with the hand kept rather high to cover the line. By careful timing it may then be possible to effect a stop hit by disengagement under the hand, angulating the blade, as the opponent attacks. The *croisé* from sixte ending at flank is an effective stroke against a left-hander or, of course, vice versa.

When one left- and one right-hander are on guard, their leading knees are more in line with the épée than when both fencers use the same hand. The knee and thigh are therefore vulnerable. Thus by judicious feints the opponent may be induced gradually to raise his sword-hand, when a redoublement at the knee is often effective. When a left-handed opponent makes a *flèche*, it is essential to hold the blade, which has been collected by the appropriate counter-parry, long enough for his point to pass the target before delivering the riposte under the arm.

It has, of course, only been possible to give some examples of general tactics. There is an almost infinite variety of methods, combinations of strokes, variations of style and cadence to be met with in competitive épée. Working out successful counter-moves, bluff and counter-bluff, in this 'game of chess at lightning speed' provides much of the fascination of épée play.

While caution is essential with the duelling weapon, the best devised moves will come to naught unless the épéeist possesses courage to risk everything when the right opportunity presents itself.

IV

The Sabre

IN the Middle Ages, the general use of armour required weapons, such as the battle-axe and the double-handed sword, to be heavy and clumsy. Sword-play was mostly confined to the use of the edge.

The invention of gunpowder in the fourteenth century rapidly led to the disuse of armour. Swords became lighter and more manageable and much attention was paid to the study of their skilful use. The Italians are credited with the discovery of the superiority achieved by use of the point instead of relying entirely on the edge of the weapon. This soon led to a universal use of the rapier.

The tradition of the cutting weapon was continued by the backsword, or broadsword, beloved of the first Elizabethans and practised well into the eighteenth century.

The modern sabre comes from the curved cavalry sabre, derived from the eastern scimitar, which was introduced into Europe in the late eighteenth century by the Hungarians for the use of their cavalry. It was soon adopted by the other Western European armies. This heavy cavalry sabre with its hanging guard and wide circular cuts was long used in the fencing schools and still had many devotees at the beginning of the present century.

During the last quarter of the nineteenth century the Italians developed a light duelling or fencing sabre, which was looked on with derision as a mere toy by those accustomed to the heavy sabre. The Italian sabre has now been universally adopted for fencing.

The famous Milanese master, Giuseppe Radaelli, is generally credited with having developed the light sabre and its technique of light, swift cuts and thrusts. In fact, this light sabre play became an academic pursuit related to the heavy military sabre in the way that the foil is related, as a practice weapon, to the épée or duelling sword. Although modern sabre fencing has become a complex game governed by similar conventions and rules to those applied to the foil, the light sabre remains a recognized duelling weapon.

Practice for a duel with the sabre in schools, or *sciabola di terreno*, is quite different to normal sabre fencing. The fencers stand in an almost upright position with a short stance and the knees only slightly bent; the sword-arm is almost fully extended and light cuts are almost exclusively confined to the wrist. In fact, *sciabola di terreno* approximates to épée fencing, the use of the edge being generally substituted for that of the point.

The writer's first introduction to *sciabola di terreno* occurred many years ago in the Salle Mangiarotti in Milan. My mentor was a stout, bearded gentleman, hero of an impressive number of sabre duels, who disdained fencing kit. He wore his elegant striped trousers and patent-leather boots in which he frequented the cafés of the Galleria, merely removing his collar and tie and substituting a pyjama jacket for his formal black coat and donning a short glove and a mask. He had a wonderful sense of distance and almost any normal sabre movement was met by a light cut at wrist from the most improbable angles. He naturally regarded anything so inelegant as a feint head cut at chest as a severe breach of etiquette.

A quite different form of sabre duelling is practised in Germany and some Central European countries with the heavy, basket-hilted *schläger*. This form of fencing is mostly practised by officers' clubs or in the student fencing clubs. The latter are a form of secret society and are most exclusive in membership. They have impressive uniforms and closely guarded, secret rules and great prestige attaches to membership. In 1922, while I was at Cambridge, I was privileged to witness some practice bouts at a student club in Prague, because I was also a student-fencer. Even on this occasion the doors of the *salle* were carefully locked before fencing commenced.

In a *schläger* duel the two combatants face each other in an upright position at close quarters and must not move their feet or bodies during a bout. The swords are very heavy with elaborate basket hilts (rather like Scottish military swords), held above the head when on guard so that the forearm is in front of the face. Owing to the close quarters, cuts are made exclusively at the head and shoulders of the opponent, while defence is exercised by the hilt of the sabre and the forearm which is well padded. No mask is, of course, worn except in a practice bout; the eyes are protected by steel goggles, while a leather band protects the jugular veins in the neck. One-minute rounds are fenced and each combatant has a second to hold his sword-arm during the rest periods between rounds, since otherwise he must not move from his on-guard position. A President starts the bout and stops it by striking up the duellists' swords with his own. The duel continues until loss of blood from the cuts on head and cheek forces one of the duellists to retire. The scars of cuts received in duels on the head and face (which, it is said, are best preserved by rubbing in white wine while they are healing) were venerated as signs of courage—and were much admired by the ladies.

The Italians established their method of classical sabre fencing during the 1860s. Their school is based on the control of the weapon by the hand and forearm, the elbow acting as a pivot, and with little wrist movement. Cuts are 'carried' on to the target, the wrist and forearm acting in one plane with the blade; parries are similarly formed by movements of the forearm pivoted from the elbow to move the sabre to the required position.

The Italian school of sabre fencing is akin to foil fencing in its position on guard and its classical movements. Its beautifully controlled, swift and complex movements, performed with a feather-light hand, build up lightning-quick phrases which are a joy to watch.

Sabre fencing has been completely revolutionized during the past thirty years by the emergence of the Hungarian school. This rapidly proved superior to the Italian school in world competition and it has now virtually replaced it in every country—even, during the last five years, in Italy.

In the Hungarian method, the fundamental difference from the Italian school is that hits and blade movements are entirely controlled by finger play, with a flexible wrist and a minimum of arm move-ments. Greater stress is laid on mobility, opportunism and speed of footwork, rather than complex phrasing, and a wide measure is usually maintained on guard with the sabres rarely engaged.

In a word, Italian sabre has much in common with foil fencing, while Hungarian sabre is tactically more akin to épée fencing.

THE TARGET AND CONVENTIONS

At sabre hits may be made with the whole of the front edge of the blade or the last third of its back edge (cuts) as well as with the point.

The target consists of the arms, head and body (trunk) above a horizontal line drawn between the tops of the folds formed by the thighs and the trunk of the fencer when he is in the on-guard position. This line is therefore some way below the waist. The half-round sabre guard protects the fingers of the sword-hand from cuts.

The clothing used at sabre should be made of more robust material than that required for foil, as a protection against cuts which can be painful. For ease of movement, many sabre fencers favour the short foil type of jacket. The sword-arm sleeve of the jacket may be lightly padded and it is wise to wear a leather or quilted elbow-guard at all times. A hard cut on the elbow is not only extremely painful and may, indeed, paralyse the sword-hand for a time, but can cause an injury which will prevent one fencing for weeks or months.

Sabre fencing is governed by rules and conventions similar to those used at foil. However, the wider target, which necessitates constant vigilance against a stop hit at arm, introduces into sabre fencing many of the elements of épée play. For example, the distance usually maintained between two fencers at sabre is greater than at foil and simpler methods of attack, those with preparation on the blade and second-intention attacks, are mostly used at the cutting weapon.

The use of cuts as well as thrusts introduces a special variety into sabre play and gives an advantage to the attack over the defence, which is particularly marked at this weapon.

Timing and sense of distance are as important at sabre as at épée.

F

Normally, when on guard, the fencers take their distance from the nearest part of their opponent's target which is the forearm, and are thus out of distance to land a hit on the body or head simply by lunging. The *sabreur* is constantly faced with the problem of getting within distance for his attack to land without receiving a stop hit. Balance and mobility are therefore of special importance and the *balestra* and *flèche* are much used when attacking or riposting.

Speed of footwork, physical endurance and strength of leg are essential at sabre.

The reasons for learning the basic technique of fencing with the foil before adapting it to specialize at the other two weapons were fully elaborated in the previous chapter. These arguments apply with rather less force to sabre, with its complete and basically different technique, than to the épée. Good results can be obtained when the novice is started with the sabre, but the writer remains of the opinion that the best results are generally obtained if the groundwork of fencing is learned with the foil, if only because of its lightness and greater manoeuvrability.

The fencing technique described for the foil is largely applicable at sabre. It is not proposed to repeat it in detail in the present chapter, but rather to show how it must be adapted to suit the basic difference between the two weapons, caused by the use of the edge as well as the point and the more extensive target at sabre.

Although some of the technique of the Italian school will be mentioned, the method of sabre fencing described below is based on the Hungarian school which has been adopted by the National Training Scheme of the Amateur Fencing Association in this country.

HOW TO HOLD THE SABRE

In the Italian school the grip is very similar to that used at foil, but with the hand generally in full or half-pronation. The blade is, however, manipulated mainly by 'carrying' it to the desired fencing position, with the hand and forearm moving together. Finger play is little used to control the blade and is mostly confined to applying the edge to the target, once the blade has reached the appropriate position.

This grip has now generally been abandoned in favour of the Hungarian grip, which gives suppleness to the wrist, while relying on finger play to direct the blade.

To hold the sabre, grip the handle between the second phalanx of the index finger and the ball of the thumb, which rests on the back of the handle (that is, that part which is furthest from the curve of the guard). The first phalanx of the index finger is wrapped round the side of the handle. The thumb is thus not lying flat along the handle as at foil, but only the ball, or last joint, rests thereon. The last three fingers of the sword-hand are wrapped round the side of the handle, which then lies along the second phalanges of these fingers. When these last three fingers are closed, the handle of the sabre rests against the upper end of the fleshy part, or heel, of the hand (see plate VIII).

With this grip, finger play is effected by pushing or pulling or rolling the handle with the manipulators (thumb and forefinger) assisted by the little finger. Finger play with the sabre is exactly similar to that used at the other two weapons, except for the auxiliary rôle of the little finger.

Although with this grip blade movements are mostly directed, and hits applied, by finger play, the wide target at sabre and the necessity to present the edge to the target require more movements of the arm than at foil. It is, however, essential to maintain relaxation and elasticity of the muscles of the arm and shoulder, so that free, light strokes come from the sword-hand and heavy, slow, punching movements are avoided. The Italians aptly describe this as 'a hand of steel on an arm of rubber'.

With this grip it is possible easily to change the position of the handle in the hand, while maintaining a supple wrist. By such changes of grip the blade may be brought into an almost perpendicular position, used in certain parries, or the reach may be lengthened so that the fencer obtains the feeling of transferring control of the weapon to the tip of the blade.

THE ON-GUARD POSITION

The attitude of the body and legs in the on-guard position is similar to that adopted at foil.

In the Italian school the legs are well flexed and the body is markedly effaced, by keeping the rear shoulder well back, in order to present as little of the target as possible to the opponent. The sabre is held in third, with the elbow well tucked in and the forearm and the sabre forming one straight line, the point being about level with the opponent's eyes (plates IX and X).

The Hungarian school adopts a rather shorter and more upright stance than is usual at foil, in order to give ease of movement and mobility of footwork. The sword-hand is usually placed in low third, that is, about level with the fencer's hip, with the point directed in the general direction of the opponent's head. The blade is thus almost vertical and, while the flexing of the wrist keeps the outside lines covered by the guard, the blade is placed diagonally across the body.

This blade position is important because it enables an attack to be launched, or the sabre to be moved to any of the parries, with equal ease. For this reason this on-guard position is called the 'offensive-defensive' position of third (plates XI and XII).

A rather more upright position of the body and head is maintained, especially when lunging, than is customary at foil, because the head is of course included in the sabre target.

At sabre the unarmed hand is part of the target and must be kept out of the way of cuts. It is therefore not raised as at foil or épée, but flexed downwards and tucked well back, with the hand resting lightly on the hip. Some *sabreurs* have the habit of gripping their waist with the unarmed hand; but it is better merely to rest the knuckles lightly on the hip, so that the rear arm is not cramped but can be used to some extent to assist balance when lunging.

LINES OF ENGAGEMENT

The line of engagement is the position in which the hand of the fencer is placed when he is in an on-guard position, so that he protects some part of his target with his weapon. Each line, of course, corresponds to the parry of the same name.

There are six lines of engagement at sabre. At foil and épée these lines are usually called in this country by their traditional French names, prime, quarte, sixte and so on. At sabre, however, the lines are usually named in English, probably because in the late nineteenth century, when fencing was revived in this country, sabre was mostly practised in the Army and the manuals produced for Army physical-training courses so named them.

The lines of engagement at sabre are first, second, third, fourth, fifth and sixth. The position of third may be taken in two ways, either with the hand held just below shoulder-level and the blade and forearm in one line (which is the normal on-guard position in the Italian school), or with the hand low, almost level with the hip, the wrist bent and the sabre almost vertical (which is the on-guard position in the Hungarian school). The latter is sometimes regarded as a supplementary position, called low third.

Although in theory a fencer may come on guard with his sabre in any of the six positions and all are sometimes adopted as an invitation, in practice second, third (or low third) or fourth are normally the only ones used. When on guard covered in any of these lines, more particularly in second or third, a *sabreur* is in the best position for attack or defence.

THE FENCING MEASURE

The wider target at sabre, since it includes the sword-arm, necessitates a wider fencing measure when on guard than is normally required at foil. The fencing measure at sabre is approximately the same as for épée, that is to say, the fencer maintains a position from which he can reach the opponent's forearm, not his body or head, with a lunge.

As at épée, the wide measure when on guard causes sabre fencers normally to fence with absence of blade. Only in the Italian school do *sabreurs* usually come on guard with their weapons engaged.

At sabre the fencer has to be prepared for attacks made either with the edge or the point and the former require wider defensive movements with the blade than are necessary at foil or épée. To guard against surprise and force the opponent to prepare his attacks, *sabreurs* usually maintain an even wider measure when on guard than is required at épée. As we shall see, a *sabreur* is constantly preoccupied with the problem of getting within distance for an attack and preventing his opponent obtaining this advantage.

MOBILITY

Mobility on the *piste* is of particular importance at sabre because of the wide measure usually maintained between fencers, the necessity to recover after an attack to obtain sufficient room for defence and the constant vigilance required against surprise attacks or stop hits.

Sabre tactics are largely based on an exact judgment of distance, without which the most carefully devised attacks are likely to fail. The *sabreur* is constantly on the move, either to get within distance to attack, or to maintain a measure which will make it more difficult for his opponent to do so. As has been mentioned above, attack has a marked superiority over defence at this weapon and the *sabreur* uses mobility and variation of the fencing measure to increase the efficacy of his defence.

He must move lightly and quickly on the balls of the feet and yet maintain perfect balance, in order to be able to lunge or launch a *balestra* or *flèche* attack when required. The shorter stance and more upright position used at sabre facilitates these movements and enables an attack to be launched with a minimum of effort and with as little notice as possible to the opponent.

Sabre fencers should pay great attention to footwork, including the lunge, *balestra* and *flèche*. They must develop strength and elasticity in ankles, legs and thighs (exercises for this purpose have been described in the previous chapter, on pages 115-116).

The *flèche* is much used at sabre both for offensive and for counter-offensive actions. It should be practised from immobility or after a step forward or a step back. It will be remembered that the *flèche* starts with a loss of balance forward over the leading leg, and that the hit should land as the rear foot reaches the ground. Much of the success of a *flèche* depends on the speed with which the rear leg can be swung past the front foot in the initial step. This step should be as far beyond the leading foot as the fencer's suppleness and length of leg allow, but care must be taken not to check the momentum of the *flèche* by an exaggerated turn of the hips.

Although the *flèche* initially includes a loss of balance, the whole movement forward should be smooth and controlled, with rapid acceleration. During a properly controlled *flèche* attack it is quite possible to effect several blade movements such as parry, riposte and counter-riposte or a counter-time action—but this, of course, requires perfect timing and balance.

However successful it may be, a *flèche* is always something of a gamble. If it fails there is no chance of recovery and one is often at the mercy of the opponent. At its inception it is usually vulnerable to a counter-attack. To have the best chance of success, a *flèche* must have an element of surprise, or the opponent will find it proportionately easier to deal with. It is obvious, therefore, that this movement should only be used sparingly and at the right psychological moment. Constant use of the *flèche* as a habitual method of attack or riposte will soon be noted and turned to good account by one's opponents.

Simple attacks, as at all weapons, are most safely executed with a lunge either from immobility or, more usually, after a step forward or a *balestra*. The mechanism of the lunge has already been described in the chapter dealing with the foil, but at sabre the vulnerability of the head to a direct riposte requires that both body and head be maintained in a more upright position while lunging with this weapon. A rapid recovery from the lunge position will greatly assist the parrying of a riposte if the attack has failed.

While it is, of course, possible, and often necessary, to execute parries, counter-ripostes and other blade movements while fully extended on the lunge, the variety of ripostes with edge or point available to the opponent at sabre makes such movements particularly difficult and dangerous. In consequence it is wise to practise and form the habit of making an automatic recovery from the lunge while performing these movements. The lunge and recovery must be practised until it is a smooth movement like the stretch and recoil of a well oiled spring. Care should be taken that the lunge is fully developed, as there is often a tendency for it to be short owing to the fencer's anticipation of the recovery.

THE HIT

At sabre hits may be made with the point, with the whole of the edge, or with the third of the back edge which is nearest to the point of the blade.

Hits with the point are placed exactly as with the foil; that is to say, the point is fixed on the target by finger play and the arm provides penetration by its smooth extension, the hand rising as the blade bends. At sabre, hits with the point are usually made with the sword-hand in pronation and almost exclusively at the opponent's body.

In the Italian school cuts are generally delivered with the sabre, wrist and forearm forming one straight line. The blade is carried on to the target and, at the moment of contact, a crisp, light cut is delivered by compression of the fingers of the sword-hand.

The different grip and flexed wrist of the Hungarian school requires a different technique when delivering a cut. To make a hit, the sword-arm is extended and the edge of the sabre presented at the target. At the moment when the arm reaches its full extension, a contraction of the last fingers of the sword-hand, combined with a downward flexing of the wrist, delivers a light, crisp cut.

It is important to appreciate that a cut involves two distinct movements—the presentation of the blade to the target to achieve the required direction, and the delivery of the cut. When making a cut, control of the blade is shared by the fingers and the wrist. To use the wrist alone will cause the cut to be heavy and slow, whereas it is essential that a cut should be swift and light and should rebound from the target. A light hand and flexible wrist will enable the sabre to move quickly and easily to the next stroke after a cut has been made.

Heavy hitting is usually caused by excessive use of the forearm and neglect of wrist and finger action. It is bound to lead to slow, wide movements which will expose the forearm to stop hits or give the opponent time to form a parry.

Control of the sabre by the fingers is what is meant by 'sabre in hand', which is a cardinal virtue in sabre fencing. Sabre in hand can only be achieved if the sword-arm and shoulder remain supple and relaxed. It means conservation of strength and imparting control and elasticity to blade movements, which enables the fencer to check the edge of his sabre at a desired point when making a cut or a parry. Italo Santelli, the founder of the modern Hungarian school of sabre fencing, used to say to his pupils: 'The sabre is your pen— write with it finely and with grace—write with it as you would to your *fiancée.*'

Cuts must be delivered with the edge; hits which are made with the flat of the blade will be disregarded by the judges. Similarly an attempt to hit with the point, which does not fix but merely grazes the target, cannot count as a good hit even if the edge of the blade is subsequently pressed along the target. A graze cannot be converted into a cut.

It often happens that when a cut is made at the forearm, the blade makes contact with the opponent's hilt as well as with the target. If the attacker's blade reaches the target before, or at the same moment as it makes contact with the hilt, this counts as a good hit. If, on the other hand, the attacker's blade meets the opponent's guard before it reaches the target, there is said to be 'broken guard' —the hit does not count as good and the opponent has the right to riposte. Similarly if a cut arrives on the target at the same time as it meets the parry, the parry is regarded as insufficient and the hit will be good. However, a heavy cut which forces its way on to the target through a correctly formed parry is not regarded as good and does not annul a riposte.

THE ENGAGEMENT

At sabre the engagement is usually made in third with the sabres edge to edge and the guard protecting the wrist and forearm, thus covering this line.

This is the normal engagement in the Italian school in the on-guard position. An engagement may also be made in second or fourth, but is rarely made in any other line except as an invitation.

In the Hungarian school, in which the normal on-guard position is with the sword-hand in low third and the sabre in the offensive-defensive position, *sabreurs* are usually out of distance for an engagement with the blades, that is to say, they are generally on guard with absence of blade.

ATTACKS

The wide target, including the arms, body and head, and the use of the edge as well as the point provide a considerable variety of attacks at sabre. The defender must make much wider movements to protect every part of his target than are necessary at foil. These factors give the attack a marked advantage over the defence at sabre.

The targets for sabre attacks may be classified as follows.

(I) Target for cuts:

(1) Flank.

(2) Right cheek.

(3) Head.

(4) Left cheek.

(5) Chest.

(6) Sword-arm, or the advanced target (which may be subdivided into outside of forearm, top of forearm, upper arm, inside forearm and under forearm).

(II) Target for attacks with the point: mostly made at the body.

Before a cut is made, the edge of the sabre is presented towards the part of the target which it is intended to hit. The angle at which the edge is presented in this way will, of course, depend on the position of the sword-hand. This will vary according to the part of the target attacked in the following ways:

(1) In pronation: for cuts at flank, right cheek, outside of forearm and upper arm, and for hits with the point.

(2) In half-pronation: for cuts at head, chest, top of forearm and under forearm.

(3) In supination: for cuts at left cheek, chest, belly and inside forearm.

It follows that with the hand in these positions cuts will be made:

(1) Vertically: at head or top of forearm.

(2) Laterally: at right or left cheek.

(3) Vertically or laterally or at an angle between the two: at flank, chest, outer and inner forearm, or upper arm.

(4) Upwards: at flank or under forearm.

The foregoing is a very general classification designed merely to indicate the most usual ways in which hits are made at sabre. They will naturally be varied or combined according to circumstances. For example, a hit to the under side of the arm may be made upwards, with the hand in half-pronation, and delivered with the back edge of the sabre, or it may be a cut made laterally or upwards with the front edge as the opponent raises his hand. A hit to the opponent's left cheek may be delivered with the front edge of the sabre, with the hand in supination, or with the back edge with the hand in pronation, and so on.

When attacking at sabre it is essential to obtain maximum protection from the guard of the weapon; this is particularly important because of the predilection of the modern *sabreur* for the stop hit at arm. This protection is achieved by maintaining the level of the sword-arm and hand, as far as possible, breast-high, at whatever part of the opponent's target the attack is aimed, and presenting the sabre at the target solely by rotation of the wrist and the use of the fingers.

The finger play required to present the edge of the sabre in the way already described consists of pressing or rolling the handle of the weapon between the thumb and forefinger, assisted by the little finger which is hooked round the handle. It is just as important to direct the blade with the manipulators at sabre as with the other two weapons, although the little finger plays an important auxiliary part in the movement. Accuracy in the direction of the blade will be lost if the weapon is controlled from the heel of the sword-hand.

Considerable practice is required to make this finger play automatically, smoothly and accurately, so that the edge of the sabre is presented correctly, for perpendicular, lateral or upwards cuts, solely by a rotation of the wrist and without bending the sword-arm at the elbow. Only in this way can one ensure that cuts are delivered with maximum protection from the guard, without exposing the forearm to counter-offensive actions.

It will be realized that the method of delivering cuts just described is the opposite to that used in the classical Italian school, where the wrist and forearm moving together are pivoted from the elbow. The Hungarian school evolved the method of attacking with extended arm and finger and wrist action, precisely to prevent exposing the forearm to stop cuts which was the weakness of the Italian school. It has been treated in some detail because of its vital importance as the basic method of delivering cuts in modern sabre fencing.

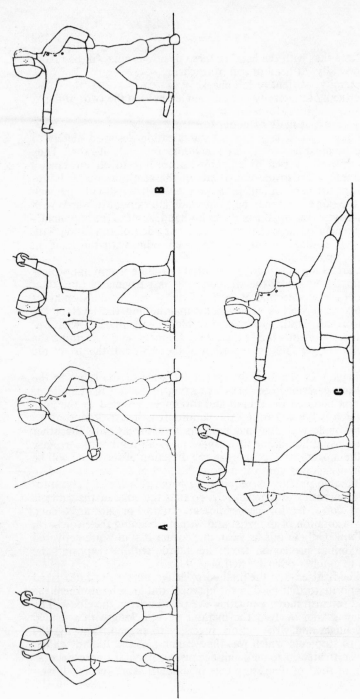

Fig. 51   The Cut at Flank

A. Fencer on left has his flank exposed
B. Attacker on right extends his arm and presents the cutting edge at flank
C. Attacker completes his cut at flank

DIRECT ATTACKS

Direct attacks with point or edge should naturally be launched when the opponent's sabre and sword-hand are farthest from the part of the target which it is intended to hit. Ideally, they should be made when the opponent's hand is moving *away* from the line into which one intends to attack, to gain maximum time and distance for the attack over the defence.

This is easier to accomplish with the sabre than with the foil, because with the former the defender has a much wider area to cover and defence against cuts requires wider movements than defence against attacks with the point. At sabre the area which must be protected, known as the defensive area or defensive box, is contained in a figure bounded by lines on the right and left of the fencer's body, joined by horizontal lines at the top of his head and below his waist (see Fig. 58, page 174).

(a) **Direct Cuts.**

(i) *The Cut at Flank.* This can be made when the opponent's blade is in first, fourth or fifth position. The sword-arm is extended breast-high, with the hand in pronation and the point of the sabre rather higher than the hand. In this position the hand, forearm and upper arm on the outside are protected by the guard. The cut is delivered laterally or slightly upwards if it is necessary to pass the blade under the opponent's arm.

(ii) *The Cut at Right Cheek (or Shoulder).* This cut is best made when the opponent's blade is in first, second or fourth position, or when a parry of third is incorrectly made, without covering with the whole blade. A cut at cheek is delivered laterally after extending the sword-arm breast-high, with the hand in pronation and the point raised level with the opponent's cheek.

(iii) *The Cut at Head.* It can be made when the opponent's blade is in second, third or fourth position. The head is particularly vulnerable at sabre because the parry of fifth, which alone is used to protect it, requires a wide arm movement and many fencers fail to raise their hand sufficiently when forming this parry. To make a cut at head, the sword-arm should be extended breast-high with the hand in semi-pronation, that is, with the edge of the blade vertical and the point raised sufficiently to clear the opponent's head. Having thus presented the edge, the cut is made vertically on the top of the mask by finger and wrist action.

Care must be taken not to raise the hand while presenting the edge at head, in order not to expose the arm to stop cuts. However, the sword-hand should be raised as the vertical cut is completed, to prevent the attack being parried by a badly formed fifth parry.

(iv) *The Cut to the Left Cheek.* This is best made laterally with the front edge of the blade, which necessitates rotating the wrist to bring the hand to the supinated position. At close quarters or after a third

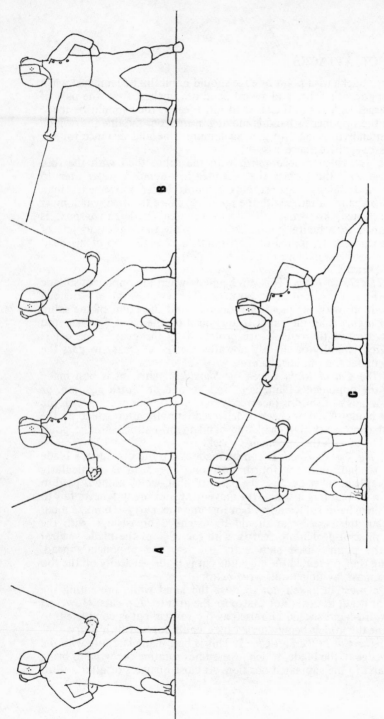

Fig. 52 The Cut at Cheek

A. The fencers on guard in third
B. Fencer on right extends his arm and presents the cutting edge at cheek
C. Atacker completes his cut at cheek

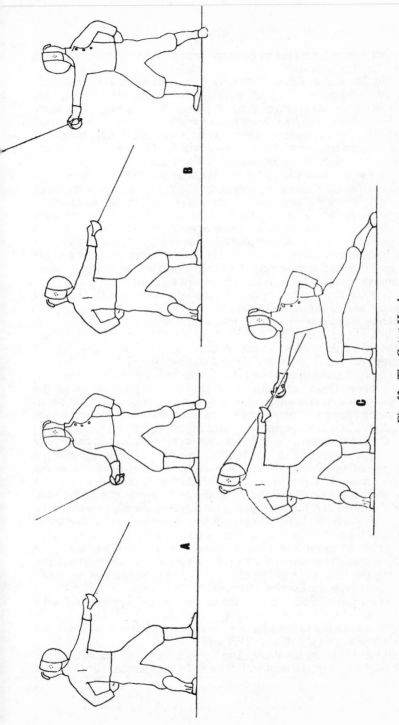

Fig. 53   The Cut at Head

A. Fencer on left has his head exposed
B. Attacker on right extends his arm and presents the cutting edge at head
C. Attacker completes his cut at head

parry, this cut can also be executed with the back of the blade, with the hand in pronation.

(v) *The Cut at Chest*. Generally it is made when the opponent's blade is in second or third position, or in fifth, or as a cut-over riposte from the parry of third or fourth. The cut at chest is made with the hand in supination or half-supination and the cut is delivered laterally or sometimes almost vertically. One can distinguish between the cut at chest, which lands at about the level of the left breast, and the cut at belly which arrives in the lower line.

In the classical school the cut at chest, the *banderole*, was made with a flowing, slicing movement, in which the arm drew the blade lightly across the target with a smooth follow-through to return to guard. This was a spectacular movement which was a joy to watch. This method has, however, been abandoned because it tends to expose the forearm and encourage wide blade movements. The cut at chest is now made, as are all cuts, with the arm extended and the edge presented at the target. There remains a certain flowing follow-through as the hand is rotated to return to guard.

(vi) *The Cut at Arm*. As at épée, the arm constitutes the advanced target and is the most vulnerable part of the target. Naturally a *sabreur* takes especial care to protect his arm and, in consequence, it can but rarely be hit with a direct attack except during an un-covered preparation of attack. A cut at arm usually results from a composed attack or is made as a riposte or stop hit.

Cuts are generally directed at the wrist or forearm. It is important to practise these cuts with due regard to the presentation of the blade at the correct angle, according to the part of this target which is being aimed at. This will avoid the natural tendency to make such cuts with arm movements which will expose the attacker's own wrist.

The cut at the outside of the forearm is perhaps the most commonly used cut at arm and should be made laterally, with the sword-hand in pronation. Cuts at the top of the forearm or at the inside of the arm are made vertically with the hand in semi-pronation. The cut to the under side of the arm is usually made upwards with the back of the blade and the hand in semi-supination, merely by raising the wrist without displacing the arm. When, however, a cut to the under side of the arm is made against an opponent who raises his hand, for example when making a badly executed attack at head, it may be made laterally or upwards, with the sword-hand in pronation, and using the front edge of the blade. Hits to the upper arm are made laterally or, more usually, vertically.

The accurate and swift placing of cuts on the forearm and wrist requires considerable experience in timing and judgment of distance. Ability to land hits on the opponent's arm is as important at sabre as at épée (plates XVII and XVIII).

(*b*) **Attacks with the Point.** Attacks with the point, generally made at the body, are executed with the hand in pronation. Hits with the

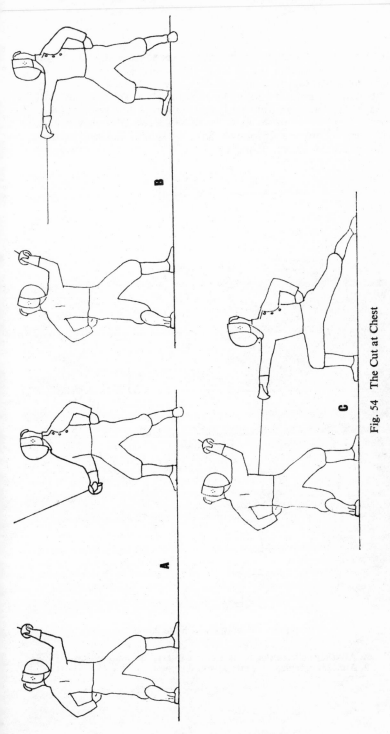

Fig. 54 The Cut at Chest

A. Fencer on left has his chest exposed
B. Attacker on right extends his arm and presents the cutting edge at chest
C. Attacker completes his cut at chest

point are more easily fixed on the target if the sabre is angulated from the wrist. This directs the point at the body, while maintaining maximum protection with the guard.

Hits with the point do not come so naturally at sabre as cuts with the edge. They are relatively easily parried with a direct or a counter-parry and are therefore likely to be most successful if they contain an element of surprise. It follows that they should be used sparingly to preserve their unexpectedness.

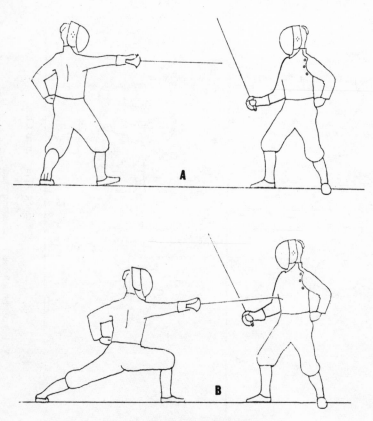

Fig. 55   The Attack with the Point

A. Attacker on left extends his arm and directs the point at chest
B. Attacker completes his attack with the point

INDIRECT ATTACKS

At all weapons the direct attack is at a disadvantage against the parry as regards time and distance. At sabre this is aggravated by the wide measure usually maintained by the fencers when on guard. This usually makes it necessary for the attack to travel the maximum distance and facilitates proportionately the possibility of a successful parry.

Indirect attacks include one blade movement passing under or over the opponent's blade. They have a greater chance to succeed than the direct attack, because they can be timed to land as the opponent's blade is moving away from the part of the target which the attacker intends to hit. For example, as the opponent moves his hand from third to fourth, an attack by disengagement to third will catch him moving in the wrong direction for a third parry.

At sabre indirect attacks are based on the disengagement, the circular cut (cut-over) over the blade and the counter-disengagement. The *sabreur* today is generally on guard with absence of blade. From that position his indirect attacks are usually more in the nature of changes of blade position, than movements closely related to his opponent's blade. Examples of such attacks are the circular cut at flank from a guard in fourth, or a circular cut at chest from a guard in third.

When making indirect attacks at sabre, finger play, in the foilist's understanding of the term, is limited by the grip and by the normal pronated position of the hand. For this reason indirect attacks made with the edge are easier to perform and more commonly used than attacks with the point, and the circular cut, or cut-over, is a more natural movement than the disengagement. For the same reason, movements from high to low lines, or vice versa, are usually made by disengagement, while movements from one side of the target to the other are generally made by a cut-over.

The degree to which the forearm has to be flexed when making an indirect attack at sabre will vary according to the distance existing between the fencers. It should obviously be kept to the minimum, so as not to expose the attacker to a stop hit.

If an indirect attack is properly timed (that is to say, is launched at the correct distance to allow the necessary blade movements to be made successfully) the attacker should be able to make his disengagement or circular cut and present the blade at the target solely by finger play and rotation of the wrist, as the arm is extending in its correct, breast-high position. There should be no necessity to bend or withdraw the arm in order to get round the opponent's blade.

COMPOUND ATTACKS

At sabre, any attacking movement, especially one made with the edge, carries the inherent danger of momentarily exposing the arm to a stop hit. For this reason, and because of the greater distance usually maintained between fencers, it is generally unwise for the *sabreur* to attempt the compound attacks of great complexity which can safely be made at foil. It is best to use the least possible number of feints to achieve one's aim of circumventing the opponent's right choice of parry.

No feint at any weapon can be counted effective unless it forces the opponent to move to parry it. To be successful it must appear to be a simple movement of attack. For example, a simple extension of the arm when on guard will be disregarded by anyone except a most inexperienced or nervous fencer, unless it is made with sufficient conviction, that is to say, unless the blade is carried sufficiently close to the target to convince the opponent that he will be hit by it.

There are two ways in which a compound attack can be made. The method taught by the classical school was to make a feint, observe the opponent's reaction to it and conclude the movement in the appropriate line. With this method, the lunge or *flèche* is usually reserved until the final movement of the compound attack and, indeed, this final movement, certain of its objective, comes almost as an anticlimax of effort. To succeed, the feints must be very convincing and exact choice of time and distance is essential because, under the rules, a mere contact of the opponent's blade during a feint will give him the right to riposte.

The method favoured by the modern school is to make the feints progressively, that is to say, at the same time as the lunge or *flèche*, so that the attacker's blade is moving ahead of the parry and thus gaining time and distance for the attack. With this method it is obviously essential correctly to anticipate the parry which the defender will take. Once launched, the plan of the progressive attack can rarely be altered and, unless the attacker has a very considerable superiority in speed, his attack is almost bound to fail if the defender does not react as anticipated to the feints.

Both methods, therefore, have advantages and disadvantages and, in the writer's opinion, neither can claim absolute superiority over the other. The sabre fencer will be well advised to study and practise both methods of making composed attacks. He will certainly find that sometimes one and sometimes the other will prove most effective against the variety of opponents he will meet. The ability to use either method of attack will enrich his game and certainly make his attacks more varied and effective.

At sabre, comparatively wide blade movements have to be made when moving from one parry to the other, certainly much wider than are necessary at foil, because of the large area of the defensive box and the necessity completely to oppose the blade in parrying cuts. If, therefore, a correctly executed feint succeeds in drawing the anticipated parry, the subsequent movement of the attack has a correspondingly greater chance to land before it can be parried. At sabre it is a cardinal rule to make feints as deep as possible, that is to say, to bring the attacker's blade as close to the opponent's target as possible in the feint.

The *sabreur's* constant preoccupation with the fencing measure has already been mentioned. This is equally true with regard to compound attacks and it is generally necessary to precede or combine feints with a step forward or *balestra* or, by constant variations of gaining and breaking ground, achieve a required distance before launching the attack.

When extending the sword-arm to make a feint, the hand must be maintained breast-high, as for a simple attack, and maximum cover for the arm must be obtained from the guard of the weapon. Once the arm has been thus extended, it must not again be retracted or bent at the elbow during the course of the attack. Subsequent blade movements, whether additional feints or the final movement of the attack, must be made by altering the presentation of the blade to the desired part of the opponent's target purely by finger and wrist movements, so as to uncover the forearm as little as possible.

The rhythm of compound attacks may be varied to much greater advantage at sabre than at the other two weapons. For example, a feint cheek—feint flank—cut at cheek may be made in the rhythm long-short-short, or short-long-short, or long-long-short, and so on. In this example the use of the words long and short of course refers to time and not to distance. Again, a broken-time attack, for example making a pause before delivering the final movement, can be very effective in deceiving the opponent as to the attacker's intention.

The use of the point, either as a feint or as a final movement after feints with the edge, often proves disconcerting to the opponent. *Sabreurs* rarely fail to react to a convincing feint with the point.

The comparatively wide movements which, as already noted, are required in defence at sabre make it particularly important to ascertain an opponent's cadence and adapt the rhythm of a compound attack to it. For example, a one-two attack made very fast against an opponent who reacts slowly will often fail, because the attacker returns to the original line to complete his attack before the defender has had time to react at all. The attacker is surprised to find that he is lunging into a closed line which, in fact, has never been opened, because he did not allow the necessary time, when making his feint, for his slower opponent to attempt to parry it.

When fencing an inexperienced *sabreur*, one must always use compound attacks with circumspection. There is a temptation to dazzle such an opponent with a multiplicity of feints, but it is dangerous to depart from the cardinal rule that a compound attack should only be used if an opponent cannot be hit by a simple one. The natural reaction of the inexperienced or nervous *sabreur* is to slash wildly at his attacker. Such reflex actions have a disconcerting habit of landing on the attacker who needlessly complicates his attack.

As at all weapons, variety in feints and rhythm are of the essence of success in making compound attacks, in order to make it as difficult as possible for the opponent to anticipate correctly the final movement of the attack.

Fig. 56   The Compound Attack

A. Fencer on left has his head exposed
B. Fencer on right presents the cutting edge to feint at head
C. Attacker on right makes his feint at head as he begins to lunge. The defender is drawn to parry fifth
D. Attacker deceives the parry of fifth as he continues his attack at flank
E. The attack is completed by a cut at flank

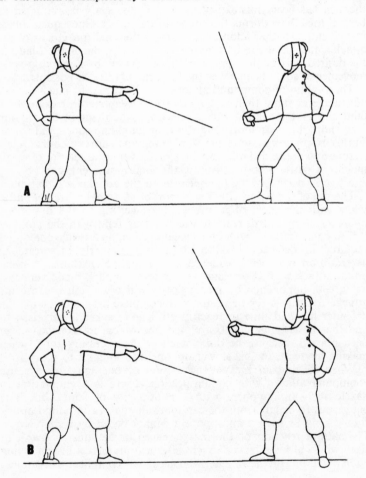

COUNTER-ATTACKS

Counter-attacks consist of the stop hit and the time hit. As at foil, a counter-attack at sabre, to be valid, must be delivered on an opponent's offensive action, which may be an attack or a riposte, in such a way as to gain a period of fencing time on the completion of the opponent's action.

This question of time does not, of course, arise in the case of the time hit since, by definition, the offensive movement cannot in any case land if the time hit is made correctly. The stop hit, on the other hand, must arrive a period of fencing time before the attack arrives. It will be remembered that a period of fencing time is the time required to perform one simple fencing action. For example, in a compound attack consisting of a number of feints and a final movement, the stop hit to be valid must arrive before the final movement is commenced, that is to say, at latest during the last feint. If it is made thereafter, the attack will, under the rules, be given priority if both hits arrive.

The inclusion of the sword-arm in the target increases the opportunities for stop hits over those possible with the foil. While stop hits are usually made on a compound attack or during a preparation of attack such as a step forward, at sabre almost any offensive movement if incorrectly executed, or made out of time or distance, may present an opportunity for a stop cut at arm or head or a stop point at the body.

The wide measure normally maintained at sabre generally requires the attacker to shorten the distance before, or during, his attack and increases the opportunities for a stop hit to be made. Indeed, the ever-present possibility of a stop hit against almost any offensive action introduces that element of caution into sabre play which makes it tactically more akin to épée fencing than to foil to which, technically, it approximates more closely by the similarity of its rules and conventions.

Stop hits at sabre may be made with the front or the back edge of the blade, or with the point, and are applied to the target in exactly the same manner as already described for the simple attacks.

Time hits are usually made only with the point. This is because the time hit is in fact a parry and riposte made in one movement; that is to say, it is equivalent to a stop hit made covered in such a way that the opponent's attack is completely deflected from the defender's target.

It is obvious that the extension of the arm required to cover the line, when making a time hit, will bring the attacking and the counter-attacking blades parallel to each other. If both are trying to make a cut, the attacker will be likely to force his way through the defender's blade. When, however, the time hit is made with the point, it will be possible to angulate the blade and deflect the attacking blade with the guard, whether the attack is made with the edge or the point.

Stop cuts are usually made at the wrist, forearm or head, which are the parts of the target most likely to be exposed during an attack or riposte. Against a wide attack in the high lines, the stop point in the low line, made while flexing the legs sharply, can be most effective.

The stop cut must be a crisp, light movement applied with the fingers and wrist as rapidly as possible. Much practice is required to attain timing and accuracy in applying a stop cut and to develop the light hand and blade control which will enable the fencer to continue the phrase should his stop hit fail. Sabre in hand is the essential factor as a basis for this control. It is rarely possible to cover the line when making a stop cut, as can be done when the stop hit is made with the point. The *sabreur* should therefore develop the habit of forming a parry immediately after he has made a stop cut.

Stop hits are generally made on an offensive movement when the attacker is shortening the measure very rapidly, probably with a *flèche* attack. The defender must, therefore, always be prepared to retire or jump backwards to restore the fencing measure for subsequent defensive movements, if his stop hit fails to land.

Here again, considerable practice is required to co-ordinate the stop hit with the step or jump backwards. It is obvious that the defender must reach forward as far as possible when making a stop hit, in order to gain the maximum time and distance on the attack. This will be nullified if the defender starts to retire too soon and the stop hit will probably land on the attacker's guard or miss altogether. Balance and footwork should enable the step or jump backwards to be made immediately after the stop hit has landed (or failed) but not before.

The most common, and the most natural, time hit with the point is made in the third position. The safest time hit is the one made in the low line with a *croisé* from second. With the hand in second position, the opponent's blade can be gathered and firmly held while it is deflected downwards and off the target.

The natural reaction when a hit is aimed at one with any weapon is to hit back. The fencer learns to control this impulse and to use it judiciously and selectively. The counter-attack must not be used indiscriminately. Constant stop-cutting on the opponent's every move is useless, and worse, it will be used by an experienced fencer for effective attacks in counter-time.

RENEWED ATTACKS

Renewed attacks, as their name implies, are new offensive actions immediately following an attack which has failed to score, because it has been parried or otherwise avoided.

Under the rules governing foil and sabre fencing, once an attack has been parried or avoided the attacker has lost the right of way, or priority, which passes to his opponent for an immediate riposte. A renewal of the attack can therefore only be valid if the defender fails to riposte, or loses time by delaying his riposte, or making a compound riposte, that is to say, does not make an immediate riposte. In the two latter cases, the attacker's renewed attack must arrive at least one period of fencing time before the riposte hits him, if it is to obtain the necessary priority to be counted valid under the rules.

Because parries at sabre require wider arm movements than are necessary at foil or épée (it is impossible, for example, to form the parry of fifth without exposing the whole of the sword-arm), renewed attacks are much used, especially to the forearm or the head. The unavoidable exposure of these targets when parries are formed, provides opportunities for them. Such renewed attacks often have the character of stop hits made on the opponent's riposte.

All renewed attacks may, of course, be made with the point or the edge, but the latter is more generally used, especially at the arm or head.

Whether made as a premeditated or as an opportunist stroke, the renewed attack must be made swiftly, lightly and accurately and the attacker should always be prepared to form a parry and continue the phrase, should his renewed attack fail to score. Bearing in mind the rules mentioned above, it will be obvious that the timing of a renewed attack is all-important unless the opponent fails to riposte at all.

When practising renewed attacks, the *sabreur* should form the habit of immediately forming a parry after he has made his renewal and returning to guard or stepping or springing back, in order to restore the fencing measure to facilitate subsequent movements in the phrase. The timing and co-ordination of these movements are the same as have already been mentioned when discussing counter-attacks (page 167).

Although the renewal of the attack is a movement much used at sabre, care must be taken that it does not become an automatic or habitual stroke. Forewarned, the defender can easily circumvent it, either by making an immediate riposte or by taking two successive parries before riposting.

There are three types of renewed attack:

(*a*) The remise.
(*b*) The redoublement.
(*c*) The reprise.

(*a*) **The Remise.** The remise is a new cut or a replacement of the point, made in the same line as the original offensive movement without withdrawing the arm. A remise may follow an attack or a riposte or a stop hit.

As the sword-arm must remain extended, the remise must be made purely by finger play and wrist action, without altering the direction of the blade or bending the elbow.

After an attack, the remise may be made while on the lunge or while returning to guard. The attacker should, in any case, normally return to guard immediately he has made his remise, while parrying the riposte. A useful alternative is to spring backwards from the lunge. When the remise follows a riposte or stop hit, the fencer should similarly step back or spring back, as appropriate, to obtain the best fencing measure for subsequent movements.

At sabre, a remise is generally made with the edge and is usually directed at some part of the wrist or forearm. Although often instinctive and made when an opportunity presents itself, it will be most effective when it is a premeditated movement resulting from observation of the opponent's habits and reactions. A useful exercise to develop accuracy and blade control is to make an attack with full lunge, which the partner parries. This is followed by a series of remises on different parts of the forearm—outside, top, inside, under side—as the partner opens these lines, ending with a spring backwards to guard, taking a parry appropriate to the partner's counter-offensive action.

(b) **The Redoublement.** The redoublement is similar to the remise, except that instead of being made in the same line as the original movement without withdrawing the arm, it includes some simple or composed blade movements. When made following an attack there is no return to guard before its execution. It may, of course, follow a riposte or a stop hit.

The remarks made above, regarding the advisability of following a remise immediately with a parry and regaining an appropriate fencing measure to continue the phrase, apply with equal force to the redoublement.

Like the remise, the redoublement at sabre is usually made by a cut to some part of the forearm or at head, although any part of the target may be vulnerable. The fencing measure existing when the redoublement is made will determine to what extent it is necessary to bend or withdraw the sword-arm, in order to disengage or make a circular cut. It is obviously desirable that such arm movements should be kept to a minimum and that the blade should be controlled by the fingers and wrist, to make the movement as light and as swift as possible.

An effective redoublement can often be made with the point, for example by one-two. When it is made as a premeditated movement the attacker can, with advantage, keep his lunge rather short, so that he has a little extra length in hand to give penetration to his redoublement by disengagement or one-two with the point.

A redoublement may be made in broken time, that is with a slight pause before one of its movements, and it can, of course, include more than one feint. Obviously, as for compound attacks, the number of feints used in a redoublement should be kept to a minimum. This is of particular importance owing to the close quarters at which the fencers usually find themselves and the probability of the defender scoring a hit, even inadvertently, if the redoublement is over-complicated.

Like the remise, the redoublement is likely to be most successful in gaining the vital advantage in fencing time if it is a premeditated action. A vigilant opponent can easily turn it to his own advantage if it becomes a habit and it thus loses its essential element of surprise.

(c) **The Reprise.** The reprise is a remise or a redoublement made after a return to guard, either forwards or backwards. It is the (even momentary) return to guard which distinguishes the reprise from the other forms of renewed attack. After the return to guard the reprise can be completed either with a lunge or with a *flèche*.

The choice of whether the return to guard is made forward or backwards will be determined by the distance existing between the fencers and usually depends on whether the opponent retires when parrying the attack or not.

The reprise forward, by bringing up the rear leg after the lunge to launch a new attack, is usually a premeditated movement, made when it is anticipated that the opponent will retire while parrying.

The reprise backwards is often made by an attacker who recovers to guard normally after his attack has failed; observing that no riposte is made, he immediately renews his attack by lunge or *flèche*.

While returning to guard the attacker should keep his arm extended, in order to cover the line with his guard. The renewed attack may be simple or compound. In the latter case the feints are designed, by forcing the opponent to parry, to increase the attacker's chance of ensuring right of way for his renewed attack. Similarly, a renewed attack may be prepared by actions on the blade.

The reprise is most likely to succeed if it is a premeditated movement. Much of its success will depend on an exact judgment of distance.

SECOND-INTENTION ATTACKS

The second-intention, or counter-time attack consists of drawing a stop hit which is parried, and scoring with a riposte. The first intention, which consists of an invitation, a feint or other offensive movement, is not designed to hit the opponent but to induce him to make a stop hit so that it may be parried and the final movement, or second intention, is the scoring stroke.

Counter-time is a tactical move used as frequently at sabre as it is at épée and for the same reason, namely the predilection of fencers at both weapons to attempt stop hits. It is a premeditated action and success depends on inducing the opponent to make a stop hit in a desired line.

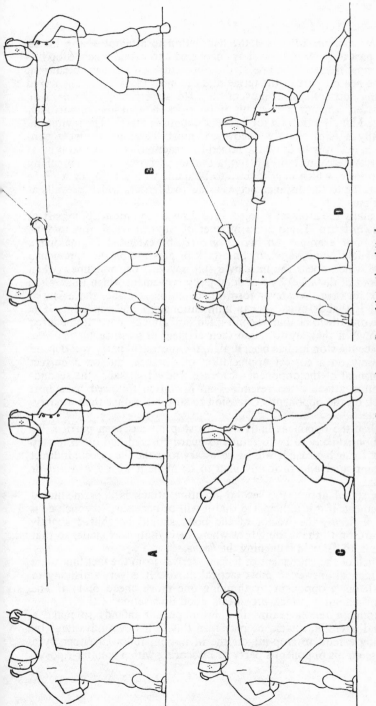

Fig. 57 The Counter-time or Second-intention Attack

A. Fencer on left has his flank exposed. His opponent makes a feint at flank
   with a step forward
B. Fencer on left makes a stop cut at head as his opponent advances
C. Attacker on right parries the stop cut
D. Attacker completes his second-intention attack by a cut at flank

Few *sabreurs* can resist the temptation to attempt a stop hit on any part of the target which is uncovered and within reach. Stop hits are most frequently made at the opponent's sword-arm, because it is the nearest part of the target and the most likely to be uncovered during any offensive movements. No experienced *sabreur* will, however, attempt a stop hit if he suspects that the opportunity offered him is a trap set for a second-intention attack. The invitation, usually a feint slightly uncovered, must therefore be made convincingly if it is to draw the hoped-for reaction. Once the stop hit is drawn, there must be no hesitation in parrying it and launching the riposte, which may require to be made with a lunge or a *flèche* according to the distance between the two fencers which prevails at the time.

Usually the attacker's object is to draw a stop hit at some part of his sword-arm. There are a number of ways in which this may be done. For example, an invitation may be extended by making a feint slightly uncovered, by an attack or pressure on the opponent's blade which opens the line, by a step forward or sometimes (when just out of distance) by a sudden jerky movement which throws the trunk forward. Whatever form of invitation is made, the essential point is that it must appear unintentional to the opponent. It is therefore obvious that second-intention attacks have to be used sparingly if they are to retain their element of surprise.

Once the stop hit has been drawn, the successful parry will depend not only on a correct appreciation of distance, but on a correct assessment of the opponent's cadence. Indeed, at sabre the second-intention attack often resembles an invitation followed by a beat attack on the opponent's extension to stop-hit, rather than a parry-riposte.

When the opponent finds that his stop hit has been parried, his reaction is likely to be to return to guard covered and often to step back. In such a case it will be necessary to make the riposte indirect or compound and probably also to combine it with a *balestra* or *flèche*.

As stated above, the second-intention attack is a premeditated movement. If it is anticipated that it will be necessary to conclude it with a *flèche*, the weight of the body should be shifted slightly forward on to the leading foot when the invitation is made, so that there is no delay in launching the *flèche*.

Much of the enjoyment of fencing derives from the fact that there is a tactical answer to most tactical moves. It is very satisfying to outwit one's opponent by thinking one move ahead of him. The second-intention attack provides a good illustration of this.

Should a fencer realize that his opponent intends to make a second-intention attack, he may turn this to his own advantage by making a feint to stop-hit on the invitation, followed either by a remise on his opponent's parry or by scoring with a counter-riposte.

INVITATIONS

Invitations, the intentional opening of a line to expose some part of the target to induce a reaction from the opponent, are much used at sabre.

Invitations at sabre generally consist of opening the line to draw an attack or counter-attack, or an extension of the sword-arm designed to induce the opponent to make a preparation on the blade. We have already noted how invitations are used when making second-intention attacks. They are also used to test an opponent's reactions.

No experienced *sabreur* will, of course, react to an invitation if he recognizes it as such, or he will react in such a manner as to draw his opponent for a counter-move to his own advantage.

Subtlety is therefore the first essential in making an invitation. It may take the form of a relaxation of the engagement, a pressure, an absence of blade or even an advance within distance. Whatever form it takes, it must be a deliberate mistake—but not so appear to the opponent.

DEFENCE

Defence is effected by placing the blade in such a position that the attacker's blade does not reach the target. This is called the parry.

PARRIES

At foil and épée it is sufficient to parry in such a way that the line is closed so that, if the attack continues, the attacker's point will be deflected past the target. At sabre, in addition, the defender has to ensure that a cut is prevented from reaching the target.

The principle of defence is to oppose the forte of the defender's blade to the foible of the attacker's blade. At sabre this is done by opposing the cutting edge to that of the attacker. When forming a parry in this way, if the attacker's cut is made with force, his blade will slip down towards the defender's guard and thus progressively fall into the forte of the defender's blade.

At sabre, parries often have to withstand cuts which are made with considerable force. They must therefore be made firmly. This is ensured by the grip of the thumb and first finger on the hilt, notably assisted by the little finger which brings the handle firmly against the heel of the sword-hand.

A strong cut which is made on the foible of an opponent's blade will often be forced through on to the target and an insufficient parry will result, to the detriment of the defender. The question of whether a parry is sufficient or insufficient frequently arises at sabre, especially when hits are made at the arm. The rule is that if a cut hits the target before, or at the same moment, as it meets the opponent's blade or guard, the hit is valid. If a cut meets the guard or blade before it reaches the target (often as a whip over the guard) the cut has been parried and the defender has a right to riposte.

The Hungarians go so far as to distinguish between the parts of the blade on which a beat is made. Thus if a beat, used as a preparation of attack, is made on the forte of the blade of a fencer correctly on guard covering the line, they consider that the beat has been parried and subsequent movements made by the attacker are counted as renewals of the original attack. In consequence, in such circumstances if the defender makes a counter-offensive movement, or riposte off such a beat, the Hungarian judges would award it priority over the attack. If in the course of a similar movement the beat is made on the foible of the defender's blade, this is not considered to constitute a parry and the attack will be given priority over any counter-offensive movement made by the defender after such contact of blades.

The International Federation has not, so far, agreed to this distinction. As the rule stands, if a beat is made even on the forte of the defender's blade in a closed line, the defender must parry the subsequent movement of the attack before obtaining the right to the riposte.

Attacks with the point are parried by opposition of the blade in much the same way as at foil and épée, the wrist being angulated in order to obtain maximum protection from the guard, especially when the parries of second and third are taken.

Fig. 58
The Defensive Box
at Sabre

The *sabreur* has to defend a defensive area or defensive box which is bounded by a straight line on each side of his body and horizontal lines at the top of his head and just below his waist. When forming parries against cuts, he has to place his blade generally along these boundaries, which entails wider movements of the sword-arm in defence than are necessary at the other two weapons where attacks with the point alone have to be dealt with. When a succession of parries are made, it is only necessary to oppose the blade firmly to the line of the attack. Care must be taken to check the blade when it reaches the proper position for the parry, even if the opponent is making wide movements in his attack. Any attempt to follow the opponent's blade outside the defensive box, or to strike the attacking blade aside rather than oppose it, will lead to wide, slashing movements which can easily be deceived by the attacker.

Against cuts, it is important that the whole of the edge of the defender's blade should be opposed to the attack, so as completely to cover the line in which the parry is formed. Especially when taking a succession of parries, or when raising the hand to the parry of fifth, there is often a tendency to let the hand overrun the blade. As a result, while the hand reaches the correct position for the parry, the blade does not completely cover the line and remains more or less diagonally across the body. This is a fruitful source of insufficient parries, because the attacker who makes a strong cut will be able to force his blade through the parry on to the target, instead of it slipping down to the forte of the defender's blade as will occur if the blade is correctly placed.

There are six parries at sabre, covering every part of the target. They correspond, of course, to the six fencing positions which have already been studied when discussing the lines of engagement. These parries are called first, second, third, fourth, fifth and sixth. In practice, sixth is rarely used because the position of the hand makes it difficult to execute the riposte—it will be disregarded hereafter. One may distinguish between the normal third position, with the hand level with the breast, and low third, where the hand is level with the hip. Low third is sometimes called a supplementary parry, but it is in fact merely a variation in the method of forming this parry and such variation also occurs, although less markedly, with a number of other parries. Indeed, many of the older books on fencing gave a large number of parries at sabre, since they distinguished between high and low quarte, high and low seconde and so on. Traditionally the parry of fifth was known in England as the St George parry.

It will be recalled that cuts may be divided into those made laterally or vertically or at angles approximating to one or other of these directions. Vertical cuts are parried by first, second and fifth, lateral cuts by third and fourth.

The defensive area at sabre is thus protected by parries which can be arranged in two distinct triangles:

(a) The triangle formed by first, second and fifth deals with vertical cuts.

(b) The triangle including third and fourth deals with lateral cuts, while fifth is also added to complete this triangle. (See plates XIII to XVI.)

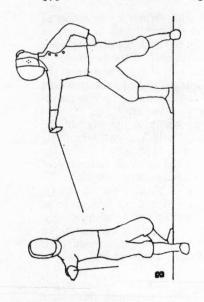

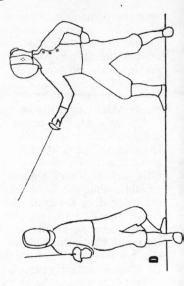

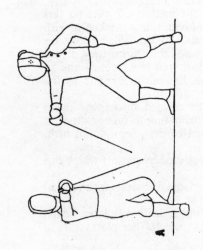

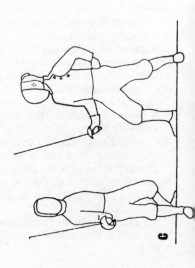

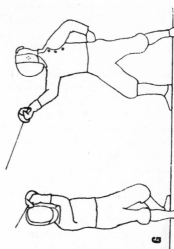
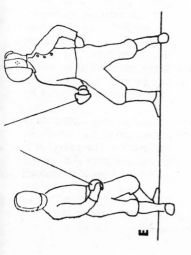

A. First   B. Second
C. Low third   D. Third
E. Fourth   F. Fifth
      G. Sixth

Fig. 59   The Sabre Parries

(a) The First Triangle (First, Fifth, Second).

(i) *First Parry*. So called because it is the natural defensive position of the sword as it is drawn from a scabbard worn on his left hip by a right-handed fencer. It protects the inside lines from hip to shoulder from vertical or semi-vertical cuts made at the chest or left shoulder.

When forming the first parry, the arm should be almost fully extended with the hand rather higher than the shoulder, level with the chin. The sword-hand is turned so that the knuckles are outwards, that is away from the body, which brings the front edge of the blade facing forward and outwards. The blade is angulated forward and to the left so that the point is towards the ground, well outside the leading leg.

Care must be taken not to raise or contract the shoulder as the hand is raised, or the forearm and elbow will be exposed. Lack of elasticity in the sword-arm will also be caused by contracted shoulder muscles which will make subsequent movements, such as the riposte, stiff and slow. It is important to angulate the blade sufficiently, by turning the hand, to present the edge to the attacker's cut which may otherwise force its way through the parry.

(ii) *Second Parry*. Protects the outside lines against cuts made upwards at the flank and is much used to parry attacks with the point. When used as a semicircular parry from third, it will gather an attack with the point directed on the quarte side and deflect it safely off the target.

The position of second is often used as an alternative to third when on guard, especially in the Italian school.

When forming the second parry, the arm is almost fully extended breast-high. The sword-hand is in pronation, with the elbow tucked in and the blade held well forward and to the right so that the point is about level with the opponent's thigh. In this position, provided the elbow is kept tucked in, the forearm is protected by the guard and the front edge of the blade is facing the outside of the target area and slightly angulated forward to resist strong cuts.

The second parry can easily be taken from the normal on-guard position, with the hand in low third, merely by carrying the sword-hand forward and slightly to the right, while lowering the point by bending the wrist slightly downwards.

As in all parries which are taken with the sword-arm almost fully extended, there is always a tendency to contract the muscles of the shoulder and arm in an effort to achieve strength in the parry. It is particularly important to avoid this fault when taking the second parry because, with the hand in second, the high lines are exposed and only by maintaining a supple and relaxed arm and shoulder will it be possible to move swiftly and easily to another position to protect them. Firmness in the parry must come entirely from the fingers and the correct presentation of the edge of the blade to the attacker's cut.

(iii) *Fifth Parry.* Common to both defence triangles, the fifth parry protects the head from vertical cuts.

To form the fifth parry, the sword-hand is raised upwards and forward until it is slightly higher than the head, but still just to the right of the line of the shoulder. The arm will be slightly bent with the elbow kept in. The blade will follow the horizontal line bounding the top of the target, that is, it will be almost parallel with the ground but with the point a little higher than the hilt. The sword-hand will be held turned to the front, with the finger-nails towards the opponent, so that the edge of the blade is slightly angulated forward in the path of vertical cuts directed at the head.

When taking a fifth parry the sword-hand should be raised in a smooth movement, achieved by keeping the shoulder down and the arm and shoulder muscles relaxed. Here again there is a natural tendency to keep the arm stiff which must be avoided, or the subsequent riposte or succeeding parry will be slow. When the fifth parry is formed, the defender is always exposed to a remise to the forearm. A relaxed, supple arm is essential if he is to make a smooth, swift riposte or move rapidly to another parry to circumvent this manoeuvre.

The parry of fifth does not come naturally to most people. If it is not correctly formed an insufficient parry is bound to result, more especially because hits aimed at the head often arrive with some force. Common faults are raising the hand too high or keeping the point below the level of the hand. Much practice is needed to place the blade correctly by a smooth, relaxed movement, while achieving a firm parry by angulating the blade and controlling it entirely with the fingers.

The parry of fifth is perhaps the most important parry in the *sabreur's* defensive repertoire, because the head is one of the most vulnerable parts of the target especially when on the lunge. There is no alternative to this parry to protect the head from a vertical cut.

(b) **The Second Triangle (Third, Fifth, Fourth).**

(i) *Third Parry.* The hand is held low, with the wrist well bent and the blade almost vertical. It protects the outside lines from hip to cheek against lateral cuts.

In the Italian school the third parry was normally taken with the arm half extended, the hand breast-high and in pronation and the forearm, wrist and blade in one straight line. Low third was regarded as a supplementary parry. The normal third parry did not completely protect the outside lines and the parries of low third or second were required to deal with cuts aimed at flank.

In modern sabre fencing, low third is the only form of third parry in general use, because it gives complete protection to the outside lines and does not expose the forearm.

To form the third parry the sword-hand is held level with the hip, with the forearm almost parallel to the ground and the elbow just touching the hip. The hand is in half-pronation with the wrist flexed outwards, so that the blade is angulated at about forty-five degrees from the line of the *piste*, which will present the edge to the path of lateral cuts. The blade is held almost upright but the point must be slightly forward and to the right of the hand. This blade position is important, as it will help to ensure that a cut causes the attacker's blade to slip into the forte of the defender's blade. If the blade is too upright a strong cut may be forced through the blade on to the target.

The low position of the hand and the turning of the wrist give maximum protection from the guard and ensure that cuts made upwards towards the flank do not slip under the guard.

The third parry as given above cannot be made correctly unless the sabre is held in the modern fashion described earlier in this chapter. It will be observed that the position of the hand is that adopted for the on-guard position in the Hungarian school; but, in the parry, the blade is angulated to cover the outside lines, instead of being diagonally across the body in the offensive-defensive position used when on guard.

(ii) *Fourth Parry*. Here again, the almost vertical blade protects the inside lines from hip to cheek against lateral cuts to the quarte side.

To form the fourth parry, the sword-hand is placed well to the left of the body, level with or just below the left hip; the forearm thus lies across the body, and the elbow is close in to the right hip in much the same position as it is when the third parry is formed.

The sword-hand is in half-pronation, with the finger-nails to the left, and slightly forward, so that the guard and blade are angulated in the path of a lateral cut arriving from the defender's left side. While the blade is almost vertical, the point must be slightly in front of the hand, in order that a heavy cut directed at any part of the blade may tend to slip down towards the guard. The low position of the hand, with the wrist very slightly flexed back to present the edge correctly, ensures protection from the guard and prevents cuts aimed in the low line from slipping under the guard.

A common fault when taking the fourth parry, more particularly when moving the hand from third, is to place the hand correctly but allow the point of the weapon to remain centrally to the body. Unless the blade is placed correctly as described above, a strong cut will be forced through on to the target—in other words, the parry will be insufficient. The lateral movement from third to fourth, or vice versa, is a very common stroke at sabre. The fencer should have the feeling of moving his hand and blade in one piece from one side of his target to the other, by directing his forearm from the elbow, while angulating his blade by a slight flexing of the wrist, and checking the hand immediately it reaches the correct position to cover the line.

COUNTER-PARRIES

At sabre, counter- or circular parries are generally used against attacks with the point or when, at close quarters, there is insufficient time to move to another simple parry. They are only practicable in third, fourth or second position.

Counter-parries are made by a circular movement of the wrist, aided by the fingers to a lesser extent than at the other weapons. Care must be taken not to use the forearm during these movements, or wide, slow parries will result. The circle described when taking a counter-parry will of course be the one which gathers the attacker's blade away from the target. Thus counter-third will be a clockwise circle, while counter-fourth or second will be made anti-clockwise.

The circle described by the defender's point when taking a counter-parry must be sufficiently large to ensure that the attacker's blade is gathered and brought back into the forte of the defender's blade.

An example of the usefulness of the counter-parry at sabre is when an attack is made by pressure or beat with the back of the blade inside the opponent's blade when he is on guard in third, followed by a direct cut at cheek. This form of attack is often used and, when properly timed, it is very difficult to parry directly, as the cut at cheek rebounds directly off the reverse beat with the attacker's blade inside. The counter-parry of third is the only effective way to gather the opponent's blade and carry it off the target.

THE RIPOSTE

A riposte is an offensive action made by the defender after an attack has been successfully parried. Ripostes are similarly named to the attacks already described; that is to say they may be direct, indirect or compound.

The riposte at sabre may be delivered with the edge or the point; either immediately or after a pause; from the static position, *à pied ferme*, or with a lunge or a *flèche*.

Sabre parries are usually parries of detachment rather than of opposition. This facilitates lightness and speed of riposte. A riposte, whether with point or edge, must be made with the finger and wrist actions already described for the hit. A relaxed and supple arm and shoulder will ensure that it is light and swift and not a wide, heavy movement which the opponent can easily parry or avoid, or on which he can make a remise or stop hit.

DIRECT RIPOSTES

The direct riposte with the edge should be an instinctive reaction from the contact of the blades in a parry. It often gains speed by rebounding from the opponent's blade as soon as the parry has been successful.

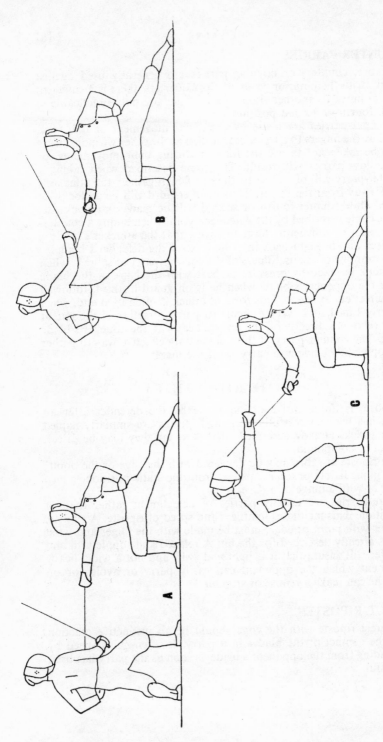

Fig. 60 The Direct Riposte
A. The attack from the right is parried by fourth
B. Defender presents his blade to cheek as he extends his arm

As its name implies, the direct riposte travels to the target by the most direct route from the particular parry formed. The most usual ripostes with the edge of the sabre are:

(1) From first to flank.
(2) From second to right cheek.
(3) From third to head.
(4) From fourth to right cheek.
(5) From fifth to flank.

While these are the direct ripostes most commonly used, others may, of course, be substituted, largely depending on the opponent's reaction after his attack has been parried. For example, it may be more appropriate to riposte from second to flank rather than cheek if the opponent raises his arm.

From the parry, the direct riposte is made by a smooth and very rapid extension of the arm, directing the hand towards the chosen part of the target. During this extension the necessary finger and wrist movements are made to present the edge to the target, after which the hit is made by finger play, as is usual for making any cut.

Speed and accuracy are essential factors in the direct riposte, to overcome the opponent's instinctive reaction when his attack has been parried. Any stiffening of the arm during the riposte will slow it down and probably cause it to be short.

A direct riposte may be immediate, that is, a reflex action from the parry in order to hit the opponent before he recovers or has an opportunity to cover the line. Often at sabre, however, the riposte is delayed by a distinct pause after the parry before being delivered. This delayed riposte, like the broken-time attack, is more commonly used at sabre than at the other weapons, for two reasons. When recovering from guard the opponent may uncover the line for the direct riposte; alternatively, a *sabreur* who has the habit of forming a parry in the path of the usual direct riposte after his attack has failed, having a wide defensive box to protect, is liable to leave the line in which he has formed his parry if the riposte does not arrive there as expected. Delaying a riposte gives the opponent the necessary time to react in either of these ways, which will leave the path open for the direct riposte.

The direct riposte to flank from the first parry is an awkward movement because of the position of the sword-hand in this parry. As we shall see later, the more usual riposte from this parry is the *molinello* to the head.

From second to cheek or from third to head are particularly fast and natural ripostes, requiring little redirection of the blade or hand. When made with a supple and relaxed arm, they fly to their objectives so fast that the opponent will have considerable difficulty in parrying them when he is committed to his attack.

From fourth to cheek is also a natural reaction, but it requires a rapid rotation of the wrist to present the edge of the blade to cheek.

This riposte can be so fast that only a counter-parry by the attacker can hope to gather it.

From fifth to flank requires a conscious dropping of the sword-hand and arm in order to pass the blade under the attacker's arm. This is usually necessary to make this riposte successfully because the *sabreur's* natural reaction, after a cut at head has been parried, is to drop his hand.

While ripostes are mostly made at the opponent's body because his arm is usually covered by his guard, ripostes at the arm can sometimes be very effective, especially against an attacker who recovers very rapidly after his attack has failed. When making a riposte at arm, it is often necessary to angulate the blade quite markedly in order to avoid hitting the guard, and to present the blade at right angles to the arm and not parallel with it.

Direct ripostes are often very effective when made with the point, particularly from the parries of second and third and, to a lesser extent, from first. The natural reaction from a parry at sabre is the riposte with the edge. It is therefore most commonly used and the form of riposte usually expected by an opponent. A riposte made with the point will often achieve surprise.

The riposte by point is made with the hand in pronation; the point is directed, usually at the body, by the fingers, with the blade and guard covering the arm as it extends. From second and third some angulation of the blade helps to fix the point on the target.

INDIRECT RIPOSTES

Indirect ripostes, like indirect attacks, can be made by disengagement, by a circular cut (cut-over), or by counter-disengagement.

The indirect riposte of course widens the choice of target, and the use of point or edge adds variety to such counter-offensive movements at sabre. For example, from the third parry the riposte may be made by circular cut at head or chest, by disengagement, or by counter-disengagement with point or edge. From each of the five parries there is generally a choice of riposte at head and at chest or flank.

The counter-disengagement, with point or edge, deceives a counter-parry. At sabre it is very frequently used to deceive a semicircular parry from third to second or vice versa.

It is generally necessary to bend the arm when making an indirect riposte to avoid being caught up in the attacker's blade. The amount the forearm has to be retracted will, of course, vary according to the distance existing between the two fencers. It should be kept to the minimum required to clear the blade, because use of the arm leads to wide, slow movements during which the defender is always vulnerable to a remise or stop hit.

The circular cut at chest, a movement much used with the sabre as a riposte, should be made with the least possible arm movement.

It is made by a rotation of the wrist, reaching well forward, to present the blade at the target before applying the cut by finger play. The natural follow-through from this slicing cut is used, again by rotation of the wrist, to return the hand to the pronated position to cover in third.

The most effective riposte from first is the circular cut at head, or *molinello*. The *molinello* is often used in lessons as an exercise to give strength, control and mobility to the sword-arm. To execute the *molinello*, the blade is drawn back, by a circular movement of the wrist and forearm, while maintaining contact with the opponent's blade until the point is cleared, when the circle is completed to head. In this riposte the sabre describes a complete circle in a vertical plane from the first position to the cut at head. Control with the fingers and wrist is required and it is an excellent exercise for relaxation of the shoulder, without which the *molinello* degenerates into a wild, slow flailing action which soon loses accuracy and is easily parried.

The indirect riposte may be executed immediately after the parry or may be delayed, for the reasons already enumerated for the direct riposte.

COMPOUND RIPOSTES

A compound riposte includes one or more feints designed to induce the opponent to form a parry which can be deceived in order to enable the final movement of the riposte to land on the target.

After an attack has been parried, the fencers usually find themselves at comparatively close quarters. To avoid getting his blade entangled in his opponent's while making his feints, the defender generally has to keep his sword-arm bent, or even withdraw it, only extending fully on the final movement of his composed riposte.

Under the rules common to foil and sabre, when a compound riposte is made the attacker can score a remise or stop hit during the periods of fencing time represented by the feints. At sabre this is an ever-present danger owing to the vulnerability of the arm to such movements. The number of feints made during a compound riposte should therefore be kept to a minimum. The forearm is particularly vulnerable to a remise as it is lowered to make any feint from the parry of fifth.

When making feints during a compound riposte it will usually be necessary to ensure, by proper use of the wrist and finger actions, that the edge of the sabre is presented at the target so as to draw the opponent's parry.

At sabre, the defensive area is particularly wide and feints directed at opposite parts of the target, for example a feint chest cut at flank, feint head-chest cut at flank or feint head-flank cut at cheek, will ensure that the opponent has to make a relatively large movement when answering them. This will assist in uncovering his target, and the final movement of the compound riposte can then be made.

In practice it is sometimes sufficient to indicate a feint in order to draw the opponent's parry. For example, a feint at head having drawn fifth, a mere presentation of the edge towards chest, stressed by an outward movement of one's head and shoulder, may cause the opponent to open the line for the cut at flank instead of returning to second or third. Similarly if the riposte is a feint chest cut at chest, a marked circular cutting motion with the arm bent and the hand still in pronation may well draw a reaction which will open the line for the properly made cut at chest.

A feint or final movement of a compound riposte may, of course, be made with the point instead of the edge. A combination of point and edge is often very effective. This is because the introduction of the point into a sabre movement often surprises the opponent for the reasons already indicated above.

A compound riposte may be made in a series of continuous rhythmic movements which, as for compound attacks, must be co-ordinated with the cadence of the opponent's reactions. On the other hand, the compound riposte may be made after a pause following the parry, or with a pause or broken-time movement introduced at any stage.

Examples of such a change of cadence are a parry-fourth quitting the blade during the pause while the opponent covers in third, feint head cut at chest; or parry-third feint head, to which the opponent forms the parry of fifth, withdrawing the hand slightly so that the opponent does not find the blade while a pause is made during which he returns to third or fourth, cut at head. Such movements naturally require very exact timing and good blade control, because if the opponent merely makes contact with the blade during the feint or feints he will have the right of way, under the rules, for a counter-riposte. Like the broken-time attacks, an indirect or compound riposte made with a pause is one of the most spectacular, and satisfying, movements in sabre fencing. Care must, however, be taken not to exploit this method of riposting too frequently. If forewarned, the opponent can often turn this type of riposte to his own advantage with a premeditated remise, a stop hit or a counter-riposte.

COUNTER-RIPOSTES

A counter-riposte is the offensive movement made after a riposte has been successfully parried. The first counter-riposte must obviously be that made by the original attacker and the second that made by the original defender. In a phrase containing a series of counter-ripostes, the odd-numbered one, three, five and so on will be made by the attacker, while those which are even-numbered, two, four, six etc. will be made by the defender.

Owing to the relatively close quarters at which counter-ripostes are generally made at sabre, they are usually made with the edge and are either direct or indirect. They may, of course, be made exactly as described for all other ripostes and with a lunge, after recovery, or with a *flèche*.

Although sometimes used as premeditated movements, when it has been noted, for instance, that the opponent has a predilection for a certain riposte, counter-ripostes are more usually executed by reflex action at sabre. A well trained *sabreur* will always react instinctively with a counter-riposte when the opportunity presents itself. It is a thrilling and spectacular sight to see two well matched sabre champions engaged in a phrase in which they may go to the fifth or sixth counter-riposte in a series of lightning exchanges, with perfect blade control, changes of line and cadence, until one gains the point, perhaps with a delayed circular cut at chest. It is equally exhilarating to see a *sabreur* execute two counter-ripostes while in full flight of a perfectly timed *flèche* attack.

PREPARATIONS OF ATTACK

Sabre fencers today rarely remain within lunging distance of the body when on guard, or when moving up and down the *piste*. They therefore rarely have their blades engaged.

An attack made out of distance gives the defender every opportunity to parry and, since almost any feint will expose some part of the forearm, facilitates a stop hit. Feints made out of lunging distance will be disregarded by all but the most inexperienced *sabreur*, however impressively they are made. The defender will have ample time to parry the final movement of such an attack.

Between two *sabreurs* there is a distance from which neither can be hit by any offensive movement accompanied solely by a lunge. There is another distance from which such an attack can land and, for reasons already given, the attack has a distinct advantage over defence at sabre. A *sabreur* is therefore constantly faced with the problem of either keeping his opponent at the former distance to prevent surprise, or himself achieving the latter distance if he wishes to attack successfully. For this reason sabre fencers rarely remain static for long during a bout. Thus, it is hardly surprising that at sabre it is rarely possible to attack from a static position merely by lunging and that generally a preparation for an attack is necessary.

The most obvious preparation for an attack is to shorten the distance by a step forward or *balestra*, or to draw the opponent within distance by stepping back prior to launching an attack. During these movements the *sabreur* is vulnerable to a counter-attack or an attack on preparation. It is usual, therefore, at sabre to combine the step forward with a preparation on the opponent's blade, in order to distract him and make it more difficult for him to take counter-offensive action. In other words, to combine two or more forms of preparation of attack, one of which is usually concerned with shortening the distance.

Preparations on the blade fall into two categories:

(a) Attacks on the blade which include the beat, pressure and graze or *froissement*.

(b) *Prises de fer* (taking the blade) by engagement, envelopment, bind or *croisé*.

While, theoretically, all these preparations are possible at sabre, in practice attacks on the blade and the engagement are almost exclusively used. This is because the limitations on finger play already noted, due to the normal pronated hand position, and the fact that at sabre a fencer rarely remains for any time with his arm straight and the point directed at the target, make it impracticable to attempt an envelopment, bind or *croisé*.

GAINING AND BREAKING GROUND

The step forward or the *balestra* are the most obvious preparations for an attack. Once the right measure has been achieved the attack is launched with a lunge or *flèche*. Sometimes the *flèche* can do double service as a preparation and vehicle for the attack.

The constant preoccupation of *sabreurs* with the measure often makes it necessary to dissemble one's intentions when gaining and breaking ground. The tactical use of the step backwards has already been studied. At sabre gaining on the lunge, bringing up the rear foot only before launching the lunge, is also often used with the same object. Some fencers, after steps forward and backward on the *piste*, move the rear leg backwards and forwards several times, before suddenly lunging or launching a *flèche* as this foot is near the leading foot.

As already stated, the vulnerability to the stop hit at the head or the advanced target while gaining or breaking ground makes it advisable to combine this preparation with some other, usually an engagement or an attack on the blade.

PREPARATIONS ON THE BLADE

(a) Attacks on the Blade.

(i) *The Beat*. The beat is the commonest, and perhaps the most effective, preparation on the blade which is used at sabre. It may be made with the front or the back edge of the blade, but in either case it should be a firm, crisp beat effected by the fingers and the flexing of the wrist and involving the least possible movement of the arm.

The strength of the beat will vary according to the reaction required. A strong beat will be used to open the line for a direct attack; for example from third, beat-cut at arm. A lighter beat will generally induce the opponent to close the line in the direction of the beat, in other words, to answer the beat, when an indirect attack follows. A beat may also, of course, be used as a preparation for a compound attack. It will often speed up attacking movements. The blade should rebound from the beat into the line of the attack or feint.

Beats in second or third are made with the front edge of the blade. In fourth it is often preferable to beat with the back edge because, when made with the fore-edge in this line, a feint entails turning the sword-hand into half-supination. In fourth a reverse beat cut at cheek, or reverse beat cut at arm, are exceedingly fast movements which can rarely be parried except with a counter-parry.

It is preferable to make a beat on the upper half or foible of the opponent's blade. It will be recalled that the Hungarians consider that a beat made on the forte when the opponent is covering the line should be regarded as an attack which has been parried. The opponent has the right to riposte directly off this beat, while the subsequent movement made by the fencer after his beat is counted as a remise. The International Federation, however, rules that a beat is a preparation of attack wherever it is made, and the opponent must parry the subsequent movement in order to have the right to riposte.

It is true that a beat made on the forte of the opponent's blade is less likely to obtain the desired reaction. Further, should the opponent react from the beat and score a hit, there is always the danger that the jury may read his movement as a parry and riposte and the original attacker's hit made after the beat as a remise. This is, of course, wrong, but the misreading of the phrase is very liable to happen—which is not very surprising in view of the difficulties of a jury's task in fast sabre play. It is always wise to avoid making the jury's task more difficult than necessary and a correct application of the beat to establish the attack is one way of helping them.

(ii) *The Pressure*. The pressure can only be made when the blades are engaged. This occurs comparatively rarely when on guard at sabre. However, when the occasion presents itself, a pressure with front or back edge is a useful stroke to induce the opponent to close the line.

(iii) *The Graze or* Froissement. The *froissement* is a useful alternative to a beat. It is mainly used to force the opponent's blade aside to open the line. By flexing the wrist as the arm extends, a strong glancing movement or graze is made from the foible to the forte of the opponent's blade. The graze should be made with the front edge of the blade. The graze should not be used too frequently or it will lose the element of surprise on which its success largely depends.

(b) *Prises de Fer*. Except for the engagement, the *prises de fer* are seldom practicable at sabre. A bind, an envelopment or a *croisé* can only be successfully executed against an opponent who maintains an extended arm offering resistance and this rarely occurs at sabre. Further the pronated position of the hand and the sabre grip are not conducive to the finger play required for *prises de fer*. The *croisé* can sometimes be used from second for a riposte or time hit with the point.

THE DEROBEMENT

The *dérobement* is the action of evading an opponent's attempts to take the blade when the arm is straight with the point threatening the target.

At sabre, the wide measure usually maintained between fencers when on guard invites the use of attacks with preparation on the blade, in order safely to get within distance for an attack.

If a fencer offers the blade by making a series of feints with the arm extended, his opponent may be induced to attempt to take the blade, when a well timed evasion, or *dérobement*, will cause the opponent to impale himself on the point which he has failed to gather.

Although a *dérobement* may be made with the edge, it is best made with the point. It is particularly successful against an opponent who makes the mistake of lunging with his preparation of attack.

ATTACKS ON PREPARATION

As has already been noted, most attacks at sabre have to include either simple or combinations of preparations of attack, for example, a step forward and a beat. While he is carrying out a preparation for his attack a fencer is particularly vulnerable, firstly because he is coming within lunging distance and secondly because he is momentarily concentrating on attack rather than defence.

This is therefore an excellent psychological moment to launch an attack. The fencer who carries out this manoeuvre must take great care to attack during the preparation and not into the attack itself. In the latter case, at best, the judges will give a simultaneous action, but in fact the attack should have the right of way. Correct choice of time, distance and cadence are essential if an attack on preparation is to be successful—and to be so regarded by the judges.

SABRE EXERCISES

There are a variety of exercises which can be used very profitably for training at sabre.

The *molinello* following the first parry is a valuable exercise to develop strong and flexible arm muscles and sabre in hand. It may be executed very rapidly from the static, on-guard position, or combined with the lunge. Thus: first parry—*molinello* to head—return to first—*molinello* to head with lunge—return to guard—step forward with first parry—*molinello* to head—step forward—first parry—*molinello* to head with lunge—return to guard—repeat the whole length of the *piste*—one final *molinello* with lunge—jump back from lunge—recommence series of movements. The great Italian master, Beppe Nadi, used to conclude a hard lesson of anything up to half an hour by requiring his pupil to carry out this exercise, riposte by *molinello* with lunge, thirty or more times without a pause—a test of stamina, control and accuracy indeed.

Exercises in stop hits and remises are used to develop lightness of hand and blade control with the fingers and wrist. Thus a stop cut is followed by several more in quick succession at the same target, gradually increasing speed and rhythm while retiring on the *piste*.

Similarly a succession of stop hits while retiring and remises while advancing, alternating edge and point, may follow a pattern of targets. For example, at outside arm—upper arm—shoulder—cheek—head—cheek—chest—inside arm; and so on, in gradually accelerating rhythm. These exercises are co-ordinated with leg movements: step forward or back, lunge, *balestra* and *flèche*.

There are several series of rhythmic sabre exercises designed to practise all the sabre movements arranged in groups. These exercises are first taken slowly and then repeated with accelerating rhythm at full speed. Many will recall the beautiful exhibition of these exercises given to music by Professor Bela Balogh and Bela Mikla at the Festival of Britain gala in 1951. These exercises were:

(*1*) Simple attacks: firstly from immobility, then including all leg exercises (lunge, *balestra* and *flèche*).

(*2*) Simple parries and ripostes: the first triangle (first, second, fifth) and the second triangle (third, fourth, fifth).

(*3*) Finger-play exercises: rhythmic hits, e.g. to wrist, forearm, upper arm, cheek, head, cheek, chest.

(*4*) Attacks on the blade: made as opportunity presents itself—from out of distance and from varying distances.

(*5*) All the ripostes and counter-ripostes from parry of fifth: firstly from immobility, then with leg exercises.

(*6*) Attacks including one feint: from varying distances, as opportunity presented, and out of distance.

(*7*) Co-ordinating exercises.

(*8*) Four different *flèche* attacks.

(*9*) Counter-attacks with parries and ripostes.

(*10*) Recapitulation including all the above movements.

Each exercise commences in slow time and is worked up rhythmically to full speed.

Fencers can derive much benefit from practising such exercises together, in addition to the regular lessons received from their masters. The writer has seen members of the world-famous Hungarian sabre team practising together in the *salle* for hours on end to perfect their strokes. For example, one would stand with his rear foot against a wall and parry, say, third or fifth, up to fifty times, with varied ripostes and at highest speed. He would then change places with his companion, who would carry out the same movements while he attacked.

NOTES ON COMPETITIVE PLAY

The sabre combines the conventional orthodoxy of the foil with the opportunism of the épée. Sabre fencing requires more athletic qualities than either of the other two weapons.

The use of the edge as well as the point, combined with the comparatively large target area to be defended, ensures that there is a wide variety of strokes available. However, the inclusion of the arm in the target and its constant vulnerability to a stop hit tend to restrict sabre play. It is, for instance, rarely safe to make any attack with more than one, or at most two, feints. The covering of the arm with the guard of the sabre during offensive movements is almost as important at sabre as at épée.

The importance of the measure, or choice of distance, at sabre cannot be over-stressed. Normally when on guard *sabreurs* maintain a measure from which it is very difficult to launch a successful attack, or at any rate to achieve surprise with one. The object for the defender is to maintain this measure, so as to have every advantage for stop hit or parry if his opponent attacks. The attacker must, by his footwork and preparations, endeavour to gain a measure within which his opponent will find it more difficult to parry the attack; in other words where the marked advantage of the attack over the defence which exists at sabre has the greatest scope.

This constant jockeying for position is a feature of sabre play and leads to constant movements on the *piste* by both *sabreurs* during a bout. Lightness and speed in footwork and a proper sense of balance through a sound on-guard position are obvious essentials. False attacks are much used to distract the opponent while gaining ground in order to obtain the proper measure, even momentarily, to successfully launch an attack under the best conditions. Variation of the length of steps backwards and forwards is used for the same purpose, steps backwards often being designed to draw the opponent within distance.

Variation of cadence, or rhythm, is important at all weapons but is particularly used at sabre. For example, the deliberate slowing down of some movement so as to deliver an indirect or compound attack or riposte in broken time can be an effective tactical move, especially against an opponent who is superior in speed to oneself. Tactically this variation of cadence can be used in two ways. In a composed attack, for example, one may find that one's opponent is correctly anticipating the form of attack and, being superior in speed, can move just ahead of one's movements. A delay in delivering either a feint or, more usually, the final movement—so to speak, missing a beat—may disconcert him and cause him to reopen the line in which the movement is completed, which would have been closed had the rhythm of the attack been constant. Similarly in an indirect riposte, the opponent covers the line in which he expects the riposte to arrive as soon as his attack has been parried; if this riposte is delayed he may, not finding the blade as expected and knowing the wide defensive box he has to protect, reopen the line as he moves to some other parry. The delayed or broken-time indirect riposte then has a clear path to its objective.

Speed is, of course, important but it will often defeat itself unless it is related to the cadence of the opponent's reactions. We have already noted how an attacker, even when making a simple movement like a one-two attack, can, by moving too fast for his opponent's reaction, return to the line before the defender has left it and in fact parry himself. One of the first things a fencer needs to discover about an opponent is the latter's rhythm, or the cadence of his movements, which is of course based on his speed. The fencer will then be able to make his strokes within that limitation, while keeping in hand his own superiority of speed of stroke, so that he can move just ahead of the opponent's reactions and impose his own cadence during the bout.

In fencing, speed and timing are complementary, and speed in delivering a stroke will lose most of its effectiveness unless the stroke is properly timed. Many fencers fail to appreciate how much true speed depends on economy of movement. This is, of course, because of the elementary, but often neglected, principle that the shortest distance between two points is the straight line. Non-fencers are often impressed by the apparent speed of the flamboyant *sabreur* who dazzles them by a series of resounding, and seemingly lightning, cuts. They are astonished when their hero is beaten by an apparently lethargic opponent whose light, almost lazy cuts seem only to travel a few inches. A slow-motion camera would show that the first *sabreur* in placing his hits makes unnecessary movements (such as withdrawing the blade or arm when delivering a cut) so that, while each blade movement travels very fast, it travels further than it need do and therefore must take longer in actual time. The second *sabreur*, by eliminating all unnecessary movements, delivers his stroke by the shortest possible route and thus achieves superiority in actual speed.

The novice is often much more difficult to deal with in a competition at sabre than at either of the other two weapons. This is not only because he may make unco-ordinated movements and fail to respond normally (or at all) to orthodox feints or other forms of attack, but because his wild, instinctive movements are quite likely to catch somewhere on the opponent's target from the most unorthodox angles. This danger will be aggravated if his main asset is a good sense of distance.

Such beginners should always be treated with respect and kept at a distance until one has been able to make some assessment of their cadence and sense of distance. Generally their usual reaction is to take a cut at any part of the target which appears to be within reach. This can, of course, be dealt with either by well timed simple attacks which will obtain the right of way, or by second-intention attacks. Such fencers can rarely rely on adequate defence and it is generally possible to induce them to attack either out of distance, or in a desired way, by pressing them with determined feints and judicious variation of the fencing measure.

Heavy hitting must always be avoided. It is not only unpleasant, but leads to wide, slow movements and impairs speedy recovery to a sound defence if the attack or riposte fails. Sabre in hand and blade control, that is, the correct presentation of the blade when a cut is made, will prevent hard hitting.

Professor Cavaliere Léon Bertrand gives his excellent book on sabre fencing the sub-title 'The subtlety of the sabre'. Indeed, modern sabre fencing is based on subtlety of conception and speed of execution. It is the subtlety and tactics which provide much of the fascination of the fighting weapons and enable persons widely dissimilar in physical or temperamental make-up to fence together on level terms.

Nevertheless, height and reach are of greater advantage at sabre than at foil or épée. There are two reasons for this. Firstly, the tall man has the whole target (including the body and head) within his reach, while his much shorter opponent, using the same effort, has to concentrate his hits on the arm; and secondly, the sabre fifth parry is less natural to many people than the other parries and, consequently, often less well formed than the lateral parries. As a result the tall man has an obvious advantage for his vertical cuts.

The need to prepare most attacks at sabre by a step forward generally accompanied by a preparation on the blade, in conjunction with the wide measure which necessitates such preparations, means that an attacker is often vulnerable to a counter-attack or to an attack on preparation. Even more than at épée, almost any attacking movement is liable to uncover the forearm to a counter-attack. The stop hit, especially the cut at arm, is therefore very frequently used. Often made as the opponent initiates his movement, it is perhaps most effective when judiciously introduced as opportunity arises during the course of a phrase, because it is then most likely to achieve surprise.

Besides making his stop hit accurately, the *sabreur* has to take care that he has a clear priority in time over the arrival of the attack. If this priority is not manifest the jury will almost certainly give right of way to the attack or, at best, nullify the hits on both fencers, on the grounds that they resulted from simultaneous actions. For this reason the *sabreur* is well advised to form the habit either of stepping back out of distance or parrying as soon as his stop hit has landed.

The prevalence of stop-hitting at sabre invites the use of second-intention attacks, because the latter are the proper answer to the former. If a stop hit can be successfully drawn and parried, the completion of the movement by a well timed *flèche* is a most effective type of counter-time. On the other hand, this tactical move can be exploited even further if it is suspected that the invitation is a prelude to a second-intention attack. A feint of stop hit having drawn the parry, the stop-hitter is prepared to parry the final movement of the attack, preferably with a counter-parry.

Renewed attacks are also much used at sabre. The wide defensive area, and the necessity to make somewhat wider arm movements when forming parries with the sabre than are necessary to deal with attacks exclusively made with the point, give the attacker many opportunities to exploit the remise or redoublement. Such opportunities are also given by some parries, notably the fifth, which cannot be made without exposing the arm. The reprise forward is much used to overcome the difficulty of obtaining or maintaining the necessary measure which always faces the attacker.

Although governed by conventions and rules, the sabre is a fighting weapon and gives some scope for individualism. There is always a temptation to rely overmuch on a small repertoire of favourite strokes which particularly suit one's temperament or physical advantages. This must be resisted if one is to progress beyond a few initial successes in competition and, indeed, to enjoy sabre fencing with its subtlety, speed and variety to the full. Especially at an academic weapon, a fencer cannot hope to raise himself progressively from junior class to senior, and from senior to international, unless he is able to exploit a wide variety of strokes and tactics, even though some movements will always suit his game best.

In competitive sabre fencing the difficulties of the jury should always be borne in mind. Although much work is being done at present to produce a satisfactory electrical judging apparatus for the sabre, it is likely to be some time before such an apparatus is perfected and adopted for universal use. Even when that is achieved, the responsibility of the President to read the phrase will, as at foil, almost certainly remain.

Presiding at sabre is particularly difficult, not only on account of the speed and variety of movements with this weapon and the frequent use of counter-attacks, attacks on preparation, renewed attacks and so on, but because the sabre presents a 'second dimension' to be taken into account, as against the other weapons where the point alone is used.

This provides another good reason why over-complication of attacking movements should be avoided, and why the *sabreur* will be well advised to phrase his movements as clearly and distinctly as possible and strive to maintain the ideal of hitting without being hit. It is extremely galling to have one's beat attack read by the President as a parry-riposte, or to find a stop hit made out of time nullifies a perfectly good attack because the phrase is read as a simultaneous attack. Some experience in judging and presiding sabre will soon show one how often such mistakes are due to the imperfections of the fencer's technique rather than to the carelessness or inefficiency of the jury.

Finally, courage and decision are essential factors to success in competitive sabre fencing. The final movement of the attack, the stop hit or the riposte, must be made without fear of the opponent's parry, counter-time or counter-riposte. Timidity will make one's movements short or slow and play into the opponent's hands. Take every care in devising and preparing a stroke, but once you decide to use it put every ounce into it without a second thought. After all, if your attack is parried you can still continue the phrase with, for instance, a counter-riposte—if that fails then you must start again.

V

Tactics

A FENCER must reach a fair standard of technicl ability before he can apply tactics successfully. The basic technique of the weapon used must be mastered by lessons, exercises and loose play so that the various fencing strokes are made automatically as required. Only then can the mind be concentrated on discovering the opponent's reactions, anticipating his intentions and devising the strategy and tactics required to beat him.

Fencing is a highly concentrated form of physical exercise and this alone, as in many other sports, brings a sense of well-being which is a source of satisfaction to its devotees. The fascination of fencing derives from the high degree of co-ordination of mind and body required and the speed of thought and reaction it develops.

It is the tactical application of fencing movements which provides much of the absorbing interest of a fencing bout. This requires cool judgment, anticipation, opportunism, bluff and counter-bluff and the ability to think at least one move ahead, combined with courage and controlled reaction of muscles and limbs which enables the fencer to carry out simple or complex movements with his weapon as required by the situation at any given moment.

It has been said that, for the fencer, to think and to act must be like one flash of lightning. Co-ordination of mind and body is certainly the secret of success in competitive fencing. Mechanical perfection is useless in fencing without the ability to think—the most intelligent analysis of an opponent's game will not ensure success unless the requisite fencing stroke can be devised and applied in the proper manner. The ability to think and act immediately, at the speed required when engaged in close combat with light weapons, can only be achieved by constant practice and considerable competition experience.

In competitive fencing the essential attributes are, firstly, the choice of the right stroke and, secondly, the ability to execute it not only correctly, but at the right moment and the right speed or cadence.

ANTICIPATING THE OPPONENT'S REACTION

It will be recalled that, when studying the various weapons, we found that at fencing the form of an attack is generally dictated by the form of defence used by the opponent against it. In other words, between opponents of approximately the same standard, an attack can rarely be successful unless it deceives, or outwits, the defence. For example, an attack made with a circular movement, such as a *doublé*, cannot succeed if the defender meets it with a simple or lateral movement in his parry.

It is therefore essential correctly to anticipate an opponent's reaction if an attack is to succeed.

An opponent's reactions are explored during a bout by feints, simple attacks, false attacks often with a half-lunge or preparations on the blade and by feeling his reactions on one's blade (the *sentiment du fer*). Most fencers have certain strokes which they favour. By these exploratory methods during the bout, one seeks to find out what they are in order to be able to devise one's tactics accordingly.

It follows that, when meeting an unknown fencer for the first time, it is unwise to start with preconceived ideas and rush into one's favourite moves without giving oneself time to study the opponent's game.

Much can be learned by watching opponents when they are fencing with other competitors in the match or pool in which one is engaged. By observing the way in which they score hits or are hit, one can gain some insight into their habits when fighting. For example one competitor may show a predilection for a certain form of defence, another for constant offensive action or renewed attacks, yet another may be an adept at stop-hitting or may frequently exploit the *flèche*. Such advance information will be invaluable when it is one's turn to meet these competitors during the pool.

Never spend the time between bouts in idleness, adjusting equipment or talking to friends. Concentrate on the job in hand and watch your next, and next-but-one opponent, learning all you can of his idiosyncracies before you meet him. It is wise always to have a copy of the order of bouts beside you, so that you know not only how long you have for rest, but which competitor you are to meet next.

Valuable as is such advance information, one should still approach each unknown opponent with caution. It is generally fatal to start a bout with a set plan, for instance on the basis that so and so always attacks, or never ripostes direct. Advance information must be supplementary to actual experience, because even the most stereotyped fencer is liable to react quite differently to different styles.

VARYING THE GAME

Knowing that opponents are constantly trying to note one's habits and weaknesses, it is obvious that a conscious effort must be made to give variety to one's game. Many fencers, especially at épée and sabre, find (generally because of some personal asset such as height, speed or a sense of distance) that certain strokes come particularly easily to them, and they achieve considerable success by their use. There is a great temptation to exploit such strokes to the neglect of most others. While this may bring initial successes, it is unlikely to enable one to gain regular results in the highest-class competitions. All too soon one's opponents will find the answer to a limited game; a routine system of defence, for instance, plays into the hands of an observant opponent.

There is an opportunity here to exploit a counter-bluff. By reacting to an opponent's exploratory moves in one definite way, it is often possible to induce him to use a particular stroke. Knowing the nature of this stroke, it will not be difficult to turn it to one's advantage.

TIMING, SPEED AND DISTANCE

Attacks and ripostes, however well designed and executed, will generally fail unless they are delivered at the right moment and at the right speed.

A simple example of the right choice of time is provided by an attack by disengagement. From the normal on-guard position at foil, a disengagement can be parried by a lateral movement of the sword-hand which travels a matter of a few inches, while the attacker's point has to travel several feet to reach the target. Under these conditions the fastest attack should be parried by even a slow defensive movement, and this disparity in time will be aggravated if the attack is directed towards a side of the target towards which the defender's blade is already moving to close the line. It is obvious that the attack should be timed to move towards a part of the target from which the opponent's blade is moving away, that is into an opening rather than a closing line, if it is to have the best chance of overcoming the disadvantage of time and distance to which it is always subject.

Similarly, an excellent moment to launch an attack is when an opponent is himself preparing an attack. His attention and blade movements will then be momentarily concentrated more on attack than defence.

The speed at which a stroke is delivered is of equal importance. Generally, except in the simple attacks or ripostes, it must be related to an opponent's cadence. It follows that yet another ingredient of success is to ascertain the opponent's speed or cadence in addition to his normal reactions. This is studied during the initial feints, false attacks and so on, already mentioned.

Ideally a fencer should seek to impose his cadence on an opponent. This may be achieved by intentionally varying the cadence of his movements. For example, he can deliberately establish a certain rhythm in his feints in a composite attack, until the defender is induced to follow that cadence. A sudden speeding up of, say, the final movement will often achieve a valuable measure of surprise. Similarly a broken-time attack or riposte can be very effective, particularly at épée or sabre.

A marked superiority in speed over an opponent is, of course, a great asset, but it can defeat its own ends unless judiciously used. Thus a very fast feint may fail to draw the desired reaction from a slow or inexperienced opponent. We have already seen how a very fast one-two attack may fail through ending in the closed line which the defender has not had time to open, because he has never moved to parry the feint.

A sense of distance, or fencing measure, comes more naturally to some fencers than to others, but it can be developed by practice in loose play and competitions. An attack can rarely succeed unless one can 'lodge' oneself at the correct distance at the moment it is launched. A parry is most likely to succeed if it can be made just as the opponent is at the end of his lunge. Many a chance to riposte is missed by the defender stepping back out of distance when he parries. To these examples must be added the obvious importance of choosing the correct measure when making a counter-attack by stop hit or time hit.

The tactical use of changes of measure, that is stepping forwards and backwards, should also be studied. Variations of measure will make it more difficult for the opponent to time his attacks or preparations. A fencer with a good sense of distance, or one who is difficult to reach to launch an attack, may often be brought to the desired measure by progressive shortening of a series of steps backward or by the movement known as gaining on the lunge.

MATCHING THE OPPONENT'S TACTICS

In boxing it is said that one should box a fighter and fight a boxer—this principle is equally applicable to fencing, in the sense of opposing the opposite tactics to those favoured by the opponent. It is obviously unwise continually to attack a fencer who relies on his defence, while one should attack without respite the opponent who himself favours strong and speedy attacks. Counter-time is the answer to the stop-hit addict, and the stop hit the counter to the fencer who uses many feints.

A fencer with a long reach, or who continually makes renewed attacks, or attacks with a *balestra* or step forward, generally requires a wide measure. It is a mistake to step back on the attack or preparation, since this will help the opponent to obtain the space which he requires to manoeuvre. Such an opponent will probably be disconcerted, and lose his precision, if the measure is shortened by a step forward into his attack.

One often meets fencers, especially at épée, who habitually attack with a preparation on the blade which they time to perfection. At épée it is often difficult to time the ceding parry or counter-riposte against a forceful opponent who is an expert in such attacks. Fencing with absence of blade and varying the measure, in preference to giving the blade, will often disconcert the opponent and severely limit his game.

Some épéeists have the habit of continually beating the opponent's blade. To submit to this will tire the sword-hand and slow down one's reactions. Against such an opponent it is obviously necessary to fence with absence of blade or, holding the weapon firmly, to block the beat, leaving the point in line for a stop hit at wrist.

Sometimes, when meeting an opponent for the first time, one is unable to analyse his game and receives several hits without quite knowing how they have been made. In these circumstances it is wise to increase the distance, to gain more time to study the opponent's methods and perhaps force him to make mistakes.

It is sometimes difficult to deal with the patient épée fencer who remains on guard well covered, keeps out of distance and evades attempts to make preparations on the blade. Such fencers generally make very accurate stop hits at wrist; it is unsafe, therefore, to attack directly at the hand, because their well covered position requires the attacker to angulate his blade and thus expose his own wrist. The obvious answer is to draw the stop hit and complete a second-intention attack, taking the blade. It is sometimes hard to effect this because of the angle of the blades and the good sense of distance of the opponent. Another method is to make a number of feints and false attacks at some part of the hand until the opponent has been induced, quite unwittingly, to displace the position of his sword-hand on guard sufficiently for an attack by disengagement to be made at the uncovered part of his wrist. The safest way of carrying out this movement is not to make the attack by disengagement as described, but, after the feint, to make a stop hit, by angulating the blade, on the opponent's stop hit. In other words, to direct the point to the wrist and allow the opponent's action to impale his wrist on the point. This, of course, requires very exact timing, but it is usually more successful than the attack as the opponent will have no chance to parry.

Before attacking an opponent who fences with absence of blade, false attacks or well marked feints can be used to draw his reaction. If this is a stop hit, one can proceed in counter-time, preferably taking the blade. If he reacts with a parry one can complete a compound attack or score by counter-riposte. On the other hand, the effect may be for him to return to engagement, when an appropriate attack can be used.

Some opponents, particularly at foil, have the aggravating habit of attacking into the attack hoping to cause it to miss. The object must be to draw this attack prematurely in order to score with counter-time or a counter-riposte. This can be done by a false attack with a half-lunge or it may be sufficient to jerk the trunk forward sharply without lunging at all.

Fencing at close quarters can be practised very effectively at foil, provided one has mastered the necessary blade control. The wider target makes it unsafe to indulge in this form of in-fighting with the épée or the sabre. At épée, when one finds oneself at close quarters, it is best to force the *corps à corps* immediately, but care must be taken not to jostle the opponent while so doing.

The *flèche* attack is often effective at all weapons, but especially at épée and sabre. It will only achieve success if perfectly timed and executed at maximum speed, or rather with maximum acceleration. It must, of course, be used sparingly because otherwise it will lose much of its essential element of surprise. The *flèche* which has been anticipated is easily parried or avoided or gives the opportunity for a counter-attack. If it fails the attacker rarely has a chance to avoid the riposte or continue the phrase; at épée it may well result in a double hit.

The *flèche* may be used very effectively as a riposte against an opponent who makes a rapid recovery when his attack has been parried, or to conclude a second-intention attack. If such is the intention, the weight of the body should be shifted forward on to the leading leg as the parry is made, in order to be able to launch the *flèche* with the least possible delay.

The circular or counter-parry is the safest one to use against a *flèche*. The blade should be held momentarily after the parry, to ensure that the attacking blade has been deflected past the body, before making the riposte. This is particularly important at épée in order to avoid the double hit.

When one finds that an opponent is able to land his attacks because he is superior in speed to oneself, it is sometimes possible to disconcert him and regain the initiative by making several changes of engagement in varying *tempo*.

The tactical use of the *piste* is important. If a fencer is confident in his defence, he may induce a cautious opponent to attack by retiring to the warning line. It is, however, usually wise when forced to give ground to take every opportunity to recover the lost ground. Otherwise one will find oneself cramped for room, which plays into the hands of the aggressive opponent seeking to lodge his attack. One often sees inexperienced fencers wasting the *piste* by retiring continuously and quite unnecessarily as soon as the bout is started. This is particularly unwise at épée and sabre, where it is always as well to preserve adequate room to manoeuvre.

A fencer is usually particularly vulnerable to a counter-offensive action while he is recovering from the lunge, more especially, of course, if he commits the fault of bending his arm during the recovery. If one finds oneself being hit in this way owing to the opponent's superior speed or timing, the spring backwards from the lunge should be used in preference to the usual recovery.

Left-handed fencers often present particular difficulty to all but the most experienced right-handers. This is of course because there are more of the latter than the former in most clubs and the left-handers get far more practice against right-handers than vice versa. For the same reason a left-hander usually encounters similar difficulties when opposed to another left-hander. It is likely that, except for very experienced fencers, the left-hander has an advantage of about one hit in five when meeting a right-hander of equivalent standard for the first time.

It is obviously wise to take every opportunity to fence against left-handers until one gains the necessary experience to deal with them as effectively as with a right-hander. When possible, take lessons from time to time from a left-handed master. This is, of course, equally necessary for the left-hander, so that he can gain the necessary experience to deal with his fellow left-handers.

One of the chief difficulties is the necessity to reverse the angle at which hits, especially with the point, are directed on to the target. Left-handers usually have a marked preference for the parry of quarte, or for bringing the opponent's blade into quarte, because in that line they obtain the top of the blade and therefore have control over it. This can often be counteracted by use of the counter-disengagement or by attacking into sixte on the outside of the opponent's sword-arm.

Left-handers are often vulnerable to attacks or ripostes which terminate in the low line, particularly at flank, because they usually find the parry of octave difficult to execute. Feints into octave often induce a left-hander to leave his quarte or high lines open to attack.

A favourite stroke with many left-handers at épée is a beat followed by an attack on the outside or top of the arm. This can often be circumvented by gripping the weapon firmly and blocking the beat, leaving the point in line for a stop hit on the top of the arm (if the beat was made on the outside) or angulated to the under side of the wrist (if the beat was made on top of the blade).

Much of the fascination of fencing derives from its almost infinite variety of movements, and the different problems set by each opponent one meets. Obviously only a few broad tactical moves can be indicated here. Each opponent must be observed and studied and his game analysed before the tactics required to beat him can be ascertained.

A golden rule is never to use more complex movements than are necessary to achieve the desired result. Start with simple movements and only introduce composed ones when you cannot otherwise succeed. To hit a worthy opponent with a complex movement is satisfying, and shows one's mastery of technique; to hit the same opponent by a simple movement is a sign of greatness.

VI

Training

FENCING is a complex art. The stance, footwork and finger play do not come naturally to most people and require the development of certain muscles in a way different to that required by other sports or for normal movement.

Fencing cannot be learned from a book. Regular lessons from a competent master or leader are the only way to lay the foundation of a sound technique. Indeed, throughout his career a fencer requires regular lessons to maintain his standard and to correct faults.

The system of class instruction recently evolved for the Amateur Fencing Association's National Training Scheme has done much to remove the tedium from learning the groundwork of fencing. Nevertheless, one's early lessons may be tiring and even painful for the undeveloped muscles. It is certainly worth persevering because while minor successes may be achieved, without a sound basic technique the full enjoyment will never be derived from fencing.

Fencing is undoubtedly harder to learn than most sports, mainly because considerable application is necessary even to acquire the basic movements without which one cannot practise it at all. A boy can be shown the correct way to kick a ball and immediately get quite a lot of exercise and fun, and learn a good deal of ball control while playing about with his friends—he can later be taught the technique of football and team-work. The aspiring fencer must spend several weeks or months learning to hold his weapon and manipulate it, to come on guard, advance, retire and lunge, before he can (or should) attempt loose play.

If fencing is hard to learn, it has the advantage of being a game which, when once acquired, is a lasting joy and fascination for most of one's life. One can fence well, and derive benefit therefrom, for far longer than one can practise most other sports. There are many examples of fencers who remained in championship class well into their fifties and a good fencer, when well on in years, can often hold his own successfully against much younger and faster opponents by reason of his experience and technique.

CHOOSING A MASTER

Since lessons are so essential for the learning, or perfecting, of a fencer's technique, the choice of an instructor is obviously of the greatest importance. Happily there are now throughout the United Kingdom many masters and leaders who are fully qualified to give adequate and interesting lessons to quite an advanced standard. If, however, the fencer aspires to reach the top class in competitive fencing, he must obviously learn from a master who is capable of developing his technique and tactics to the full—such masters are comparatively rare.

To choose a master, one can either take the advice of an experienced fencer who has himself a successful record in competition, or examine the records published annually by the Amateur Fencing Association, noting which masters have produced the pupils who have become eminent in recent years in senior competitions and international events. It is these who have the ability to lift a fencer above the 'ceiling' of the good club fencer into championship class.

To change one's master is often difficult, more especially because it may also mean changing clubs. Many fencers feel that it is disloyal to abandon the teacher who has brought them to their first successes, even though they are not too sure that the master in question can give them more advanced teaching than they have already received.

The writer feels strongly that this is a false attitude and one which a good master should not expect even his favourite pupil to adopt. Club loyalty should not be pressed to the detriment of a promising fencer's personal progress.

As in all branches of teaching, masters vary greatly in their ability to develop and inspire their pupils. There are many instructors who can interest a beginner and attend with patience and understanding to his development; they are meticulous in correcting detailed faults and can bring an aspiring fencer rapidly to junior-championship class. They do not, however, possess the vital experience to take their pupil beyond that class. Conversely, there are great masters who can inspire and develop a good fencer to reach championship and international class, but who simply have not got the patience to deal with a beginner as successfully as their more limited colleagues. This fact must be recognized by professional and amateur alike, and questions of personal loyalty must not be allowed to obscure the issue. The aspiring fencer must take his lessons from the master whom he considers best fitted to develop his talents at the stage at which he finds himself. No considerations, other than, of course, economic ones, should be allowed to influence his choice or prevent him changing his master or club when he is convinced that this is necessary to his improvement.

Once a master has been chosen, a fencer must put himself unreservedly in his hands and follow his instructions and advice. Above all, disregard the comments and advice of well-meaning friends if these conflict with the views of the master. Every experienced master has his own slightly different interpretation of details of tactics and technique. Provided his basic technique is sound, such variations of detail will probably be of minor importance. In any game as complex as fencing there is room for many interpretations and it is a great mistake to imagine that any one school or method is the ideal and that all variations from it are useless.

To sum up, choose the best master you can find (and afford) regardless of any other considerations, place yourself unreservedly in his hands, give him your confidence, heed his advice and finally work with him as regularly and as often as you can.

PRACTICE WORK

Besides lesson training, a fencer can do a great deal by exercises, either alone or in company with a friend, to develop his or her technique. Such exercises are valuable, in the initial stages, in developing balance and forming the fencing muscles, and later serve to improve co-ordination and the accuracy of execution of various strokes. Exercises are excellent as a supplement to lessons but they can never replace them.

Advancing and retiring, lunging, the *balestra*, gaining on the lunge, the jump backwards and the *flèche* can all be practised by the fencer on his own in any reasonably large room. A long mirror is most helpful to enable one to correct faults. By such exercises one can develop balance and the feel of the *piste*, and build up muscles and body control until the position on guard and the various details of footwork become natural and automatic.

Valuable and interesting training can be undertaken by two fencers of approximately the same standard working together. In the early stages such practice, preferably under the supervision of the master, will be much more advantageous than attempting loose play. Later these exercises can be used to perfect the timing of various strokes. Working in pairs, fencers should start with simple movements such as direct attacks, simple parries and ripostes, later working up to more complex movements. Alternating the rôles of attacker and defender in turn, the fencers in fact follow the lines of a routine lesson, correcting each other's faults and developing the rhythm and accuracy of the various movements they are studying. A variation may be introduced by closing the eyes when carrying out certain movements. This will develop the sense of touch and the feel of the blade—*sentiment du fer*. Some groups of exercises have been indicated in the chapters dealing with épée and sabre, as well as special exercises to strengthen the wrist, fingers and legs (on pages 115–116 and 190–192).

TRAINING FOR COMPETITIONS

Training for competitions is as necessary in fencing as in other sports. Physical fitness is, in many ways, as important as technical training.

Fencing competitions, being based on the pool system, usually take a considerable time to complete. A competitor often has long waits between bouts or rounds, but must be able to produce his maximum effort and concentration in the relatively short periods of actual fighting. Further, each round becomes progressively harder as the lesser competitors are eliminated, and the greatest effort has to be produced in the final which will, of course, come at the end of a long and tiring event. All this is a considerable strain on the nervous system, quite apart from the physical effort which has to be furnished in each bout. Physical fitness will do much to counterbalance these cumulative strains and, by enabling the competitor to relax, make it possible for him to keep his mental alertness during a long and tiring competition.

These conditions apply particularly to the major international competitions such as the Olympic Games or the World Championships. In these events the competitor, often after a long journey, has to submit to living conditions and food which are strange to him. He may have to remain in the atmosphere of the stadium from early morning until after midnight for several days running while the events in which he is engaged progress and, of course, has to increase his effort as round succeeds round. Mealtimes vary widely and, should he reach the final, his maximum effort will be required at earliest on the night of the second day of intensive competitive strain. Only the physically fit can produce their best under these trying conditions.

Most people have had the experience of putting up an excellent performance in some match or pool, with very little training and after a sleepless night or even a 'night out'. This is because, on that occasion, the circumstances produced a high degree of relaxation which is as great an asset at fencing as at most other competitive sports. One should not be misled by such an experience. It may come off now and then, but it certainly cannot be relied upon to do so—nor will it enable one to resist the fatigue of a major competition. To obtain regular and consistent results in competitions, mental and physical fitness are essential. In championships, all things being equal, the fittest man usually wins.

Fortunately fencing does not require the rigorous training necessary, for example, for boxing or rowing, nor the disruption of normal life which training for these sports entails.

Training for a competition should be undertaken according to a planned programme over a period of six weeks to two months prior to the event, phased so as to work up progressively to peak form at the date of the event. The famous Italian Olympic Champion, Gustavo Marzi, used to time his training programme so as to allow the early rounds of the championship in which he was engaged to complete his preparation and put the edge on his form—but one must have great experience and considerable confidence to do this.

A training schedule should include a programme of physical training and one of fencing training which should be complementary. Each training schedule should commence with physical training and continue with fencing training. The emphasis in the early stages should be on the former, the time allotted to the latter being progressively increased in the later stages.

Physical training is designed to develop stamina and strength of wind and limb, and build up general physical fitness which will, in turn, tone up mental and nervous reactions. A physically fit competitor is much less likely to suffer from strains, pulled muscles or cramp during a competition than one who has paid little attention to physical training during his preparation.

The physical-training programme has two facets: firstly, the general exercises designed to develop bodily strength, stamina and reflex action; secondly, fencing exercises to develop balance and co-ordination of the special muscles used in fencing movements.

There are a variety of tables of exercises available for general physical fitness and these can easily be adapted for fencers. One should always start with general warming-up exercises and then run through a series of general exercises which cover every part of the body. For example, neck rolling, arm swinging sideways with the body upright and bent from the waist, trunk rolling, bending and stretching exercises for shoulders, back and loins, knee bending, abdominal exercises and so on. Alternate with skipping, rhythmical jumping and arm-stretching movements and 'running on the spot'. Fencing requires lissom muscles allowing reflex action, rather than the great muscular development such as, for instance, the weight-lifter needs.

Many people find such physical-exercise programmes tedious to perform, more especially when they are preparing alone for some event for which they have entered. Recently 'circuit training' has been applied to fencing and many will find their physical training much more interesting if it is arranged in this way.

Briefly, circuit training consists in arranging a series of exercises, or circuit, containing, say, ten steps on to and off a chair with each foot, body rolling ten times, arm stretching and knee bending eight times, chest expanding using light weights ten times, and so on up to six or eight exercises, performed a set number of times each and the series completed without a pause. The fencer carries a stop-watch and times each complete circuit. He will be surprised to find how rapidly he can reduce his overall time as training progresses. It is important that some brief limbering-up exercises be performed before the circuit is attempted, to obviate muscular strains. As training progresses the circuit may be varied by performing each exercise a different number of times or by adding new exercises.

Besides the general physical exercises mentioned above, it is important to include in the programme exercises which are particularly applicable to fencing movements. Advancing and retiring, lunging, gaining on the lunge, the *balestra*, the reprise forward, the *flèche* and the leap backwards have already been mentioned. To these may be added exercises in balance: for example, balancing on a plank or chair while performing body bending and arm exercises, or horizontal balancing movements performed on each leg alternately.

Simple home-made apparatus may be used to assist with some exercises. For example a broom-stick weighted with a sand-bag tied at each end may be placed across the shoulders when doing knee-bending exercises to ensure an upright carriage and strengthen the back. A couple of flat-irons can be used to help the chest-expanding exercises, a short plank may be placed under the heels for bending and stretching leg exercises and so on.

It is wise to seek the advice of an experienced physical educationalist before deciding on one's circuit or physical-training programme. More harm than good may be done if exercises beyond one's physical capabilities are attempted. The importance of limbering up before any training is attempted has been stressed. Naturally physical exercises should be commenced slowly, with suitable rests to prevent strain or stiffness, and should be increased in intensity as training proceeds.

As regards fencing training, it has often been said that fencing is the best training for fencing. Indeed, regular lessons and loose play, either in one's club or at team-training sessions, form the basis of all training for fencing competitions.

Most people, at any rate in this country, have to carry on their normal vocation while they are training and can only devote some hours in the evenings or at week-ends to their training programme. Such a programme may run as follows.

Each training evening begins with a short session of limbering-up exercises followed by the physical and fencing exercises or circuit, gradually increased according to a predetermined programme as described above. For, say, the first two weeks of training the fencer will concentrate on lessons only twice, or preferably three times each week.

Then, after the lessons, bouts of loose play will be added against the greatest variety of opponents available. While it is obviously beneficial to fence against the best fencers, bouts with less advanced fencers should not be neglected. They will be valuable for teaching the adjustment of cadence and speed and variation of tactics. When undertaking loose play during training, it is preferable always to fence for a set number of hits which should, especially during the later stages of training, be the number of hits which will be fenced in bouts during the competition in view. This will develop concentration and the will to win and be far better tactical training than long bouts of loose play without counting hits. When possible one should

H

visit other clubs to widen the variety of one's opponents and meet fencers who are less familiar than one's own club mates. This will, of course, help to develop tactics and the ability to analyse an opponent's game.

During loose play the opportunity should be taken to practise and perfect certain strokes and this can be supplemented by joint practice with a friend on the lines discussed above. Every opportunity should be taken of participating in club matches or pools in order to acquire experience of competition atmosphere and the will to win, as well as to maintain interest and obviate staleness. When possible training sessions should be increased from two to three each week, to every other day or every two days with a break of one day between, during the last two weeks of training.

Individuals react differently to training and only general methods are indicated here. Each fencer must find by trial and error the programme which suits him best, with the sole proviso that the programme must be progressive and designed to bring the competitor to peak condition, physical and technical, at the time of the competition.

Since training for competitions is generally ancillary to one's usual work and activities, it is best not to depart unnecessarily from normal habits and routine. Indeed, to do so often has an adverse effect by making one irritable and nervous. It is obviously necessary to exercise moderation. For example, if you are a smoker it will probably do more harm than good to try to give it up completely. Over-indulgence in tobacco will, of course, have a bad effect on wind and stamina, so one should try to moderate one's smoking (especially cigarettes) and concentrate it preferably after, rather than between meals.

Rest is one of the most important things during training, because one will expend a great deal of energy through physical and fencing training, in excess of that used in one's normal work. Late nights should be avoided, particularly during the last weeks of training. Individuals vary greatly in the amount of rest they require and it is no good trying to have ten hours' sleep each night if normally you are a person who requires an average of six or seven—or vice versa. It will usually be found best to budget for about an extra hour in bed during training, beyond one's normal requirements.

Some people experience difficulty in sleeping during training. The use of drugs for this purpose should be avoided. It is often helpful to have a hot bath in which one should soak for a maximum of five minutes, dry without friction and go straight to bed without reading before attempting to sleep. It is very common to experience difficulty in sleeping the night before a competition or an important final. This should have little adverse effect provided regular hours have been kept. It is helpful to remember that lack of sleep is not particularly harmful, provided one relaxes in bed and avoids nervous tension induced precisely by worrying about not sleeping. The first thing is not to worry and the second is to try consciously to relax each part of the body in turn, and to have the feeling that one is 'falling through the bed'.

Over-eating must also be avoided but no special diet is required for fencing training. Cut out over-rich or starchy foods and include plenty of protein, such as meat or fish, and fresh vegetables and salads. A fencer should find, by trial and error, his best weight for competitive fencing and try to reach and maintain that weight as early as possible in his training programme.

Maximum benefit is derived from the food taken about eight hours before a competition. A substantial meal should not be eaten within two hours of an event. After meals it is better to stroll about or to lie prone, rather than remain in a sitting position.

Many fencers find it beneficial to have a glass or two of light claret with their evening meal. Here again it is a question of what one is used to, but in any case over-indulgence in alcohol should obviously be avoided during training and, as a general rule, one is better without spirits. Most people find it as well to drink plenty of water during training: it is better to do so between, rather than at or immediately after meals.

One of the most important points to watch during training is that the bowels are kept open and regular. It is better to achieve this by diet and exercises rather than rely on the regular use of drugs. A useful exercise is to stand with legs slightly apart and hands on hips and roll the body as far down, to the sides and back as possible, alternately clockwise and anti-clockwise.

NOTES ON MATCHES

It is often difficult to make adequate arrangements for meals during a fencing competition, because these events usually take so long to complete that little time can be allowed between rounds and even before the final. One should therefore rely on a substantial meal, including plenty of protein, some eight hours before the commencement of a competition, with a light meal about two hours before actual fencing begins.

During a competition, well sugared black coffee, raisins and glucose are valuable for replacing lost energy. If there is time for a light meal between rounds, eggs or grilled or poached fish will be found useful. Here again each fencer must find out by experience what suits him best.

A thorough check of all equipment should be made at least a day before a competition. Nothing is more disconcerting than having to search for, or repair, clothing or equipment immediately before one is due to fence. A wise fencer will ensure that the pocket of his fencing bag always contains such items as waxed thread, Elastoplast, spare shoe-laces and a spare martingale against emergencies.

Most people find it best not to fence the day before a competition, merely doing a few bending and stretching exercises. It is better to take a rest and seek distraction by a visit to a cinema or theatre.

Always arrive at the venue of a competition in ample time to change, carry out some limbering-up exercises and have a short bout before the pool or match is due to start. Having thus warmed up, keep well covered between bouts. Particular attention should be given to keeping the whole body, especially the legs and lumbar regions, warm during a competition. Otherwise one will probably suffer from stiffness and lack suppleness and co-ordination at the beginning of a bout. Fencing is so concentrated that there is rarely time to warm up during a bout; the man who comes on guard cold will be at a disadvantage.

A loose-sleeved long coat, a rug or a blanket is preferable to a blazer for keeping warm between bouts. If a track-suit is preferred, it is more comfortable to have the blouse made to close with a zip-fastener running the whole length of the front, so that it can be put on like a coat. The normal track-suit blouse, which has to be put on over the head, is not very practical when wearing a fencing jacket.

In competitions, it is wise to train oneself to concentrate solely on the fencing and avoid letting outside matters influence this concentration. This does not mean that one should be tense all the time. Indeed, relaxation between bouts is most important. What it does mean is that one should not dissipate one's energy, or allow one's mind to be distracted by, for example, conversation with friends.

Besides the necessity to obtain the greatest possible amount of mental and physical rest between bouts, it is generally advantageous to watch one's opponents during their bouts with other fencers in the pool. We have already seen that the correct choice of tactics and attacking strokes depends, to a great extent, on correct anticipation of the opponent's reactions. It is therefore obviously advantageous to glean as much information as possible about an unknown fencer before one has to meet him. Much can be learned of a fencer's habits and preferences for certain strokes or tactics by watching him fence and seeing how experienced fencers deal with him.

It is important to train oneself not to be upset by decisions of the jury. Many fencers are put out of their stride, and lose valuable hits during a bout, by real or fancied errors of the jury, or lose their concentration by fulminating against the judges between bouts.

Even the best President or judge is quite likely to make some mistakes during a competition. The faster and more complex the fencing, the more difficult is their task. A fencer can comfort himself by remembering that, with a competent and honest jury—and most are so nowadays—mistakes will usually even themselves out between the competitors during the course of a pool. He should also remember that it seems natural to fencers to recall the errors to their detriment while they rapidly forget those which are to their advantage.

If more active fencers took their turn on a jury, especially as Presidents, they would realize that the spectator often sees most of the game, and the stroke which a fencer is convinced he has performed perfectly was in fact made quite differently to the way he intended. A common example of this is the *dérobement* made on an opponent's attack. The fencer is convinced that he had his arm straight before his opponent commenced his attack and that he successfully evaded the latter's attempt to deflect the blade. He is filled with righteous, and often vociferous, indignation when the President rules in favour of the attack and regards what he is convinced was the perfect *dérobement* as a stop hit. What in fact happened was that the fencer who made the *dérobement* merely straightened his arm fully at the moment his opponent initiated his attack—and the phrase has been correctly read by the President.

A fencer must train himself to put such incidents out of his mind immediately after the decision has been made. There is, in any case, nothing he can do about it because, under the rules, the President's reading of the phrase cannot be challenged. It is foolish to allow one's natural irritation at a fancied, or even a real, error of the jury to spoil one's concentration.

It is surprising how many active fencers do not bother to familiarize themselves with the rules applicable to competition fencing and to their chosen weapon. Ignorance of the rules can quite easily cost one a vital hit which may lose a championship. For example, an épée fencer may receive a decisive hit on his guard. If this is found to be due to patches of oxidization or rust on the *coquille*, the hit will be counted against him. Again, he may score a decisive hit in a bout but it may not be registered by the apparatus, while a much later hit is registered against him. He tests his weapon and finds it does not work. If he then unplugs his weapon before the President has had an opportunity to test it he will lose the right to have his opponent's hit annulled and he will perhaps have lost an important championship from ignorance of the rules.

I remember the case of a well known international fencer who had his weapons altered so that he could use a special grip with which he practised assiduously, and with which he achieved considerable success in minor competitions. He never troubled to find out that the grip he adopted with such care was contrary to the rules. During an Olympic Games an alert President spotted the mistake and the fencer was forced to revert to an orthodox weapon with which he had long been unfamiliar. This completely put him off and he departed in an early round in an event in which he should have had every chance perhaps to reach the final.

Training will enable a fencer to achieve the concentrated mind, its co-ordination with muscular movement, relaxation and the 'ice-packed brain' which are the ideals in competitive fencing.

VII

Judging and Presiding

A FENCING bout is judged by a jury consisting of a President and four judges. When an electrical judging apparatus is used a President officiates alone.

The success of a competition, the confidence and serenity of the competitors, the enjoyment and understanding of the spectators and to some extent the standard of fencing, depend very largely on the correctness, rapidity and accuracy with which the Presidents direct the bouts.

The speed and complexity of competitive fencing makes the task of the jury particularly onerous. This was perhaps exaggerated by a writer in the *Daily Courier* in June 1896, but there was certainly some truth in his statement: 'Everyone who has watched a bout with the foils knows that the task of judging hits is, with a pair of amateurs, difficult enough, and with a well matched pair of *maîtres d'escrime* well-nigh impossible. To accomplish his responsible work satisfactorily, it is necessary for the judge to possess the eye of a hawk and the agility of the tiger in order to keep the lightning-like movements of both points well under observation.'

Most experienced fencers appreciate the difficulties of their judges. They know that mistakes, especially in seeing hits, are bound to be made, but they also know that these mistakes generally even themselves out between the competitors during the course of a pool. So long as they have confidence in the ability and integrity of the jury, they will make allowances for any mistakes which may occur. If they lose this confidence they may become restive, bad temper intervenes and fencing inevitably becomes ragged.

Fencing is a sport requiring great concentration, rapidity and control of thought and movement. Competitions generally take a considerable time to complete, and competitors are therefore subjected to much nervous and emotional strain for hours and even days. There is nothing more irritating to fencers than a jury which appears hesitating or uncertain, or a President who fails to read the sequence of fencing movements in a phrase correctly or is slow in reaching his decisions. Lack of confidence in the jury accentuates the nervous tension of the competitors and the standard of their fencing usually deteriorates rapidly.

There are, of course, fencers who always think that whatever action they have made must be the right one. There are others, I regret to say, who appear angry or aggrieved in order to impress the jury and solicit their leniency in subsequent hits. An experienced President will know how to deal with such competitors. Allowance must, however, be made for the fact that a fencer may be quite convinced he has carried out some well thought-out movement successfully, when in fact he has committed some fault of timing or execution, quite unwittingly, which has given the priority to his opponent. It is a case of the spectator seeing most of the game. In such cases the President can do much to restore the confidence, and serenity, of the competitor if he takes the trouble briefly to state the reasons for his decision. Even if he does not agree with him, the fencer will at least know that the President has seen and understood the movement.

We can add another example to those given in the last chapter. Thus a fencer may have noted that his left-handed opponent keeps his arm straight after his attack is parried, well covered against the direct riposte and seeking the immediate remise. He therefore makes what he imagines is the perfect disengagement riposte, and is infuriated to find that the President gives the remise against him. He has not realized that, when making his riposte by disengagement, he has quite unconsciously made the common fault of withdrawing his arm in order to find room to riposte. The President has seen this fault of execution and his judgment is correct. In such a case the President will be well advised not merely to give the remise as in time, but to add that this was because the indirect riposte was made in two periods of fencing time because it was executed with a withdrawal of the arm.

KNOWING THE RULES

Neither a President nor a judge can carry out his duties efficiently unless he is thoroughly conversant with the *Rules for Competitions* published by the Amateur Fencing Association. These are an exact translation of the international rules issued by the Fédération Internationale d'Escrime. A President, of course, requires a more detailed knowledge of the rules than a judge.

The *Rules for Competitions* are, of necessity, rather complex and contain nearly 700 articles. No one should try to memorize them all.

Judges should familiarize themselves with the rules governing the assault and judging, the correct terminology for fencing movements and the rules and conventions applicable to each weapon.

A President requires a general working knowledge of the rules, but should not try to memorize details, such as the specifications for weapons, dimensions of the *piste* and so on—that is, information which can be obtained by reference to the book if, at any time, it is required while he is presiding. He should concentrate on gaining a thorough knowledge of all matters which may arise during a bout and which he, as the chief official in charge, should know without having to refer to the rule book. Besides the rules and conventions for the weapon in use, these will include his powers over judges, scorers, timekeepers and other personnel, competitors and spectators, his disciplinary powers, penalties for infringement of the rules and that part of the rules dealing with organization which refers to the conduct of a bout, pool or match.

Both Presidents and judges should ensure that their personal copy of the *Rules for Competitions* is amended to date. The International Federation makes some modifications almost every year, and such amendments are always made available to the honorary secretary of each affiliated club at the beginning of each year. Every fencer should ensure that he sees these amendments and brings his own copy of the rules up to date.

All fencers, and especially those who serve on juries, should make a habit of re-reading the *Rules for Competitions* at frequent intervals. The complexity of the rules no doubt accounts for the rapidity with which details are forgotten or become distorted in one's mind. The writer can vouch for the fact that even his fellow members of the commission of the International Federation who write the rules are frequently mistaken in their recollection of details and have constantly to refer to the book in the course of their discussions. Only by frequently brushing up one's knowledge of the rules can one avoid making mistakes in applying them while presiding or judging.

All fencers would be well advised to take their turn at judging and presiding. Unfortunately many active fencers avoid doing so, presumably on the grounds that they do not find it interesting. This is a mistake, not only because everyone should take a fair share of judging—as otherwise this essential accessory function at every competition devolves on a few overworked devotees—but because judging, and especially presiding, gives valuable training in reading and analysing a phrase and quickens the eye. It provides an excellent way to train oneself to observe and read a fencer's movements without being involved in devising means of dealing with them. The lessons so learned can then be applied when one is oneself fencing.

Judging and presiding require constant practice. The best President or judge will lose his power of observation and analysis to a marked degree if he fails to officiate for even six months. To become a first-class President takes many years of experience and application and the best fencers are not necessarily the best judges. Only by regularly officiating at first-class tournaments can such Presidents and judges retain their efficiency.

THE WORK OF THE JUDGES

A judge's primary duty is to watch for the arrival of a hit on or off the target and advise the President when he has seen a hit.

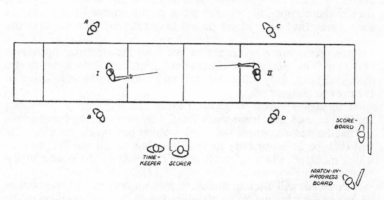

Fig. 61   The Jury

I : II Fencers
A : B Judges watching II
C : D Judges watching I

Normally he does this merely by raising his hand. If, however, the judge finds himself so placed that the President does not see his signal, he may shout 'Hit' or otherwise draw the President's attention. He must be careful not to use the word 'Halt' because this will cause the competitors to cease fencing. A judge may only call 'Halt' if he thinks that an accident is likely to occur, for example if he notices that a blade is broken, or the clothing or equipment of a competitor is in a dangerous state (for instance if the bib of the mask is raised exposing the neck). It is obvious that a judge must be conversant with the target and the definition of a hit for the weapon in use.

Indeed, the duties of a judge go far beyond merely spotting the arrival of hits. At foil and sabre, besides knowing what constitutes the valid target, he must understand what is meant by the possible extensions of the valid target; that is to say, when a hit which arrives off the target counts as good, because the fencer who receives it has displaced, or substituted a non-valid surface for, the target. Thus a judge should be able to claim a hit on the arm or head as a valid hit at foil if, in his opinion, the arm or head has been placed in front of the valid target or substituted for it in such a way that, had this not been done, the hit would have reached the valid target. The judge must also be conversant with the rules regarding the validity of hits made as the President calls 'Halt' or when one of the competitors leaves the *piste*.

While, normally, a judge is only required to see hits which arrive on the competitor who comes on guard opposite to him, he may be asked by the President if he saw a hit on the other competitor, should the competitors change sides in the course of a phrase in such a way that he is better placed to see the hit than his opposite number.

Épée events are now always judged with the electrical apparatus and therefore, except for the duties of ground judges which are discussed later, only judging at foil and sabre will be considered in the present chapter.

At these weapons a judge must know the rules and conventions applicable, and the terminology for the various fencing movements, so that he can recognize the stroke which has produced a hit. He will then be able not only to spot hits, but to tell the President at which moment, and as a result of which stroke in the course of the phrase, the hit was made.

A President will often be unable to make a correct judgment unless he can rely on his judges to give him the correct information in the course of his analysis of the phrase which has resulted in a hit, as to which fencing movement produced the hit they are claiming. Obviously the President and the judges must use the same terminology, and it is as important for the latter as for the former to be able correctly to recognize fencing strokes.

For example, the whole judgment may be falsified if the judges claim a hit as a riposte when in fact it was only a counter-riposte which arrived, or if they claim as an attack a hit which was only a remise. It is important that a judge, especially at sabre, should be able to differentiate clearly between a hit which is parried and a hit which is insufficiently parried, otherwise the President will be led to give a wrong decision.

It follows that a judge must not merely gaze at the target, but must follow the development of the phrase intelligently. Actually, it is much easier to see a hit if the judge follows and interprets the blade movements made by the fencer behind whom he is standing. It is not necessary to take one's eyes off the target of the fencer opposite in order to do this. It is quite easy, with a little practice, to keep the blade which makes the hit and the target at which it is directed in one's field of vision at the same time. In this way a judge, as it were, anticipates where a hit is likely to be made and is correspondingly less likely to miss its arrival or to misread the moment in the phrase in which it was made. Indeed, a judge should train his eye to take in the whole of the target as a main objective, and the remainder of the fencer whom he is watching and the movements of the latter's opponent as a secondary one. He will then be less likely to miss a hit, on or off the target, than if he remains with his eyes riveted on some part of the target area.

A judge must, however, remember that the reading of the phrase is the responsibility of the President, who is in the best position for it because he is placed centrally and therefore can alone get a full picture of the bout. It often happens that from one end of the *piste* this picture may appear quite differently. A judge must remember that his function is to follow the phrase in order to advise the President, who is making an analysis of it, at what moment and as a result of which action a hit has occurred; he must resist the temptation to try to impose his reading of the phrase on the President.

It sometimes happens that an experienced judge is unable to agree with the President's reading of the phrase and is quite convinced that the latter's analysis is wrong. The judge has not, of course, the right to disagree with the President's decision as to the phrasing, but in such a situation he is quite entitled to indicate his position by saying: 'There was a valid (or non-valid) hit, but I can give no opinion on the phrasing.' This is better than saying 'Yes' to a question which one believes is in opposition to the facts. It will serve, at any rate, to warn the President that all may not be well, and he can then decide whether to maintain or reverse his analysis.

The most common example of this kind of situation is when, in a complex phrase, the President starts his analysis by the original attack from the wrong side. The judge will then be in the difficult position of being asked if the attack arrived when in fact the movement which he saw was the riposte. His opposite numbers will be asked if the riposte, or the stop hit, arrived, when in fact the movement which they saw was the attack—and so on through the phrase inevitably to a wrong conclusion. The President, seeing the whole picture, may be right, but he knows that he is as fallible as anyone else and a good President will always be grateful when directing an experienced jury for the opportunity, by an indication from his judges as described above, for second thoughts.

The position occupied by the judges on the *piste*, in relation to the fencers, is important. Each judge must take up his position on the side of the *piste* allotted to him by the President. He should stand slightly behind the fencer nearest to him and at such an angle to the edge of the *piste* that he obtains the best, and least interrupted, view of the target of the fencer opposite to him. One often sees judges who stand level with, or even in front of, the fencer on their side. This is extremely dangerous and a sudden blade movement may cause them to receive a severe injury to the head and even to lose an eye. It is also liable to cramp or disconcert the fencers and may even obstruct the President's view of the whole bout.

Judges must not remain static, but must follow the fencers in their movements up and down the *piste* so as to maintain at all times, as far as possible, the ideal position just behind the fencers as described above.

When the President stops the bout because a hit has been signalled or because he thinks that one has been made, he will proceed to analyse the phrase, asking each pair of judges in turn whether each movement he described, for example the attack, riposte, or stop hit, has resulted in a hit. When thus questioned by the President, a judge should answer 'Yes' if he has seen a valid hit on the target, 'Yes, but off the target' (or on the arm or leg) if he has seen a non-valid hit, 'No' if he has seen that there has been no hit at all, or 'Abstain' if he has not seen whether in fact there was a hit or not (that is, he has no definite opinion either way).

In a long phrase, it is a great help to the President if a judge keeps his hand raised until the President, in the course of his analysis, comes to the hit which actually arrived. For example, the judges on the right of the President have seen a counter-riposte arrive and raise their hands, thus causing the President to call 'Halt'. The President will then probably ask these two judges 'Attack from my right?' to which they will reply 'No', but will keep their hands raised. The President will then ask the other pair of judges 'Riposte?' to which they will reply 'No'. He will then return to the first pair of judges, who still have their hands raised, and ask 'Counter-riposte?' to which the reply will be 'Yes', and it will be so awarded.

The abstention from voting is often misused by judges and may well cause a completely false judgment. A judge *must* abstain whenever he is unable to see clearly whether a hit has arrived or not. At foil the judge placed on the sword-arm side of the fencer opposite to him has a restricted view of the target, as compared with his partner who is on the 'open' side. He will probably be unable to see the arrival of the majority of hits made on the chest or the inside of the arm. His fellow judge will likewise be unsighted for hits which arrive on the back or the outside of the arm. Some judges fear continually to abstain in such circumstances, as they would be fully justified in doing, lest the fencers or spectators should think that they are inattentive. It is far better to say 'Abstain obscured' or 'Abstain hidden by the arm' than to risk giving a false judgment.

It must be appreciated that when judging fencing the abstention has an importance which differentiates it from 'No'. Thus if two judges abstain, the hit in question is regarded as doubtful and no subsequent hit can be counted against the fencer whose hit is established as doubtful, although he may score a subsequent hit provided he himself has not been hit meanwhile. It is therefore obviously necessary not to confuse the value of the negative and the doubtful or treat them as synonymous.

A judge must guard against any tendency to follow the lead of his fellow judge when the President interrogates the latter first about a hit. Fearlessly he must answer according to his own observations and, if he has no opinion, he must abstain. Similarly, he must treat each hit on its merits and neither be overawed by a protesting competitor nor attempt to favour a fencer whom he thinks had bad luck with a previous hit.

As already mentioned, all épée bouts are judged with the electrical apparatus. Judging at that weapon is now confined to ground judges. Two ground judges are appointed whenever fencing takes place on a non-insulated *piste* or, at the discretion of the President, when there is a possibility of hits arriving outside an insulated *piste*.

Ground judges have a somewhat negative rôle. They are not required to spot hits on the target or take part in the judgment, but merely to see when a hit, signalled by the apparatus, has been made on some surface other than that of the fencers or their equipment.

Each ground judge takes up a position slightly behind the fencer at one end of the *piste* and they are on opposite sides of the *piste*. They must not sit at each end of the *piste*, but must follow the fencers in their movements up and down, so as to maintain a clear view of the blades throughout the bout.

It must be confessed that the function of a ground judge is not a particularly enthralling one, and he may well be liable to get bored and lose his concentration. It will help him to maintain interest and carry out his job efficiently if he follows the blade movements during a phrase. This will help him to anticipate when a hit, say on the ground, is likely to occur. When interrogated a ground judge answers 'Yes', 'No' or 'Abstain'. These votes have the same value as in other judging, that is to say, each judge has one vote and the President has one and a half votes or, in other words, a casting vote if the two judges disagree.

A ground judge must remember that he is not only required to watch for hits made by the fencer on his own side of the *piste*: both ground judges are expected to watch all the play and to see any hit off the target made by either fencer during the bout.

THE WORK OF THE PRESIDENT

The President of a jury has a most responsible task and enjoys wide powers. He alone directs the bout and, while he is in charge of an event, controls the fencers, judges, officials and spectators. He alone can award hits.

The smooth running of an event and the correctness and justice of the results largely depend on the impartiality and efficiency of the President.

By his calm, firm approach and quick, confident analysis, a President can set the tone for an event and often bring serenity to the most explosive situation. Quietly but firmly a President must impose the authority of his position, and he must not allow the fencers, judges or spectators to usurp it. Naturally the first essential to enable a President to do this is that he should have a thorough knowledge of the *Rules for Competitions*.

There are many experienced fencers who have attained the highest honours in competitions but are unable to become good Presidents. They may have a good manner and be able to control a bout perfectly, and of course they know by experience exactly what has happened during each phrase, but to make a coherent analysis is beyond them. This is generally because, while they follow the phrase with diligence and form a correct impression against which fencer the hit should be scored, they have not the gift of registering the sequence of movements which build up the phrase in their mind and reconstructing it verbally for the benefit of the judges, fencers and spectators.

Such people, when they preside, generally get the result of the bout right in the end, but they cause a lot of bewilderment to their judges and irritation to the fencers and their supporters, because no one can get any idea from their analysis by what process of thought they have arrived at their decision. As already mentioned, fencers, especially in the later stages of an important competition, are inclined to be nervous and to imagine that the hits which they make should be awarded even when in fact they are wrongly made under the rules. Their serenity and discipline are not enhanced if the President cannot explain, briefly but clearly, how he has arrived at his decision. In presiding as in the law, it is not sufficient to do justice, but justice should appear to be done.

The gift of analysis when presiding, by which is meant the ability to note and remember each movement in a fencing phrase in its correct sequence and immediately repeat it clearly to the jury, is possessed by comparatively few fencers. It is akin to the ability to think and speak at the same time. Provided one's mind is capable of functioning in that way, the ability can be developed by practice. Indeed constant practice is essential for every President. It is remarkable how quickly the best President can lose his touch—a few months away from fencing will suffice.

Audibility is another quality which a President should possess. Nothing is more irritating than a President who mumbles, and he is obviously unlikely to obtain satisfactory answers from his judges unless they can hear and understand his questions. Here again justice will not appear to be done unless the fencers are favoured by a President who produces an audible and clear analysis leading to his decision.

This was not always the case. The writer well remembers taking part in major competitions over thirty years ago, when it was the habit for the President to halt the bout and award a hit without any explanation at all, sometimes merely consulting the judges by a slight raising of his eyebrows to which they replied with a nod. In those halcyon days, if a complicated phrase had occurred, the President sometimes beckoned to the four judges and they would form a group in earnest discussion for some minutes, while the two fencers either retired to the end of the *piste* or had a pleasant chat together.

Eventually the jury would return sedately to their positions and the President would award a hit, again without any explanation of how the decision had been reached.

The verbose President is almost as irritating as the inaudible one, though he will perhaps be less likely to make mistakes. The President's analysis should be a brief but clear summing-up of what has happened in the phrase, not a long-winded description of how every movement was made. The fencing is the important part of a competition—the deliberations of the jury are necessary, but should always be ancillary to the fencing.

When presiding with a jury, the President should take pains to place his judges to the best advantage. He must ensure that the fencer called first takes up a position on his right hand or, if one of the fencers is left-handed, he must place him so that he, the President, has a direct view of the open sides of the targets of both fencers.

If in a team match competitors have to judge, the President will see that the judging is equally divided between the members of each team and that a member of each team is alternately on his right and left hands. When all four judges are competitors he will ensure that a member of each team is watching the open target of each competitor.

With neutral judges, a President will soon form an estimate of their relative worth and experience. He should not hesitate to move his judges around so as to balance his jury, that is to say, so as to have (as far as possible) equal efficiency on both sides. If the President realizes that there is a weak or unreliable judge and is unable to have him replaced, he will be well advised to position him on his own side of the *piste*, watching the open target. In that position the President will most readily control and, if necessary, overrule such a judge. A President must, of course, never hesitate to ask the organizing committee to replace a judge whose competence or impartiality he has reason to doubt.

It is common practice for the judges to move round in a clockwise direction between each bout; this is known as a revolving jury. Provided all four judges are neutral and of approximately the same competence, this practice has much to commend it. A change of position maintains interest and prevents two of the judges being placed permanently on the 'blind' side of the target, that is in the position from which the target is largely hidden by the fencer's arm. A President should never, however, consent to his jury revolving in this way unless he knows their relative efficiency. His first consideration must be to have a well balanced jury.

A President should stand equidistant between the two fencers and at such a distance from the edge of the *piste* that he has a clear view of the whole of the movements performed by both fencers. He should, as far as possible, maintain this position by following the displacements of the fencers up and down the *piste* during the bout.

He must ensure that the judges maintain their correct positions just behind the fencers, so that they neither run the risk of being accidentally hit by a wide blade movement, nor disconcert the fencers, nor impair his own view. When the fencers change ends half-way through a bout, if one is a left-hander, the President should cross to the opposite side of the *piste* in order to maintain his direct view of the open sides of both targets. If for any reason (such as a raised *piste* or lack of space) he cannot himself cross to the other side in this way, he should ask the judges on both sides to exchange positions, which they should do from right to left and vice versa without crossing the *piste* diagonally.

A fencer is allowed to acknowledge a hit as soon as he has received it, although he is under no obligation to do so. The President is not obliged automatically to award this hit. He should always seek confirmation from his judges. In no circumstances must a President allow a competitor to acknowledge a hit after the jury has reached its decision or to comment in any way on that decision.

A President must be particularly careful not to put leading questions to his judges. He must remain strictly impartial and not indicate by word or gesture his personal opinion regarding the materiality of a hit until the judges have expressed their opinions. Thus the question 'Did the attack from my right arrive?' is correctly framed. 'The attack arrived didn't it?' is not correct.

In the course of his analysis, a President must be careful not to bypass any of his judges just because they have not raised their hands to signal a hit. They may well wish to abstain when, if he has no opinion himself, his whole judgment may be altered. For example, it may happen during a bout that both judges on the President's right hand raise their hands to indicate that they have seen a hit. The President stops the bout and starts his analysis by asking these judges 'Attack from my right?' to which he receives a negative reply from both judges. Since the judges on the President's left hand have given no signals, he may ignore them and again ask the judges who are still signalling a hit 'The remise (or counter-riposte)?' and, receiving affirmative replies, award the hit against the fencer on his left.

This, in fact, may be incorrect because, had he interrogated the judges on his left, they might well both have abstained as to whether a riposte had arrived or not on the original attacker. If he himself had no opinion regarding this hit, the President could not then have awarded the remise or counter-riposte made by the original attacker, because the hit which the latter might have received was doubtful.

A President must use his discretion regarding the order in which he interrogates his judges. If he observes that one of the pair of judges on one side is weak and inclined to follow the lead given by his partner or, as sometimes regrettably happens, awaits his partner's reply in order to influence the decision by a negative or by an abstention, he should make a point of questioning that judge first so as to ensure that he has to give an independent opinion.

In deciding the materiality of a hit, the President can override one judge (since each judge has one vote and the President one and a half votes) but he cannot override both judges if they are agreed. When aggregating the votes, a President must be careful always to cast his own vote last in order not to influence his judges in any way.

A President is, however, ill-advised constantly to watch for the arrival of hits. His primary duties are controlling the bout and reading the phrase. An alert President will certainly see a number of hits arrive, but if he is concentrating on doing the judges' work his reading of the phrase is bound to suffer.

He should also avoid stopping the bout whenever he thinks a hit may have arrived. This will spoil the continuity of the bout and is very irritating to the competitors. A President should rely on his judges to spot and signal hits, and he should only stop the bout on his own initiative when he is quite sure he has seen a hit which his judges have missed.

Some Presidents have a tendency to stop the bout whenever the fencers are at close quarters. Provided there is no *corps à corps*, and the fencers are wielding their weapons correctly, fencing at close quarters should be allowed to continue until either a hit results or the phrase becomes so confused that, even if hits were scored, the President would be unable to award priority to either competitor. Fencing at close quarters is a tactical manoeuvre favoured by many good fencers and is perfectly legitimate. Not to allow it to continue may gravely disadvantage one competitor and give an undue advantage to his opponent—it is not only at boxing that one can be 'saved by the bell'.

The analysis of the phrase is the most important part of a President's duties. On his correct interpretation of the phrase, the result of a competition may well depend. The analysis of the phrase consists of an audible, clear and concise repetition of the various fencing movements made by the competitors leading up to a hit. This calls for considerable concentration, the ability to recognize fencing strokes and to remember and repeat the sequence of movements which have occurred.

At foil and sabre a President is assisted in establishing the materiality of hits either by his judges or by an electrical judging apparatus. The President alone is responsible for the decision regarding the priority between hits, according to the rules and conventions of the weapon concerned. If he misreads the phrase the final result is likely to be wrong.

A President must firmly resist any natural inclination he may have to be garrulous; above all he must avoid any tendency to show off his knowledge of fencing technique! Otherwise he will probably confuse his judges, and he will certainly irritate the fencers. It is often necessary to name a stroke in the course of an analysis to make sure that the judges know about which movement they are being questioned. It is best, however, to avoid too detailed an analysis and the object should always be to present a clear, concise picture of the phrase to the jury. As a general rule, it should only be necessary to name the stroke made if there is a possibility of the judges mistaking it for another stroke. Thus at sabre it would be unnecessary to describe an attack by feint head cut at flank as such—it will be quite sufficient to ask the judges if the attack arrived. If an attack is preceded by a beat, there is the possibility that the judge, standing on one side of the *piste*, may read the beat as a parry, whereas the President from his central position can decide that the beat was a preparation for the attack. In this case the President would be justified in framing his question as 'Attack by beat cut at arm, did it arrive?'

Similarly if there has been a long, indecisive exchange of movements ending in some clear strokes resulting in a hit, it is not necessary to try to recapitulate everything which has happened since the word 'Play'. One should concentrate on the final effective movements, taking care, of course, that the jury realize that one is doing so.

Just as clarity and conciseness in analysis will save time, so unduly long pauses should also be avoided when putting the fencers on guard. The proceedings must not be unduly rushed, but a good President will usually get a pool over far more quickly than an inexperienced one. Clear, decisive presiding undoubtedly has a psychological effect on the fencers who, in their turn, tend to fence confidently and without wasting time.

Sooner or later even the best President comes to a moment when hits are signalled on both competitors and he is quite unable to establish a phrase clearly in his mind. The President must not seek assistance in this matter from his judges and to guess is fatal. The President must have the courage to accept the position and replace the fencers on guard again.

Presiding at foil with the electrical judging apparatus presents special problems and requires a good deal of experience to master its technique. No doubt similar problems will be encountered when the electrical sabre is perfected.

With a jury, a President can rely on his judges to assist him to determine which movement during a phrase resulted in a hit. For instance, the human judge will differentiate between an attack and a remise. With the foil judging apparatus, the only priority indicated by the machine is when a hit off the target is followed by a valid hit. Thus if a coloured and a white light appear on one side of the apparatus, the President knows that a non-valid hit has preceded a valid hit on that fencer, because the apparatus does not register non-valid hits after valid hits on the same side. Otherwise every hit scored on or off the target by either fencer will be registered, by a coloured or a white light respectively, without any regard to the sequence in which the hits are made in the phrase.

At first sight one might imagine that the task of the President in such circumstances would be fraught with almost insuperable difficulties. How, for example, can he be expected to see whether it is the attack or the remise which has caused the apparatus to signal a hit made on the fencer who has his back to the President, with much of his target hidden by his sword-arm? In practice, the difficulties of presiding with the foil apparatus are nothing like as formidable as might be feared, once one has acquired the necessary experience.

The task of the President is certainly harder without the help of judges in confirming the phrasing, but this is largely compensated by the certainty he enjoys that every hit which is correctly made will be registered by the apparatus. This enables the President to devote all his attention to the phrasing. The difficulty, in the writer's experience, is not in reading the phrase so much as in the amount of concentration which presiding without judges requires. For this reason a President should have frequent rests during a pool. There should be two Presidents who should alternate every six or seven bouts.

An analysis made a few years ago of several pools, comprising leading foil fencers judged with the electrical apparatus, produced the surprising information that on average about seventy per cent of the hits scored during a pool are judged by the apparatus without the President having to intervene. That is to say that in seventy per cent of the hits made only one fencer was hit (on or off the target) and therefore only one light was shown on the apparatus.

When only one hit is indicated in this way, the President should award it, if on the target, or annul it, if it is off the target, without wasting any time in making an analysis of the phrase. When, however, lights are shown on both sides of the apparatus, it is not sufficient for the President to award one hit or annul another, however clear the phrase may be to him. To award hits regularly in this way without explanation may save time, but it certainly will not add to the serenity and confidence of the fencers. A short analysis should always be made, so that the justice of the President's decision is apparent to all. Whether they agree with him or not is an entirely different matter!

The analysis should be made in the normal way, starting with the attack and following the phrase through, but using the lights shown on the apparatus to confirm whether a hit has resulted in place of the replies of the judges. In no case can the President award a hit which he thinks he has seen unless it is registered by the apparatus, but the rules provide a number of instances in which the President can annul hits so registered.

Basically there is no difference between presiding with a jury or with the apparatus, the reading of the phrase is exclusively the President's responsibility. Considerable experience is, however, required in presiding with the apparatus before the President can acquire the necessary degree of concentration on the phrase and learn to do without the help he is used to receiving from the judges in establishing at which moment in a phrase a hit occurred—for example, whether it is the attack or riposte or the remise of either movement which caused the hit, whether a parry was insufficient or not, and so on.

A President can only judge successfully with the apparatus if he concentrates primarily on the blade movements made by the competitors. At first, especially if he is used to presiding with the electrical épée, there is a great temptation to watch the apparatus rather than the fencing. This is fatal at foil because (as shown above) the foil apparatus does not show priority between valid hits. Unless he has a clear picture of the phrase, he will rarely be able to establish priority under the foil rules which does not, of course, depend on physical time.

The President must, however, always have the lamps on the apparatus in his field of vision. He will then be able to stop the bout as soon as the apparatus registers a hit and often avoid having the situation complicated by other lights being shown by immediately following hits. It is stressed that the President must train himself to make his observation of the lamps secondary to his observation of the phrase. This is not as difficult as it sounds, especially if extension lamps are fitted to the apparatus. Without extension lamps the President often has to place himself farther from the competitors and, when they are fencing near one end of the *piste*, to place himself at a distinct angle in order to keep the lamps constantly in view.

As has been stated, the foil apparatus is not designed to show priority between hits made on different sides, as is the case with the electrical épée. The foil apparatus is, however, so constructed that there is a time lag of two seconds after a hit is registered before the apparatus will fail to register a hit made on the other competitor. This time lag at épée is of the order of one twenty-fifth of a second. When there is an appreciable difference of time between two such hits, the lamps on the foil apparatus can give a valuable indication of this difference. The President must, of course, be careful not to confuse this actual time with the conventions relating to fencing time, which may be quite a different thing.

As an illustration of this, one can take a case when the President forms the impression that a stop hit, if it arrived immediately, would have priority over an attack. This impression may be confirmed by the lamp signals, that is by the actual time which they indicate. If the light registering the stop hit appears appreciably before the light registering the attack, the President's impression will be confirmed. If both lights appear simultaneously, he will know that the stop hit did not arrive immediately and the attack will have priority.

The electrical foil apparatus has now been used in major competitions for several years. Most experienced Presidents are agreed that presiding with this device does not present the particular difficulties anticipated with such apprehension at its inception. All that is required is experience and a thorough knowledge of the special rules applicable to the use of this apparatus.

Presiding with the electrical épée apparatus presents no difficulty at all. The apparatus establishes not only materiality of hits but also their exact priority. This can be done because the épée is not a conventional weapon like the foil or the sabre. The difference between hits is determined entirely by physical time—if a hit arrives one twenty-fifth of a second or more before the competitor making it is himself hit, the apparatus will only register the first hit; if both hits arrive within one twenty-fifth of a second, both hits are registered and a double hit is scored.

This simplicity often leads organizers of competitions to imagine that anyone can preside at an electrical épée match, provided he keeps awake sufficiently to start and stop the bout when required and warns the competitors when they are approaching the limits of the *piste* or when time is running out. This is far from true. An inattentive or untrained President can commit a surprising number of faults, even with the electrical épée box.

Besides correctly warning the competitors as to their position on the *piste* and applying the rules regarding retiring to the limits (necessitated by the fact that electrical épée bouts can never be fenced on a full-length *piste*), he must note exactly when a competitor leaves the *piste* and watch for hits made outside it. He must apply the rules regarding fencing at close quarters and *corps à corps* and all those generally applicable to the direction of an event. He must be fully conversant with the somewhat complex rules governing the annulment of hits registered by the apparatus, the responsibility of the fencer for his personal equipment, the detection of errors and breakdowns in the apparatus or the fencer's equipment and the use of weapons which do not conform to the rules, and know the rules for dealing with quite a number of other specialized situations which may arise when using this form of judging. If there is no insulated *piste*, he must be capable of directing the ground judges.

Presiding with the electrical épée apparatus is not a sinecure, but requires knowledge of the rules and experience in their application. An inattentive or inefficient President can sometimes alter the result of a competition and, even with this foolproof apparatus, a dishonest one can often find occasion to favour a competitor or limit his opponent's legitimate tactics.

While presiding, at all weapons, the President is responsible for the work done by the scorers and timekeepers. At the conclusion of a pool or match he is required to sign the score-sheet and he is in fact certifying that it is correct. He should, therefore, check the entries on the score-sheet before he does so. In major competitions the President also signs a bout-in-progress score-sheet, on which the hits in that bout are recorded, at the conclusion of each bout. He should take particular care to check the hits before signing, because these individual score-sheets are the evidence relied on if later a dispute arises as to the score in the event as a whole.

Besides directing the bouts, a President enjoys full powers to control not only the competitors, but all officials, supporters and spectators, in fact everyone present at the event at which he is officiating. He should be familiar with his disciplinary powers. Fortunately difficulties are rarely met with but, when trouble arises, there is not usually time to refer to the book of rules, and the President who is uncertain as to the steps he is permitted to take will lose much of his authority.

The President's decision as to fact, concerning the materiality or validity of a hit, is final and no one can appeal against it. If, however, a President gives a decision which is contrary to the rules, or fails to apply the rules correctly, a competitor, or his team captain, may lodge an appeal. The rules require that such an appeal be made verbally to the President and it is only receivable if made immediately and before any decision has been taken regarding a subsequent hit. This is yet another reason why all fencers should be thoroughly conversant with the rules. If a mistake is made and the sufferer has to spend some time checking through the rule book, the event will continue meanwhile and the chance to appeal may have been lost.

Whenever an appeal is lodged in this way, the President should treat the matter with every courtesy. The point in dispute can usually be settled by reference to the *Rules for Competitions*. If he is at fault, the President should, of course, immediately rectify the error he has made. If, however, the President maintains his opinion or interpretation of the rules, the aggrieved party may refer the matter to the Directoire Technique or, eventually, to the Jury d'Appel for decision.

An efficient, attentive and courteous President will soon gain the respect and confidence of the fencers, judges and spectators and can do much by his control and general attitude to set the tone of the competition at which he is officiating. Fencers should appreciate that the President is carrying out a difficult, tiring and often thankless task and should give him the respect and consideration which are his due.

VIII

The Organization of a Fencing Club

A NY group of people can form a fencing club. One of the great advantages of fencing is that large numbers are not required before one can start. Any multiple of two can fence and foil fencing is equally suitable for ladies as for men.

FORMING A CLUB

Obviously the first essential is to find a suitable room, which may be a local hall, school or gymnasium, and obtain the services of a master or leader. It is an advantage for the club to own a small pool of equipment—jackets for both sexes, masks and foils. Prospective members will appreciate the opportunity to have their initial lessons with club equipment and, if they maintain their interest, will be prepared to purchase their own equipment when they have decided to continue fencing seriously. Second-hand equipment is rather hard to come by, but good results can sometimes be obtained by an advertisement, or an appeal for equipment, in a local paper.

Application should be made to the Section of the Amateur Fencing Association for the area to obtain the services of a coach or the address of local masters. If none is available, it may be possible to obtain the services of a physical-training instructor trained in fencing from a local Army depot or RAF station. In the London area, information as to the availability of professional masters can be obtained from the British Academy of Fencing, which is the governing body for professional fencing in Great Britain.

In the initial stages finance may be a limiting factor which makes it difficult for the club to hire premises or pay for professional tuition. It is often advantageous to apply to the local education authorities to explore the possibility of the group of people who wish to take up fencing being enrolled as an evening class. If this can be arranged and the minimum number of students required enrolled, the local authority will supply premises and an instructor at very low subscription rates. In many cases they can supply some basic equipment as well. The club can then be founded among the members of the class.

THE CONSTITUTION

Once these details have been settled, the next step is to draw up club rules. These usually fall under the following headings:

(1) The name of the club.

(2) The objects of the club.

(3) The conditions of membership, details of subscriptions and date at which the club year starts. This rule should state that all members of the club must be amateurs as defined by the Amateur Fencing Association. Under the laws of the Association, no professional is allowed to be a member of an amateur club or to take any part in its organization or administration.

(4) The constitution of the committee and description of the officers.

(5) Provisions regarding the holding of the annual general meeting, extraordinary general meetings and the quorum required at such meetings, and details as to how and when the officers and committee are to be elected.

(6) Rules required for specific purposes, e.g. club championships, the club captain and selection committee for teams, club colours and how they shall be awarded, times of club meetings and so on.

(7) Finally, the all-important rule that 'All matters arising which are not covered by these rules shall be decided by the committee'.

It is advisable to draft the rules as simply and as widely as possible. If too much detail is included they will have to be constantly amended. The rules should be for general guidance, details of administration being left to the committee. If its decisions do not please the members, the latter can change their committee at the next annual general meeting.

ADVANTAGES OF AFFILIATION TO THE AFA

As soon as the club has thus been established, it should apply for affiliation to the Amateur Fencing Association through the local Section (area organization) of the Association or through the headquarters at The de Beaumont Centre, 83 Perham Road, West Kensington, London, W.14.

The Amateur Fencing Association is the governing body for fencing in Great Britain and Northern Ireland and has area organizations, called Sections, covering every part of the country. Many Sections contain a number of county unions.

By affiliation, a club supports and is in direct touch with the local and central organization of fencing in this country. It can then participate in local and national competitions, of which there are a great many of all grades each season, and in the National Coaching Scheme and other activities, besides being in touch with other clubs in the area for matches. A club can obtain a great deal of assistance and advice from its local Section or union. Further, it receives notices of competitions and other events throughout the year and the annual report of the Association, which is a very full document containing the names and addresses of all Sections, county unions and affiliated clubs, members, official Presidents and judges, Section coaches and AFA coaches and much other useful information. Interest may be fostered in the club's district by arranging a fencing display. This can generally be organized by a Section for an affiliated club.

All persons interested in fencing, club members and their friends, should support the organization of British fencing by joining the Amateur Fencing Association as individual members. This involves a small annual subscription which is, at present, £1. If there were no governing body, there would be little fencing in this country today, no local organizations, no leaders and few other instructors. There would be no organization capable of issuing fencing rules, sponsoring instructional books, arranging coaching schemes and courses, promoting competitions and championships, selecting and training Olympic and other international teams, issuing a fencing journal, arranging publicity and performing many other services for British fencers. Thus every fencer in the United Kingdom, whatever his degree of skill, derives some benefit, directly as well as indirectly, from the work of the Amateur Fencing Association, which covers a wide field.

Like most amateur sports bodies, the Association is always handicapped by lack of funds in meeting continually rising costs. It is surely worth while helping by a small annual subscription to support the organization of British fencing.

Although this should be a sufficient reason for joining the Association as an individual member, such membership brings a number of personal benefits to a fencer. These include the automatic receipt of the amateur (international) fencing licence, notices of competitions and other events and the annual report, the right to wear the AFA lapel badge, tie and blazer badge and to obtain entry on advantageous terms to attend the finals of important competitions. Further, only individual members of the Association are eligible to enter for senior Section championships, open competitions, national competitions and training courses under the National Coach, which the Association arranges or sponsors.

Application for individual membership should be made to the secretary of the AFA at the London headquarters. An excellent plan is to include the AFA individual membership subscription in the club subscription, by adding 10s. to the latter and sending all the subscriptions *en bloc* to AFA headquarters. If all club members are thus individual AFA members, the club benefits by a rebate of one shilling per member from the Association. In other words, provided the club guarantees that all its members are individual AFA members, it need only send 19s. for each member's annual subscription to headquarters.

SOCIAL ARRANGEMENTS

It is generally advantageous to elect some well known local person as president or patron of a club. It will at least help to obtain valuable publicity for the club in local newspapers. However, as in most amateur organizations, the success of a club will largely depend on the presence of a few enthusiasts who will undertake the secretary-ship, captaincy and so on, and assist new members, arrange fixtures and club competitions and generally make the club run happily.

The social side of a club should not be neglected. Occasional functions, such as open club evenings to which members of neighbouring clubs can be invited, fencing parties, a club dinner or a dance to which members can bring non-fencing relations and friends, will help to foster the club spirit. Some clubs make a habit of adjourning to the local pub at the conclusion of their fencing evening —the hostelry generally soon comes to be known as *The Fencers' Arms*. A club tie and blazer badge may be evolved and perhaps a brassard for those members who have been awarded their club colours for prowess in matches, or another brassard to be worn by the winner of a monthly handicap pool. In these and many other ways the committee can make a club a far more enjoyable and friendly meeting place for its members than if it is merely a venue for learning fencing.

ORGANIZING COMPETITIONS AND MATCHES

RULES GOVERNING COMPETITIONS

All fencing matches and competitions are governed by the *Rules for Competitions* which are published by the Amateur Fencing Association. These rules are a translation into English of the international rules issued by the Fédération Internationale d'Escrime. They are obtainable from AFA headquarters at the address given on page 232, and the present price is 6s. per copy including postage in the United Kingdom.

The organizers of a competition may vary any provision in these rules to suit local conditions, provided that notice of the proposed changes is clearly given in the prospectus announcing the competition. For example, the time factor may require bouts to be fenced for three, instead of five, effective hits, or that promotion of fencers from preliminary pools should be on a count of hits and not by fencing off barrages. The formula usually included in a notice announcing a competition is 'The competition will be organized under the rules of the Amateur Fencing Association with the following exceptions. . . .' The organizers are obliged to adhere strictly to the published rules unless such preliminary announcement of variations therefrom is made.

The notice announcing a competition should always contain a note regarding the nature of the *piste*, linoleum, wood, rubber or insulated track, on which fencing will take place. Competitors will then know which shoes to bring. Fencing shoes with leather soles are best for linoleum *pistes* but rubber shoes have to be worn on a wood surface or on a metallized (insulated) *piste*.

The organizers are advised to make their notice announcing a competition as clear and concise as possible and to enclose with it, or attach to it, an entry form in the simplest possible wording. Fencers, and indeed most people who take part in competitive sports, seem quite incapable of reading any notice sent to them which is at all complicated. Print the closing date for entries in the boldest available type—and stick to it rigidly.

After the closing date, the organizers will draw the first-round pools as described below and it is usual to send a copy of this draw, together with exact details of venue, times for all rounds and so on, to every competitor. This notice should also be very concise and it is helpful to include a 'box' in which all particulars as to the times at which each round starts, number of competitors promoted from each round, whether by barrage or count of hits, and other essential information is clearly set out to cover the whole competition.

A special permit from the Amateur Fencing Association head-quarters is required before anyone can organize an open competition in this country. Broadly speaking, an open competition is one which is not confined to the members of one club.

Any British fencer who wishes to participate in any competition abroad must, under the laws of the International Federation, have his or her entry made through Amateur Fencing Association head-quarters. This also applies to matches arranged with foreign clubs, whether in this country or abroad. Severe penalties, including suspension, may be inflicted on fencers who compete abroad without advising the Association.

TEAM MATCHES AND COMPETITIONS

Matches take place between teams which have usually three or four a side. The captain of each team has the right to choose the order in which the names of members of his team are entered on the score-sheet. Every member of one team meets every member of the other team, according to a prescribed order of bouts which is usually printed at the bottom of the score-sheet. This order of bouts is designed to allow approximately equal periods of rest between bouts for each competitor.

Before a match begins, the team captains toss for the position in which the names of their teams will be entered on the score-sheet, either in the upper half, numbers one to three or one to four, or the lower half, numbers four to six or five to eight. The winner of the toss usually selects the upper half of the score-sheet because, especially in three-a-side matches, the upper position has the advantage of a more even distribution of rests between bouts. In three-a-side matches, the last bout in the match is between numbers three and five, whereas in four-a-side matches it is between numbers four and eight. Captains usually assign these two positions to their strongest and most experienced fencers, but opinion on the best strategy in placing the members of a team varies widely. Against a much weaker team it may be better to fence the strongest members of the team first, so that they can build up an early lead and discourage the opposition.

At the conclusion of a match, the team whose members aggregate the most victories is the winner. Should both teams score an equal number of victories, the number of hits scored against all the members of each team is likewise counted and the winning team is the one whose members have received the lesser total of hits during the match. If the total of victories and hits is the same for each team the match is drawn.

At the conclusion of a team match, it is usual for the teams to line up on the *piste*, facing each other, and give three cheers, after which all the members of each team, led by their captain, shake hands with their opponents.

If the order of bouts laid down in the rules for team matches, or for pools of various sizes in individual competitions, is examined it will be noticed that the number representing a competitor is placed according to a set pattern. For example, in a four-a-side team match, the bouts in which number one is concerned are entered as 1—7, 8—1, 1—6, 5—1. It will be remembered that, under the rules, the fencer first called for a bout places himself on the right side of the President (except in the case of one right- and one left-hander). Thus in the example just cited, number one will be placed alternately on the right and the left side of the *piste* in his four bouts. This is designed to give each competitor in turn an equal chance to benefit from any advantage one end of the *piste* may have—for example, better lighting. This is particularly important when an electrical judging apparatus is used, as competitors do not change ends during a bout. During a match or pool the apparatus may develop a slight advantage in timing on one side or the other. By the fencers being placed alternately on either side of the apparatus, such slight advantage or disadvantage will be distributed equally between all the competitors.

In a friendly match between clubs it is usual to complete all the bouts in the match. In team competitions, however, a match is often stopped when one side has obtained a winning lead, that is, has won five bouts in a three-a-side match or nine bouts in a four-a-side match. This is done to save time and obviate needlessly tiring the fencers. As a matter of courtesy, the captain of the team which has thus obtained a victory should always make a point of asking the permission of the losing team's captain before this course is adopted.

Team competitions usually follow the lines described below for individual events, that is to say, the teams are drawn into pools, usually of three or four teams. The organizers are responsible for seeding the teams so as to balance the pools at approximately the same strength. Each team in a pool normally fences one match against every other team in the pool. Each match won counts two points to the winning team, a draw scores one point to each team concerned and a loss gets no points. The team or teams (usually two from each pool) with the greatest number of points are promoted to the next round. It is usual, in a pool of three, first to fence a match between the two weaker teams, the loser having then to fence the strongest team. In a pool of four, matches are first fenced by the two stronger teams against the two weaker teams and afterwards the winners fence the losers in the other match. In this way it is often possible to save time by obtaining a result after two rounds of matches in the pool.

Sometimes team competitions start with one or two rounds of pools and, when the weakest teams have thus been eliminated, continue by direct elimination exactly as described for individual events under the system below.

INDIVIDUAL EVENTS

Individual competitions are usually organized under the pool system. In each pool every competitor meets every other competitor in turn, according to a prescribed order of bouts printed in the rules and, generally, at the foot of the score-sheet.

When all the entries for a competition have been received, the organizers plan the competition in such a way that, after the specified number of rounds, they will be left with the number of competitors they require for the final pool. There are usually several possibilities and the one chosen will depend on the object in view. If it is a junior competition with a small entry, a relatively large number of fencers, say fifty per cent, may be promoted from preliminary pools to give maximum fencing experience to the successful competitors. In a major championship, or with a large entry, it is usually necessary to promote the minimum number allowed by the rules, in order not to exhaust the best fencers before the final is reached.

Next the organizers have to arrange the competitors in a number of first-round pools, each containing approximately the same number of fencers (usually six to eight). From each pool a predetermined number of competitors are promoted to the next round, and this must be not less than one third of the number in the pool and at least three fencers. It may not be necessary to finish pools where a definite result has been obtained but, if time permits, it is always better to do so. After each round the organizers draw the competitors who have been promoted from the previous round in a fresh number

BRITISH EMPIRE & COMMONWEALTH GAMES
CARDIFF, WALES, 1958

FENCING — INDIVIDUAL EVENTS

	JURY	NATIONALITY
President	C-LdE BEAUMONT	ENGLAND
	P. MURPHY	N-I
	A. McTAVISH	SCOTLAND
	J. TAFFY	WALES.
	A. COBBER	N.Z

WEAPON _Foil_
EVENT _Individual_
POOL NO. _Final_
PISTE NO. _1_
DATE _5-August 1958_
TIME _2 pm_

Country	Competitors	No.	1	2	3	4	5	6	7	8	9	10	V.	Hits Rec.	Hits Given	Pl.
BERMUDA	J. JONES	1	■	V	D	D	V	V	V	D			4	25		III
CEYLON	P. PETER	2		■	V	V	V	D	D	D			3	28	25	VI
GUIANA	T- ROOT	3	V	D	■	V	D	D	D	D			2	30		VII
JAMAICA	O- BROWN	4	V	D	D	■	D	D	D	D			1			VIII
I.O.M	M. CAT	5	D	D	V	V	■	D	D	V			3	28	26	V
TASMANIA	J. SATAN	6	D	V	V	V	V	■	V	V			6			I
TONGA	Q- RAIN	7	V	V	V	V	D	D	■	V			5	22		II
FIJI	F. WUZZY	8	V	V	V	V	D	D	D	■			4	26		IV
		9									■					
		10										■				
	Hits Given ...				25	26										

Signature of President _____

ORDER OF BOUTS:

5 fencers 10 bouts	6 fencers 15 bouts	7 fencers 21 bouts	8 fencers 28 bouts	9 fencers 36 bouts	10 fencers 45 bouts		
1—2	1—4	1—4 3—1	1—5 6—3	1—2 3—1	1—6	7—4	2—4
3—4	2—5	2—5 4—6	2—6 7—4	2—8 2—4	2—7	8—5	6—8
5—1	3—6	3—6 7—2	3—7 1—2	3—7 5—9	3—8	10—1	7—9
2—3	5—1	7—1 3—5	4—8 3—4	4—5 6—6	4—9	2—6	5—2
4—5	6—2	5—4 1—6	6—1 5—6	1—5 7—1	5—10	3—7	8—10
1—3	4—3	2—3 2—4	7—2 7—8	2—9 4—3	7—1	4—8	1—4
2—5	1—6	6—7 7—3	8—3 3—1	8—3 5—2	8—2	9—5	5—3
4—1	3—5	5—1 6—5	1—4 7—5	7—4 6—9	9—3	1—2	9—6
3—5	2—1	4—3 1—2	1—7 7—5	6—5 8—7	10—4	3—4	7—10
4—2	4—5	6—2 4—7	2—8 6—8	1—2 4—1	6—5	6—7	
	3—2	5—7	3—5 1—4	9—3 5—3	1—8	8—9	
	6—4		4—6 2—3	8—4 6—2	2—9	5—1	
	1—3		8—1 8—5	7—6 8—7	3—10	2—3	
	5—6		5—2 6—7	6—1 1—8	4—6	6—10	
				3—2 4—5	5—7	7—8	
				9—4 3—6	9—1	4—5	
				5—8 2—7	10—4	10—9	
				7—6 9—8	6—3	3—1	

NOTE: The fencer whose number is called first places himself on the right of the President, except in a bout between a right and a left-hander without the electrical apparatus (épée).

Fig. 62   Score-sheet for Individual Events

of pools and the competition proceeds in this way, according to the original plan, until the final pool is reached.

In order to save time, a competition may be arranged with direct elimination throughout, or one or more rounds of pools with direct elimination by individual matches between the last eight, sixteen or thirty-two competitors. Although the regulations for running an event by direct elimination are included in the official rules, to hold a competition under this system constitutes an exception to the rules and must be announced beforehand with the original notice about the competition.

Under the pool system, the organizers must make every effort to draw the pools for each round so that they are, as far as possible, of equal strength and to distribute fencers belonging to the same club as evenly as possible between the pools, so that fellow club members avoid meeting in the competition until the last possible moment. This latter provision, referred to in the rules as 'nationality', is an overriding factor.

To make a draw, the organizers first 'seed' the entry, that is to say they select the competitors according to strength. There is thus a group of first seeds, one of second seeds, one of third seeds and so on, each group having the same number of fencers as there are pools in the round which is being drawn. The seeded fencers of each group are then distributed equally between the pools, but the primary consideration is always to keep members of the same club apart as far as possible.

When the pools have all been drawn in this way, the names of the competitors in each pool are entered on the score-sheet according to an order determined by drawing lots. If, however, a pool contains more than one fencer from the same club, then these fencers must be so placed on the score-sheet that they will meet each other before they fence against competitors in the pool from other clubs. Once again 'nationality' is an overriding factor.

In order to gain promotion to the next round, a fencer must have obtained more victories in the pool than anyone who is eliminated. Thus in a pool in which three fencers are to be promoted, one may find four competitors with an equal number of victories, or one or two with a superior total who are immediately promoted, leaving two or three others equal on victories for the last remaining place for promotion. The fencers who tie are said to be in a barrage and this is immediately fought off. If, after this one barrage round, two or more competitors are still equal on victories, they are divided by aggregating the hits received by each, both in the original pool and the barrage round. The competitors with the least number of hits scored against them are promoted. If, at this point, both victories and hits received are still equal, then the hits given by each competitor in the original pool and the barrage round are aggregated and the successful fencers are, of course, those who have scored most hits.

In the unlikely event of these competitors still tying, further barrages are fought until a result is obtained.

The competitors who have been promoted from the previous round are then drawn by the organizers into the predetermined number of second-round pools. The same procedure is followed in drawing these pools as for the first round, except that seeding is determined by the placings obtained by the fencers in the pools of the preceding round, provided, of course, that these pools have been fought to a finish. Thus the winners of the first-round pools are automatically the first seeds, the fencers placed second are the second seeds, and so on. Here again 'nationality' is given priority over everything else, so as to keep members of the same club apart as long as possible. Another factor which the organizers have to take into consideration is to avoid as far as possible the competitors who were drawn in the same pool in one round meeting again in a pool in the immediately subsequent round. Obviously, since there are progressively fewer pools in each round, this cannot be entirely avoided.

The competition proceeds in this way by rounds of pools, until the required number of competitors remain to form the final pool. This also is usually composed of six or eight fencers.

In the final pool, the winner of the competition is the fencer who has won the greatest number of victories in that pool. He must always have a lead of at least one victory over all other finalists to be declared the winner. When determining the first place in a final, only victories are taken into account. One never counts hits for that purpose. When several fencers tie for first place with an equal number of victories, the barrage is fought off, as often as is necessary, until one fencer has a clear lead on victories. Once a winner has been found, the other fencers who have taken part in the barrage round, or rounds, are awarded the next places in the final according to their number of victories. If these are equal, they are classified according to the aggregate of hits received, or if necessary of hits scored, in the original pool and the barrage pool or pools.

In final pools barrages are not normally fought off to determine the places other than the first place as described. Fencers who are equal on victories when the pool is concluded are divided by the numbers of hits received or scored. If still equal on victories and hits, such fencers are normally classed equal for the position concerned[1].

ADMINISTRATIVE ARRANGEMENTS

The organizers of a competition must make certain provisions before the event starts. They must obtain the use of a hall large enough to accommodate the number of *pistes* required for the first-round pools.

[1] In 1969 the International Federation adopted a new system for organizing competitions by pools throughout. Under this system the ratio between the number of victories and the number of bouts fought between the number of hits received and the number of hits scored (indicators) accumulated throughout the competition, except for the first round pools, are used not only for determining the placing in the pools in each round without any barrages, but also for drawing the pools in each round. See 'Rules for Competitions'.

These need not, of course, all be in the same room, but some space should be available round one *piste*, which will be used for the finals, to accommodate spectators. Sufficient space should be available for the 14 metre (45ft 11ins) regulation *piste* used for all three weapons with a run-back behind the back line at each end of the *piste* of 1.50 to 2 metres (5ft to 6ft 7ins) to allow a fencer to retire with both feet off the end of the *piste*. Each *piste* should be approximately two metres wide. It is essential to leave sufficient space, say ten to twelve feet, between adjacent *pistes* to accommodate the juries, and electrical apparatus.

The *pistes* may be marked out with chalk lines or strips of white one-inch adhesive tape. The centre line, on-guard lines and warning lines can be indicated by small lines of tape about six inches long at right angles to the lateral boundaries of the *piste*.

If fencing is to take place on linoleum or unpolished wood, a small heap of rosin should be provided at each *piste* in which fencers wearing leather-soled fencing shoes can rub their shoes. If the floor is inclined to be slippery, it is preferable to supply a very wet floor-cloth on which the fencers can likewise rub their shoes to get a better grip. Some chairs or benches must be available for the competitors during the pool.

It will obviously be necessary to make the best arrangements possible for changing accommodation for both sexes. Wise organizers will have a first-aid box available, or arrange with the local voluntary first-aid service to look after this. They will also require a supply of score-sheets, pencils and stop-watches. The latter item will probably be difficult, but at least one stop-watch of the start-stop-start variety should be available for use during the final pool. If arrangements can be made with a local restaurant or café for meals and drinks during the competition, this will be greatly appreciated by the competitors.

ADJUDICATING THE MATCH

The organizers must try to obtain the services of competent Presidents and, when possible, judges. The presence of at least one first-class President to take the final will make all the difference to the success of the competition. The local AFA Section will certainly help in finding such officials. A scorer and timekeeper will be required for each *piste* in use and, when the electrical judging apparatus is used, a separate person should be available to work the apparatus.

The duties of the scorer consist of calling over the competitors in a pool or match in the order in which they are entered on the score-sheet, ensuring that all are present and that each knows his number on the score-sheet. He then calls the competitors for each bout in the sequence in which they appear on the order of bouts for the event. This is important because it will be recalled that the competitor whose number is called first places himself on the right hand of the President, unless the latter otherwise directs. At the same time the

I

scorer should warn the competitors required for the next bout, saying 'Get ready X and Y'. This will save time by enabling the next pair to prepare themselves while the bout is in progress.

The scorer must enter in the appropriate square, opposite the name of each fencer actually fighting, each hit as awarded by the President and announce the score at that point in the bout in a loud voice, thus, 'Two against X, three against Y'. At the conclusion of the bout he places a V against the name of the winning competitor, just below (and not obscuring) the hits in that square, and likewise a D against the name of the loser.

If the time allotted for a bout expires without either competitor having scored the prearranged number of hits to win, a fencer leading on hits (say 1—2, 3—2 etc.) wins the bout. The scorer then adds an equal number of hits to the score of *each* competitor until the loser has received the maximum number of hits being fought for. Thus in a five-hit bout, if the score was 2—1, the final score will be 5—4; if it was 3—1, the final score will be 5—3, and so on.

If time runs out in similar circumstances but the competitors at that point are equal on hits (2—2, 3—3 etc.) then at foil or sabre the scorer makes both scores up to the maximum number of hits being fought for, less one—which, in a five-hit bout, will of course be four all. The competitors then fight for a deciding hit, without time limit, which will give the victory to the one who scores this hit. However at épée the rule is different. If time runs out and the fencers are level on hits (2—2, 3—3 etc.) then the hits against each competitor are made up to the maximum being fought for—in the case of a five-hit bout to five all—and a defeat is scored against each. If, however, by reason of a double hit the score reaches five all before the time limit has expired, the bout continues until time is called and if during this period one competitor scores a hit (double hits being disregarded) he wins the bout. The scorer must remember that he does not enter any of these supplementary hits on the score sheet but merely enters a victory or a defeat against the competitors, so that the score in such a bout will always be 'V—five hits', 'D—five hits'.

In every pool or match there must be a timekeeper, whose functions, in minor events, may be carried out by the scorer. The timekeeper should be provided with a stop-watch of the type which can be interrupted and restarted without returning to zero until the bout is completed. His duty is to keep the exact time during which the competitors are free to fence. He will start his watch whenever the President calls 'Play' and stop it whenever the President calls 'Halt'.

The time limit for actual fencing is five minutes for a four-hit bout and six minutes for a five-hit bout, at all weapons. The time-keeper must advise the President when the competitors have fenced for one minute less than the maximum time limit. When time runs out the timekeeper should call 'Halt' in a loud voice and also strike the table bell with which he will be provided for this purpose. The timekeeper must make sure that the President hears his signals. As time is running out, the fencer who is behind on hits will probably be attacking hard to try to level the score and the President will, of course, be concentrating on the phrase, while the competitor who is leading will probably be retiring to the end of the *piste*. If the timekeeper were merely to raise his hand such a signal would probably be missed—and at that point every moment is important. In these circumstances it is in fact the timekeeper's 'Halt' which stops the bout.

The scorer and the timekeeper will be best placed to carry out their duties if they are seated at a small table situated centrally to the length of the *piste*, on the opposite side to the President.

The organizers should ensure that an expert is available whenever the electrical judging apparatus is used in a competition. This expert can be responsible for setting up the apparatus and checking the competitors' weapons and equipment, he can check for faults if a break-down occurs during a bout and can probably undertake minor repairs which may be required.

When possible two persons should be provided at each *piste* to attach and detach the fencers. This can be dispensed with if necessary but it is always better to provide this service, especially in a final pool.

Each President should be provided with a testing weight, which should be 500 grammes for foil and 750 grammes for épée. These weights are usually cylindrical, with a deep hole or slot bored in one end so that the weight can be fitted easily over the point of the weapon and will so remain without being touched when the sword is held in a vertical position. The President will use these weights, to ensure that the electrical point resists the weight as required by the rules, before each bout and whenever a weapon is changed during a bout. This is important because the spring in the electrical point, especially at foil, can become weakened during use when over-light hits will be registered as good.

Presidents should remember that the spring in an electrical point must *resist* the prescribed weight. It is not, therefore, sufficient merely to depress the point with the weight but, after this has been done and the apparatus has functioned, the box should be reset while the weight remains balanced on the point, when at that stage the apparatus should not function. This shows that the spring in the point has raised the weight and is therefore in order.

PRELIMINARY PRECAUTIONS

The organizers should ensure that the weapons and equipment of all competitors are checked before a competition begins. Weapons should be measured to ensure that they conform to the rules and electrical weapons and body-wires will be checked by the experts concerned. In addition the clothing and equipment of each fencer should be checked. This can conveniently be done on each *piste* just prior to the first round when all competitors will be changed and ready to fence. Naturally a lady member of the organizing committee will be used to test ladies' clothing. Points which should be watched include the material of jackets and breeches, which must be of sufficient strength and thickness for the weapon in use and have double thickness from the elbow of the sword-arm, covering the arm-pit and breast. Ladies must use breast-protectors of rigid material. At all weapons competitors must wear a regulation plastron under their jackets, and must use an adequate glove covering the end of the sleeve to about half way up the forearm. When a short jacket is used at foil or sabre, it must overlap the breeches or skirt by at least four inches when the fencer is in the on-guard position.

It is particularly important to ensure that masks are strong and in good condition. An old, battered mask with the meshes pushed awry and probably rusted in places can cause a serious accident. A mask should be examined for displaced or broken meshes and pressed with the thumbs to test its strength.

Particularly dangerous habits are wearing a foil jacket for épée, wearing a right-handed jacket when left-handed (which means that the buttons are the wrong side and there is no reinforcement to upper arm or armpit), using a jacket which is torn or which has a low collar and exposes the neck, or wearing flannel trousers at épée.

There is little danger when fencing, provided regulation clothing and equipment in good condition is used. Otherwise a very serious accident can occur, especially when a blade breaks. Organizers of competitions should refuse to let anyone fence unless their equipment is adequate—it may disappoint and even infuriate a keen, if careless, competitor, but it will quite likely save his life.

THE MATCH PLAN

If a competition is held by direct elimination, the position in which competitors are placed on the match plan, that is to say the way that they are paired in successive rounds, is obviously most important.

In most competitions what is known as the mixed system is used, that is to say that the competition starts with one or two rounds of pools, proceeds with direct elimination with repechage until six competitors remain, and terminates with a final pool.

In such an event the results of the preliminary pools determine the position in which competitors are placed on the match plan. For each competitor the number of victories obtained in the pool is divided by the number of bouts fought to produce a first indicator. Similarly dividing the number of hits scored by the number of hits

8 Competitors	16 Competitors	32 Competitors
$\left\{\begin{array}{l}1\\8\end{array}\right.$	$\left\{\begin{array}{l}1\\16\end{array}\right.$	$\left\{\begin{array}{l}1\\32\end{array}\right.$
$\left\{\begin{array}{l}5\\4\end{array}\right.$	$\left\{\begin{array}{l}9\\8\end{array}\right.$	$\left\{\begin{array}{l}17\\16\end{array}\right.$
$\left\{\begin{array}{l}3\\6\end{array}\right.$	$\left\{\begin{array}{l}5\\12\end{array}\right.$	$\left\{\begin{array}{l}9\\24\end{array}\right.$
$\left\{\begin{array}{l}7\\2\end{array}\right.$	$\left\{\begin{array}{l}13\\4\end{array}\right.$	$\left\{\begin{array}{l}25\\8\end{array}\right.$
	$\left\{\begin{array}{l}3\\14\end{array}\right.$	$\left\{\begin{array}{l}5\\28\end{array}\right.$
	$\left\{\begin{array}{l}11\\6\end{array}\right.$	$\left\{\begin{array}{l}21\\12\end{array}\right.$
	$\left\{\begin{array}{l}7\\10\end{array}\right.$	$\left\{\begin{array}{l}13\\20\end{array}\right.$
	$\left\{\begin{array}{l}15\\2\end{array}\right.$	$\left\{\begin{array}{l}29\\4\end{array}\right.$
		$\left\{\begin{array}{l}3\\30\end{array}\right.$
		$\left\{\begin{array}{l}19\\14\end{array}\right.$
		$\left\{\begin{array}{l}11\\22\end{array}\right.$
		$\left\{\begin{array}{l}27\\6\end{array}\right.$
		$\left\{\begin{array}{l}7\\26\end{array}\right.$
		$\left\{\begin{array}{l}23\\10\end{array}\right.$
		$\left\{\begin{array}{l}15\\18\end{array}\right.$
		$\left\{\begin{array}{l}31\\2\end{array}\right.$

The Nos. 1, 2, 3, etc., indicate the places assigned to the fencers 'seeded' in order of merit. See AFA *Rules for Competitions.*

Fig. 63   Match Plans for Direct Elimination

received in the pools produces a second indicator. By using the first indicators and, where these are equal, the second indicators the competitiors can be arranged in order of merit on the match plan, the only proviso being that competitors of the same nationality or the same club are kept as far as possible to different quarters of the match plan.

Competitors who win their matches (usually two bouts for each match with a deciding bout is necessary) proceed on the right of the match plan until four are left in who qualify for the final. Those who lose their matches proceed on the left side of the match plan in the repechage which provides that no one is eliminated until he has lost twice. The last two remaining from the repechage qualify for the final which is thus a pool of six fenced normally.

When a competition takes place in public, much can be added to the interest and enjoyment of the audience if a member of the organizing committee makes a brief announcement—say, before the final begins—describing the weapon in use, the target, the number of hits being fought for, the time limit and other points of interest. It is equally important to announce the results as rapidly as possible at the conclusion of the pool. A large score-board visible to everyone in the hall also helps to this end.

IX
The Grand Salute

THE grand salute was originally a prelude to the assault, designed to give suppleness to the whole body or, as we would say today, to help limber up. It became a tradition to execute it before a gala fencing demonstration, as a salute to the audience.

There are two very similar versions of the grand salute: the military salute, or *le mur*, and the civil salute. The main difference is that the military salute is performed rather more stiffly and precisely and includes the *double appel*, two swift, short beats with the leading foot. In the civil salute special attention is paid to gracefulness in all the movements, especially those of the wrist and feet.

The grand salute requires considerable practice by a pair of fencers well matched in height and figure, if it is to be performed gracefully and with perfect timing. The writer's view is that the military salute is best adapted to a performance in costume and wig, using court swords, and the civil salute to a performance in fencing kit using foils. In both forms of the grand salute one performer acts as the *maître* and the other as his or her pupil.

THE MILITARY SALUTE

To perform the military salute, the two fencers take up a position facing, but well out of distance from each other, place their masks on the floor to their left sides and, standing erect, pivot a half-turn to the left. At the same time they extend their sword-arms upwards and to the front, with the points of the foils well above their heads.

Both then lower and bend their sword-arms so that their foils are in the position of tierce, while the rear arm is raised in a graceful curve and the legs are bent. The leading foot is then advanced a half-pace and the rear foot retired, so that both fencers have assumed the on-guard position.

The fencer who is to act as *maître* calls on his pupil to begin by saying loudly '*À vous l'honneur*', to which the pupil replies '*Par obéissance*'. The *maître* says '*Faites*' and at that moment the pupil straightens his arm and makes a full lunge, but without landing his point on the target, and both return to the upright position.

Both fencers then perform a salute to their left sides, with the sword-arm half extended at an angle of forty-five degrees. The hand is held in supination, with the point of the foil in line with their eyes, and they are looking towards the left side.

The arm is drawn back and a similar salute, but with the hand in pronation, is made to the right side towards which each looks. Both then return to the first position adopted and fall on guard with the foils engaged in quarte.

The pupil, who now becomes the attacker, takes the distance by extending his arm and rhythmically, with a full lunge, makes a disengagement from quarte to sixte. The *maître* parries this disengagement by sixte and immediately lowers his foil to seconde, but with the point level with the waist. As the parry meets the pupil's blade smartly, it causes it to swing round between thumb and forefinger so that the foil remains parallel with the ground above the shoulder, pointing to the rear and level with the ear. The pupil remains on the lunge for about two seconds with his eyes fixed on the *maître*, after which he returns gracefully to guard in sixte.

The pupil makes his next disengagement, with full lunge, from sixte into quarte. The *maître* parries quarte and lowers his foil, this time into septime with the hand in supination. The pupil's foil pivots back over his shoulder as before and he again remains on the lunge, looking towards the *maître* for about two seconds before returning to guard in quarte.

The pupil repeats these two disengagements as before and when, at their conclusion, both have returned to guard in quarte, the pupil executes a one-two. On the first feint, the *maître* parries tierce and remains in that position while the pupil completes his second feint and comes to the upright position forwards. He passes his foil over the *maître's* blade, with his hand in the position of tierce, while he moves his rear foot back to resume the on-guard position.

Both fencers then execute a *double appel* simultaneously with the leading foot and recover backwards to the original upright position.

In his turn the *maître* extends his arm to take the distance, lunges without hitting and returns to the upright position. Both then salute as before, first to their left sides and then to the right, and then come on guard slowly and rhythmically in seven movements[1] so that they are finally engaged in quarte.

---

[1] To come on guard in seven movements from the 'prepare' position (that is upright, half turned to the right, the sword-arm and foil extended, pointing downwards, with the hand in supination, the point about two inches from the ground and the rear arm hanging loosely in line with the rear leg):

(1) Raise the sword-arm until the hand is level with the eyes, with the foil pointing vertically upwards.

(2) Lower the sword-arm to the 'prepare' position.

(3) Sweep the foil backwards, by wrist action only, so that it lies parallel to the ground and is just touching the fingers of the extended rear arm.

(4) Raise both arms together, keeping the elbows down and the blade constantly in touch with the fingers of the rear arm, until the foil is lying parallel to the ground but at about the level of the shoulders, still with the point towards the rear.

(5) Lift the foil with both arms until—still parallel to the ground—it is above the head, with the arms almost fully extended.

(6) Lower both arms in a graceful curve to the classic on-guard position, bringing the foil forward to the normal position.

(7) Bend both legs, sitting well down, and advance the leading foot to the normal on-guard stance.

The *maître* now becomes the attacker and repeats exactly the movements just performed by the pupil, that is, four disengagements followed by a one-two and a cut-over as he returns to guard.

Then simultaneously both execute a *double appel* with the leading foot and return to the original upright position backwards, before again falling on guard and again making a *double appel*.

Both salute to their left and to their right and return to the upright position, with the arm straight. Finally both bend the sword-arm, with the elbow close to the body and the guard of the foil level with and close to the chin, with the finger-nails turned inwards. They then lower their foils, with the arm straight and the point a couple of inches from the ground, with the hand in pronation.

After a pause, both advance a few paces and shake hands.

THE CIVIL SALUTE

The civil salute was evolved by the Académie d'Armes of Paris in 1886.

Both *maître* and pupil take up an erect position facing each other, rather farther apart than in the military salute. They place their masks on the ground to their left and each makes a half-turn to his left, standing erect with the feet at an angle of forty-five degrees, heels touching, sword-arm straight, the hand in pronation and the point of the foil a few inches from the ground in line with the feet.

Both fencers then take a short step forward, at the same time raising the sword-arm with a graceful rotation of the wrist, to place the hand in supination with the point of the foil just above the level of the opponent's head. They then salute each other by bringing the foil down, with hand in pronation, until the point is in line with the leading foot.

Both then fall on guard with the sword-hand in tierce and immediately return to the upright position with the arm extended forwards and upwards and the hand in supination.

The *maître* then makes a slight bow with his head to invite the pupil to begin. The pupil lowers his sword-arm and foil to a horizontal position, with his hand still in supination, and lunges, returning immediately to the upright position.

Maître and pupil then salute each other with their foils; they salute to the left; again salute each other; then salute to the right and finally fall on guard engaged in quarte.

The pupil then executes a disengagement into sixte with lunge, the parry of sixte executed by the *maître* causes the pupil's foil to swing back (as in the military salute) until it is pointing backwards horizontally over his shoulder, about level with his ear. The pupil maintains this position, looking towards the *maître* for about two seconds, then returns to guard in sixte. The pupil then makes an exactly similar disengagement into quarte, returning to guard in quarte. He then repeats these two disengagements as before.

The pupil makes a one-two from the on-guard position, without moving his legs. The *maître* answers these movements and the pupil concludes by placing the sword-hand in tierce and returning to the upright position.

The *maître*, who has remained in the on-guard position, immediately extends his sword-arm, lunges and recovers to the upright position. Both then fall on guard in quarte.

The *maître* performs the four disengagements in exactly the same way as the pupil has just done, parried by the pupil. He concludes with a one-two from immobility, ending with his sword-hand in tierce as both return together to the upright position, with the sword-arm extended forward and upwards and the hand in supination.

Both together once more fall on guard with the hand in pronation and arm bent and return to the upright position forward. They salute each other; then salute to the left; then salute to the right, fall on guard and make a *rassemblement* forward—that is, come to the upright position forward by bringing the rear foot up to the leading foot, while extending the sword-arm straight but opposite the rear shoulder, looking directly towards each other.

Together they lower the sword-arm until the point of the foil is just above the ground, in line with the leading foot. Finally both step forward with the rear foot and shake hands with the unarmed hand.

The grand salute should be performed slowly and rhythmically. Much practice is needed to synchronize the movements so that they flow gracefully and the head, body and limbs all remain relaxed to give the effect of suppleness, especially of the wrist, and co-ordination throughout.

A Glossary of Fencing Terms

ABSENCE OF BLADE When the blades are not in contact, i.e. not engaged.

ACADEMIC ASSAULT A bout during a display in which hits are not usually counted.

ADVANCE To step forward.

AIDS The last three fingers of the sword-hand.

ANGULATION Bending the wrist when placing a hit, so as to present the point at right angles to the target.

ASSAULT A bout between two fencers.

ATTACK An offensive movement designed to hit the opponent.

ATTACK ON THE BLADE A preparation for an attack by beat, pressure or *froissement*.

ATTACK ON PREPARATION An attack launched when the opponent is making a preparation for an attack.

BACKWARD SPRING A leap backwards, out of distance, from the lunge.

BALESTRA A short jump forward during an attack.

BARRAGE A tie.

BEAT A preparation of attack.

BIND A preparation of attack which carries the opponent's blade diagonally across from a high to a low line, or vice versa.

BOUT An assault between two fencers in which hits are counted.

BREAKING GROUND Retiring by stepping backwards.

BROKEN TIME A pause deliberately made between two movements which normally follow each other immediately.

CADENCE The rhythm in which a sequence of movements is made.

CEDING PARRY A parry formed by giving way to an opponent who is taking the blade.

CENTRAL GUARD A position on guard when the hand is placed between two lateral lines and thus not completely covered in any line.

CHANGE BEAT A beat made after a change of engagement.

CHANGE OF ENGAGEMENT Engaging the opponent's blade in a new line.

CIRCULAR PARRY A parry in which the defender's blade describes a circle to gather the attacker's blade.

CLOSE QUARTERS When two fencers are close together but can still wield their weapons correctly.

COMPOUND ATTACK An attack which includes one or more feints. Also called a Composed Attack.

COMPOUND RIPOSTE A riposte made with one or more feints. Also called a Composed Riposte.

COQUILLE The bell-shaped guard of a foil or épée.

CORPS À CORPS When two fencers are touching so that they cannot wield their weapons correctly.

COULÉ (or Graze) A thrust in the line of engagement while keeping contact with the opponent's blade.

COUNTER-DISENGAGEMENT The action of deceiving a change of engagement or a counter-parry.

COUNTER-OFFENSIVE ACTIONS The stop hit and the time hit.

COUNTER-PARRY A circular parry.

COUNTER-RIPOSTE The offensive action which follows the parry of a riposte or of another counter-riposte.

COUNTER-TIME A movement by second intention.

COVERED A position of the sword-hand and weapon which closes the line of engagement against a direct thrust.

CROISÉ Taking the opponent's blade from a high to a low line on the *same* side as the engagement (not diagonally as in the bind).

CUT A hit made with the front edge, or the first third of the back edge, of the sabre.

CUT-OVER A disengagement made by passing *over* the opponent's blade.

CUTTING THE LINES Circular parries made otherwise than in the line of engagement.

DELAYED An attack or a riposte made after a pause.

DÉROBEMENT Evading an opponent's attempts to beat or take the blade while the arm is extended.

DETACHMENT PARRY A crisp parry, in which the defender's blade quits the attacker's blade immediately it has deflected it.

DEVELOPMENT The extension of the arm and the lunge.

DIRECT An attack or a riposte made in the line of engagement.

DISENGAGEMENT Moving the weapon from the line of engagement into an opposite line by passing under the opponent's blade.

DOIGHTÉ Finger play.

DOUBLÉ An attacking movement during which the blade performs a complete circle in order to deceive the opponent's circular parry. Basically it is a disengagement followed by a counter-disengagement.

DOUBLE *PRISES DE FER* A succession of takings of the opponent's blade.

ENGAGEMENT The crossing of the blades.

EN MARCHANT Movement made with one or more steps forward.

ENVELOPMENT Taking the opponent's blade and describing a circle to return to the line of engagement without losing contact of blades.

ÉPÉE The duelling sword.

EVASION A *dérobement*.

FALSE ATTACK An offensive movement which is not intended to score a hit.

F.I.E, THE Fédération Internationale d'Escrime.

FEINT An offensive movement made to resemble an attack, in order to draw a reaction from the opponent.

FENCING MEASURE The distance which exists between two fencers.

FENCING POSITIONS The positions in which the sword-arm and weapon may be placed to cover the lines of the target.

FENCING TIME The time required to perform one simple fencing action.

FIELD OF PLAY The *piste* and its extensions on which fencing takes place.

FINGER PLAY The method of manipulating the weapon with the fingers.

FLÈCHE   An attack made by a succession of running steps, instead of by the lunge or steps forward.

FOIBLE   The half of the blade nearest to the point of the weapon.

FOIL   The basic weapon with which the art of fencing should be learned.

FORTE   The half of the blade nearest to the guard of the weapon.

FROISSEMENT   A preparation of attack made by deflecting the opponent's blade with a strong, sharp grazing movement along it.

GAINING GROUND   Stepping forward.

GAINING ON THE LUNGE   Bringing the rear foot up to the leading foot before making a lunge.

GRAZE   A *coulé* along the opponent's blade.

GRIP   The part of the handle normally held by the sword-hand. Also the manner in which the weapon is held.

GROUND JUDGES   Two judges who look for hits made on the ground at electrical foil or épée.

GUARD   The portion of the hilt between the blade and the handle designed to protect the hand.

HIGH LINES   The parts of the opponent's target visible above his sword-hand when on guard.

HIT   The offensive action which lands with point or edge on the opponent.

IMMEDIATE   An action made without a pause.

INDIRECT   A simple attack or riposte made in another line.

IN QUARTATA   An offensive movement made while removing the body out of line by a side-step.

INSIDE LINES   The parts of the target farthest from the sword-arm.

INSUFFICIENT PARRY   A parry which does not close the line completely, and through which the opponent can land a hit.

INVITATIONS   Opening a line to offer a path to an opponent's offensive movement.

JURY   The President and judges who officiate at a fencing event.

LA BELLE   The deciding hit during a bout.

LINES   Theoretical divisions of the target, corresponding to the fencing positions.

LOW LINES   The parts of the opponent's target visible below his sword-hand when on guard.

LUNGE   The extension of the arm, body and legs used to reach an opponent.

MANIPULATORS   The first finger and thumb of the sword-hand.

MARTINGALE   A loop of tape or string used to prevent a foil flying out of the hand during a bout.

MATCH   A contest between two teams.

MEASURE   See Fencing Measure.

METALLIC OVER-JACKET   A plastron of metallized cloth worn over the fencing jacket, on which valid hits are registered with the electrical foil.

METALLIC *PISTE*   A copper-mesh strip laid over the *piste* to neutralize hits made on the ground at electrical foil or épée.

MOLINELLO   A circular cut at head made from the sabre parry of first.

ON GUARD   The position of the arms, body and feet adopted by a fencer when prepared for a bout.

OPPOSITION   A movement made without quitting the opponent's blade.

ORTHOPAEDIC GRIP A handle moulded to the shape of the fingers.

OUTSIDE LINES The parts of the target nearest to the sword-arm.

PARRY A defensive action made with the blade to deflect an attacker's blade.

PASSATA SOTTO The action of avoiding an attacker's blade by ducking below it.

PERIOD OF FENCING TIME See Fencing Time.

PERSONAL EQUIPMENT The weapon and body-wire used when fencing with an electrical judging apparatus.

PHRASE A sequence of fencing movements exchanged between two fencers, leading up to a hit.

PIED FERME, À A movement made while the feet remain immobile.

PISTE The part of the field of play within which a bout takes place.

PLASTRON An undergarment of hemp cloth worn as a safety precaution at épée.

POINTE D'ARRÊT A serrated or triple-pointed attachment to the tip of a blade, designed to fix a hit at electrical foil or épée.

POMMEL A piece of metal screwed to the end of the hilt to lock the parts of the weapon together and balance the blade.

POOL A grouping of fencers or teams in a competition.

PREPARATION FOR ATTACK A blade, body or foot movement made prior to an attack.

PRESIDENT The referee in a fencing bout.

PRESSURE A preparation of attack made by pressing on the opponent's blade.

PRINCIPLE OF DEFENCE The opposition of the forte of the blade to the foible of the opponent's blade.

PRISE DE FER A preparation for an attack in which the opponent's blade is taken by an envelopment, a bind or a *croisé*.

PROGRESSIVE ATTACK A method of executing the various movements of a compound attack, while continuously approaching the target in order to cut time and distance to a minimum. The opposite to *à pied ferme*.

PRONATION The position of the sword-hand with the finger-nails downwards.

RASSEMBLEMENT Bringing the leading foot back to the rear foot while rising to full height.

RECOVERY OR RETURN TO GUARD Coming back to the on-guard position after a lunge.

REDOUBLEMENT A renewal of an attack, while remaining on the lunge, which includes one or more blade movements.

REMISE A renewal of an attack, while remaining on the lunge, by replacing the point on the target in the same line without withdrawing the arm.

RENEWED ATTACK A remise, redoublement or reprise.

REPRISE A renewal of the attack, preceded by a return to guard forward or backward.

RETIRE To step back.

REVERSE BEAT A change beat or, at sabre, a beat made with the back of the blade.

RICASSO The flattened part of the tang of the blade, between the guard and the cross-bar, of an Italian foil.

RIPOSTE   The offensive action which follows a parry.

SABRE   The cut-and-thrust weapon.

SALUTE   The acknowledgement with the weapon which a fencer extends to his opponent at the commencement and conclusion of a bout.

SECOND INTENTION   A premeditated offensive action made after an opponent has been induced to make a movement such as a stop hit.

SEMICIRCULAR PARRY   A parry during which the blade describes a half-circle from high to low line or vice versa.

SENTIMENT DU FER   Feeling an opponent's reactions through contact of the blades.

SIMPLE ATTACK   An attack made with one movement, either direct or indirect.

SIMULTANEOUS ACTIONS   Where both fencers conceive and execute a movement at the same time.

SITTING DOWN   Bending the knees when in the on-guard position.

STANCE   The position of the feet and legs in the on-guard position.

STOP HIT   A counter-offensive action made on an opponent's attack.

STRAIGHT THRUST   A simple and direct offensive movement.

SUCCESSIVE PARRIES   A series of parries which immediately follow each other until the attacker's blade is found.

SUPINATION   The position of the sword-hand with the finger-nails upwards.

TAKING THE BLADE   A preparation of attack by a *prise de fer*.

TARGET   The area within which a hit counts as good.

TERRAIN   The field of play. Also the measured piece of ground on which a duel is fought.

TIME HIT   A counter-offensive action which anticipates and closes the final line of the opponent's attack as it is made.

TIMING   The execution of a fencing movement at the correct moment.

TOUCHÉ   The word used to acknowledge a hit.

TROMPEMENT   Offensive blade movements which deceive the opponent's parries.

TWO-TIME   A movement made in two periods of fencing time.

UNCOVERED   A position of the sword-hand and blade where the line of engagement is not closed.

VALID HITS   Hits which arrive on the target.

WARNING LINES   Lines drawn one metre (for foil) or two metres (for épée and sabre) from the rear limits of the *piste*, at which competitors are warned that they are approaching the rear limit.

A History of Fencing

Swords in a variety of forms have been used by man since long before the dawn of recorded history. Certainly by the Bronze Age recognizable swords were in current use.

Fencing may be defined as the skilful use of swords according to set rules and movements. We know that as such it was widely practised by all the ancient races such as the Persians, Babylonians, Egyptians, Greeks and Romans, both as a pastime and for single combat and war.

Probably the earliest record of a fencing match appears in a relief carving in the temple of Madinet-Habu near Luxor in Upper Egypt, built by Rameses III about 1190 BC. There can be no doubt that this is a picture of a practice bout and not of a duel or battle scene. The fencers are using swords with well covered points and are wearing masks, fitted with large bibs and padded over the ears, tied to their wigs. Some are parrying with narrow shields strapped to their left arms. The picture includes a group of spectators from Syria, the Sudan and Egypt, while in the centre the jury and organizers can be recognized by their feathered wands. A hieroglyphic inscription records one fencer as saying 'On guard and admire what my valiant hand shall do', while the spectators acclaim the victor by shouting 'Advance! Advance, O excellent fighter, O meritorious fighter'.

In the Middle Ages swords were heavy and clumsy and more strength than skill was required for their use. This was because the general use of armour until the early sixteenth century precluded speed and finesse in the use of weapons. The battle axe or the heavy, two-handed sword were used, with other fearsome varieties, to bludgeon the adversary into submission.

It was the invention of gunpowder in the fourteenth century which eventually brought fencing to an art. This was, of course, because its general use during the following century led to the disuse of armour in war. The resnlt was a sudden transformation of weapons to lighter forms more suitable for quick, neat movements and more skilful sword-play.

Guilds of fencing masters, such as the famous Marxbrüder of Frankfurt, sprang up all over Europe to study the now essential art of swordsmanship. Early methods were rough and ready, including many wrestling tricks.

The Italians are said to have been first to discover the effectiveness of a dextrous use of the point rather than relying on the edge of the sword. By the end of the sixteenth century, their lighter weapons and simple, nimble, controlled fencing had spread throughout Europe and was established as rapier fencing. Indeed, the Italians are credited with being the originators of true swordsmanship and, thanks to their lead, from then on the emphasis was on speed and skill rather than mere force. Masters abandoned most of the wrestling tricks, the lunge was discovered and fencing may be said to have been established as an art.

The long rapier, although beautifully balanced, was still too clumsy to carry out all the defensive and offensive movements required in combat. Though it was excellent for keeping the opponent at a distance and for aggressive thrusts, defence was effected by parrying with the left hand armed with a dagger, or protected by a cloak or gauntlet. Often an opponent's thrusts were avoided by ducking (*passata sotto*) or the side-step (*in quartata*). Rapier fencing was thus essentially a two-handed game, in which the fencers stood almost square to each other as they circled round seeking the advantage of light or the terrain.

In the early seventeenth century, the Spaniards evolved a highly special-ized school of rapier fencing, based on an exceedingly complex series of movements related to various lines drawn within a circle, about which the fencers moved with mathematical precision. This method never appears to have spread generally in Europe as did the Italian school.

During the seventeenth century, a change of dress produced a revolution in swords and swordsmanship. At the court of Louis XIV in France, fashion decreed the wearing of silks and satins: panniered dresses and elaborate coiffures for the ladies, silk stockings and breeches, brocaded coats and lace at throat and wrist for men. The long, trailing rapier had gone well enough with the doublet and hose, top boots and cloaks of the earlier age, but was no longer suitable for the new-found elegance of the court of the *Roi Soleil*. Every gentleman, however, must needs carry a sword, ready to defend his honour at the drop of a hat, so fashion decreed the wearing of a light, short court sword.

The French court now set the tone in Europe as surely as the Italians had done in earlier times. Proficiency with the small-sword soon became an indispensable accomplishment for every gentleman.

Here at last was a light weapon with which the fencer could perform all attacking and defensive movements, using one weapon wielded by one hand—the use of the left hand or the dagger was no longer required. Swift and subtle sword-play became a reality, hits were made with the point only and defence was effected mostly with the blade alone. True fencing, as we understand it today, emerged and the light sword of the French school soon displaced rapier fencing throughout Europe.

It is a curious fact that although, as we now know, the mask was used by the Egyptians some 2,000 years before Christ, it was quite unknown in Europe until the end of the eighteenth century. The speed with which light swords could be used at close quarters involved the risk of severe injury to the eyes—indeed it was said that no good fencing master ended his life with two good eyes. When practising, even with blunted weapons, it became necessary to impose rules and conventions to regulate fencing with the court sword or the foils, primarily to minimize this risk. Valid hits were restricted to those which arrived on the right breast; and a fencer who initiated an attack had the right to complete his movement (unless it was effectively parried) before his opponent could, in turn, attack or riposte.

Fencing became increasingly complex and formalized. The position of guard, with the unarmed hand raised to balance the body, was very like the present on-guard position, except for a marked tendency to keep the weight on the rear foot and the head well back as a safety precaution.

The 'invention' of the mask by the celebrated French master, La Boëssière, about 1780 widened the possibilities for more complex sword-play. Phrases including the remise, the counter-riposte, the redoublement and other sequences of movements became possible without undue risk of injury, once the mask was established in general use. Foil fencing as we know it today became a reality. The rules and traditional conventions already mentioned had to be maintained and gradually amplified if this complex game, at close quarters and at great speed, was not to degenerate into a brawl of simultaneous actions. These rules and conventions have endured as the basis of our modern rules governing foil and sabre fencing.

Meanwhile, however, duelling continued unabated. The complexities of foil fencing as practised in the schools, the beautiful 'conversation with the foils', became increasingly unlike the simpler play with heavier weapons, comprehensive target and absence of conventions, on the terrain.

The *épée de combat* was therefore evolved in the mid-nineteenth century to prepare fencers in the schools for the more serious encounters, against determined opponents unimpressed by the orthodox methods of the *salle d'armes*. The épée, as the recognized duelling weapon, is now used competitively as a separate weapon governed by simple rules approximating, as far as possible, to the *jeu de terrain*.

The traditions of the cutting weapons of mediaeval times were continued by the backsword or broadsword, known as the Englishman's traditional weapon in the days of Elizabeth I, well into the eighteenth century.

The modern sabre was derived from the eastern scimitar, introduced to Europe by the Hungarians in the late eighteenth century for the use of their cavalry. Its curved blade was soon adopted for their cavalry by other Western European armies. The heavy military sabre (and its counterpart the naval cutlass) with its hanging guard and wide, circular cuts, was long used in the fencing schools and still practised at the beginning of this century.

A light sabre was developed by the Italians during the last quarter of the nineteenth century and was soon universally adopted for fencing, although looked on with derision by those used to the heavy sabre. Light sabre play developed by the famous Milanese master, Giuseppe Radaelli, became an academic pursuit, with similar rules to those for foil play, even though the light sabre remained a recognized duelling weapon.

Swordsmanship has been practised in Britain from the earliest times. A statute of Edward I, enacted in 1285, forbade the teaching of fencing, or the holding of tournaments, within the precincts of the City of London. The City Fathers regarded schools of fencing as places which encouraged duelling, brawling and all manner of ruffianism.

Swordsmen continued to be regarded with disfavour and suspicion until Henry VIII, a great lover of sword-play, granted letters patent to a Corporation of Masters of Defence some years before 1540. This corporation became the first governing body for fencing in this country, included the leading English and foreign masters, was granted a coat of arms—gules a sword pendant argent—and great privileges, including the lucrative monopoly of teaching the art of fencing in the King's realms.

It was because the first organization of fencing in Britain had been established by a Tudor king that, in 1906, His Majesty King Edward VII granted to the Amateur Fencing Association permission to adopt a Tudor rose as the badge to be worn by British fencers of international rank.

Sword and buckler and the long, two-handed sword were the staple English weapons and the rapier was not fully established in this country until towards the close of Queen Elizabeth I's reign.

From about the sixteenth century until mid-Georgian days, prize fights consisted of displays and trials of swordsmanship. They were exceedingly popular with all ranks of the population and were often patronized by royalty. A stage was erected in a hall or public garden and the champions would challenge each other to bouts with a variety of weapons—often with 'sharps'—when they were most sanguinary encounters. The winner was the one who 'held the stage' until the end by defeating all his opponents, either in single combat or sometimes in a *mêlée*.

Towards the end of the eighteenth century James Figg, who besides being Champion of the Corporation of Fencing Masters was also the first British boxing champion, introduced fisticuff fights into these prize fights. Soon these knuckle fights became so popular that they ousted the bouts with the sword, and we now always associate prize fights with boxing rather than fencing. Thereafter fencing was relegated to the status of a provincial amusement, using backsword, singlestick and quarterstaff.

Fencing was neglected in Britain during the early Victorian era although a few masters, such as the famous Angelos, continued to teach the *beau monde* and the London Fencing Club was founded in 1848.

In the early sixties the military authorities recognized that gymnastic instruction had proved beneficial to the French and Prussian armies. A committee was sent to the Continent to study the methods used and, on their report, a similar system (which included fencing) was established in the British army. A class of non-commissioned officers was sent to Mr Mclaren's gymnasium at Oxford for training. Mr Mclaren, who had been a member of the committee of inspection mentioned above, wrote a book of instruction for fencing in 1862 which was adopted for use in the Army.

The revival of general interest in fencing in this country was largely due to the enthusiasm of Captain Alfred Hutton, FSA, a great authority on ancient weapons who, in the early nineties, organized displays and lectures on the subject all over England. He was assisted by the members of a school of arms which he had founded among the young officers and cadets of the London Rifle Brigade.

Colonel G. M. Fox, the inspector of gymnasia at Aldershot, brought the celebrated Italian master, Ferdinando Masiello of Florence, to England (largely at his own expense) and the Italian method was adopted for fencing in the Army in spite of furious resistance by Captain Hutton. In 1895, the War Office issued a new Handbook on Infantry Sword Exercises for use in the service, which dealt with sabre fencing only.

At that time the only fencing competition was one held annually by the German Gymnastic Society, which was judged by the fencing masters. One year Captain Hutton was invited to judge this event and, when he asked for the rules, it was found that none existed. This incident led to the organization of an amateur body to govern fencing. On 6 November 1895, the fencing members of the Amateur Gymnastic Association founded a Fencing Branch Committee with Captain Hutton as chairman and Mr (later Sir) E. Stenson Cooke as honorary secretary. Rules for fencing, drafted by Captain Hutton, were adopted in 1896 and in the same year the Association changed its name to the Amateur Gymnastic and Fencing Association.

The first amateur championships at foil and sabre were organized by the Fencing Branch Committee on 30 March 1898. The foil was won by Mr H. Turner and the sabre by Captain W. Edgworth-Johnstone.

Dissatisfied by the organization of the Association, the fencing clubs met on 3 December 1901 and decided to form a separate body. The Amateur Fencing Association was thus founded on 1 January 1902, with

Captain Hutton as president, Mr C. F. Clay as honorary secretary and Mr J. Norbury Jnr the honorary treasurer.

Fencing remained the sport of the few up to the First World War. The twenty-one clubs affiliated to the Association in 1902 had only increased to twenty-five by 1914. A few London clubs and *salles*, the larger universities and public schools and the services provided the chief centres.

Between the two wars, fencing became a more popular sport in every sense, but was still mainly confined to London and the larger provincial towns. By 1939 the Association included 109 affiliated clubs and area organizations covered Scotland and the North and Midlands.

The Second World War arrested this progress and by 1945 only fifty-one clubs remained active.

Since that time there has been a remarkable expansion of interest in fencing throughout the United Kingdom and fencing is now practised increasingly by young people of every class and calling. Besides the services, universities and schools of all categories, clubs have been formed in youth organizations, business houses and factories and in towns and villages all over the country, and there are a large number of local-education-authority evening classes for fencing. By the end of 1969 the Association included seven associated bodies and about 638 affiliated clubs, with fourteen Sections, or area organizations, for every part of Great Britain and Northern Ireland, many containing a number of county unions.

The great increase in fencing throughout this country has been very largely due to the considerable success achieved by the Association's National Training Scheme, founded in 1949, which has trained a large number of coaches or amateur instructors at all weapons to supplement the work of the masters. By this means it has been possible to provide sound basic instruction in clubs throughout the country.

The Association now maintains two full-time National Fencing Coaches (with the assistance of a grant from the Ministry of Education), issues its own publication, *The Sword*, and organizes annually a wide range of competitions at all weapons, both nationally and in Sections and county unions, for all categories of fencers, from novices and school children's events to international competitions. It also trains British teams for the Olympic Games, World Championships and other international events.

It is gratifying to note that this development of fencing has not only entailed an increase in the numbers of young people who obtain the unique advantages of this highly competitive sport, but also a rise in technical standard. This has been demonstrated by the successes achieved by British fencers in world competition. Since 1955 there has been a steady advance in this field and British fencers are now in the first flight of world competition, especially at ladies' and men's foil and épée. Miss Gillian Sheen won immortal fame by becoming the first British fencer to win an Olympic Gold Medal when she won the ladies' individual foil title at Melbourne in 1956. In 1958 Mr H. W. F. Hoskyns won the World Épée Championship at Philadelphia and in 1959 Mr A. L. N. Jay won the World Foil Championship. British fencers now regularly appear in the leading places in open competitions on the Continent.

The British Academy of Fencing was revived in 1949 on the initiative of the Association. As the governing body for professional fencing, it continues the tradition of the Corporation of Masters of Defence founded by King Henry VIII.

List of Championship Winners

THE OLYMPIC GAMES

The ancient series of games was held at Olympia (not Mount Olympus) at four-yearly intervals from 776 BC to AD 394, a period of 1,170 years. The main sports, varied from time to time, were foot racing, wrestling, boxing, pancratium (all-in wrestling), pentathlon and chariot racing.

The high ideals of the Olympic movement were revived by Baron Pierre de Coubertin at an international sports congress in 1894 and the first modern Olympic Games were held at Athens in 1896. Fencing is an obligatory sport.

MEN'S FOIL: TEAMS

	Where Held	*First*	*Second*	*Third*
1904	St Louis	Cuba	International Team	
1920	Antwerp	Italy	France	USA
1924	Paris	France	Belgium	Hungary
1928	Amsterdam	Italy	France	Argentine
1932	Los Angeles	France	Italy	USA
1936	Berlin	Italy	France	Germany
1948	London	France	Italy	Belgium
1952	Helsinki	France	Italy	Hungary
1956	Melbourne	Italy	France	Hungary
1960	Rome	USSR	Italy	West Germany
1964	Tokyo	USSR	Poland	France
1968	Mexico	France	USSR	Poland

MEN'S FOIL: INDIVIDUAL TITLE

	Where Held	*First*	*Second*	*Third*
1896	Athens	E. Gravelotte FRANCE	H. Callot FRANCE	Dankla FRANCE
1900	Paris	C. Costa FRANCE	H. Masson FRANCE	J. Boulenger FRANCE
1904	St Louis	R. Fonst CUBA	A. van Zo Post CUBA	C. Tatham CUBA
1906	Athens	M. Dillon-Kavanagh FRANCE	G. Casimir GERMANY	Ct. d'Hugues FRANCE
1912	Stockholm	N. Nadi ITALY	P. Speciale ITALY	R. Verderber GERMANY
1920	Antwerp	N. Nadi ITALY	P. Cattiau FRANCE	R. Ducret FRANCE
1924	Paris	R. Ducret FRANCE	P. Cattiau FRANCE	M. van Damme BELGIUM
1928	Amsterdam	L. Gaudin FRANCE	E. Casmir GERMANY	G. Gaudini ITALY
1932	Los Angeles	G. Marzi ITALY	J. Levis USA	G. Gaudini ITALY
1936	Berlin	G. Gaudini ITALY	E. Gardère FRANCE	G. Bocchino ITALY
1948	London	J. Buhan FRANCE	C. d'Oriola FRANCE	L. Maszlay HUNGARY
1952	Helsinki	C. d'Oriola FRANCE	E. Mangiarotti ITALY	M. di Rosa ITALY
1956	Melbourne	C. d'Oriola FRANCE	G. Bergamini ITALY	A. Spallino ITALY

	Where Held	First	Second	Third
1960	Rome	V. Jdanovich USSR	Y. Sissikine USSR	A. Axelrod USA
1964	Tokyo	E. Francke POLAND	J-P. Magnan FRANCE	D. Revenu FRANCE
1968	Mexico	I. Drimba ROUMANIA	J. Kamuti HUNGARY	D. Revenu FRANCE

LADIES' FOIL: TEAMS
(First held at Olympic Games 1960)

	Where Held	First	Second	Third
1960	Rome	USSR	Hungary	Italy
1964	Tokyo	Hungary	USSR	West Germany
1968	Mexico	USSR	Hungary	Roumania

LADIES' FOIL: INDIVIDUAL TITLE

	Where Held	First	Second	Third
1924	Paris	E. D. Osiier DENMARK	G. M. Davis GREAT BRITAIN	G. Heckscher DENMARK
1928	Amsterdam	H. Mayer GERMANY	M. Freeman GREAT BRITAIN	O. Oelkers GERMANY
1932	Los Angeles	E. Preiss AUSTRIA	H. Guinness GREAT BRITAIN	B. E. Bogathy HUNGARY
1936	Berlin	I. Elek HUNGARY	H. Mayer GERMANY	E. Preiss AUSTRIA
1948	London	I. Elek HUNGARY	K. Lachmann DENMARK	E. Müller-Preiss AUSTRIA
1952	Helsinki	I. Camber ITALY	I. Elek HUNGARY	K. Lachmann DENMARK
1956	Melbourne	G. M. Sheen GREAT BRITAIN	O. Orban ROUMANIA	R. Garilhe FRANCE
1960	Rome	H. Schmid WEST GERMANY	V. Rastvorova USSR	M. Vicol ROUMANIA
1964	Tokyo	I. Rejto-Ujlaky HUNGARY	H. Mees WEST GERMANY	A. Ragno ITALY
1968	Mexico	E. Novikova USSR	P. Roldan MEXICO	I. Rejto-Ujlaky HUNGARY

ÉPÉE: TEAMS

	Where Held	First	Second	Third
1906	Athens	France	Great Britain	Belgium
1908	London	France	Great Britain	Belgium
1912	Stockholm	Belgium	Great Britain	Holland
1920	Antwerp	Italy	Belgium	France
1924	Paris	France	Belgium	Italy
1928	Amsterdam	Italy	France	Portugal
1932	Los Angeles	France	Italy	USA
1936	Berlin	Italy	Sweden	France
1948	London	France	Italy	Sweden
1952	Helsinki	Italy	Sweden	Switzerland
1956	Melbourne	Italy	Hungary	France
1960	Rome	Italy	Great Britain	USSR
1964	Tokyo	Hungary	Italy	France
1968	Mexico	Hungary	USSR	Poland

ÉPÉE: INDIVIDUAL TITLE

	Where Held	First	Second	Third
1900	Paris	R. Fonst CUBA	L. Perrée FRANCE	L. Sée FRANCE
1904	St Louis	R. Fonst CUBA	C. Tatham CUBA	A. van Zo Post CUBA
1906	Athens	Ct. de la Falaise FRANCE	M. Dillon-Kavanagh FRANCE	Van Blyenburgh HOLLAND

	Where Held	First	Second	Third
1908	London	M. Alibert FRANCE	A. Lippmann FRANCE	P. Anspach BELGIUM
1912	Stockholm	P. Anspach BELGIUM	I. Osiier DENMARK	Le Hardy de Beaulieu BELGIUM
1920	Antwerp	A. Massard FRANCE	A. Lippmann FRANCE	E. Gevers BELGIUM
1924	Paris	C. Delporte BELGIUM	R. Ducret FRANCE	N. Hellsten SWEDEN
1928	Amsterdam	L. Gaudin FRANCE·	G. Buchard FRANCE	G. C. Calnan USA
1932	Los Angeles	G-C. Cornaggia ITALY	G. Buchard FRANCE	C. Agosťoni ITALY
1936	Berlin	F. Riccardi ITALY	S. Ragno ITALY	G-C. Cornaggia ITALY
1948	London	L. Cantone ITALY	O. Zapelli SWITZERLAND	E. Mangiarotti ITALY
1952	Helsinki	E. Mangiarotti ITALY	D. Mangiarotti ITALY	O. Zapelli SWITZERLAND
1956	Melbourne	C. Pavesi ITALY	G. Delfino ITALY	E. Mangiarotti ITALY
1960	Rome	G. Delfino ITALY	A. L. N. Jay GREAT BRITAIN	B. Khabarov USSR
1964	Tokyo	G. Kriss USSR	H. W. F. Hoskyns GREAT BRITAIN	G. Kostava USSR
1968	Mexico	G. Kulcsar HUNGARY	G. Kriss USSR	G-L. Saccaro ITALY

SABRE: TEAMS

	Where Held	First	Second	Third
1904	St Louis	Cuba	USA	—
1906	Athens	Germany	Greece	Holland
1908	London	Hungary	Italy	Czechoslovakia
1912	Stockholm	Hungary	Austria	Holland
1920	Antwerp	Italy	France	Holland
1924	Paris	Italy	Hungary	Holland
1928	Amsterdam	Hungary	Italy	Poland
1932	Los Angeles	Hungary	Italy	Poland
1936	Berlin	Hungary	Italy	Germany
1948	London	Hungary	Italy	USA
1952	Helsinki	Hungary	Italy	France
1956	Melbourne	Hungary	Poland	USSR
1960	Rome	Hungary	Poland	Italy
1964	Tokyo	USSR	Italy	Poland
1968	Mexico	USSR	Italy	Hungary

SABRE: INDIVIDUAL TITLE

	Where Held	First	Second	Third
1896	Athens	J. Giorgiades GREECE	T. Karakalos GREECE	H. Nielsen DENMARK
1900	Paris	Ct. de la Falaise FRANCE	L. Thiebaud FRANCE	S. Flesch AUSTRIA
1904	St Louis	M. de Diaz CUBA	W. Grebe USA	A. van Zo Post CUBA
1906	Athens	J. Giorgiades GREECE	G. Casimir GERMANY	Caserano ITALY
1908	London	J. Fuchs HUNGARY	B. Zulawski HUNGARY	Gophold v. Lobsdorff BOHEMIA
1912	Stockholm	J. Fuchs HUNGARY	B. Bekessy HUNGARY	E. Mezaros HUNGARY
1920	Antwerp	N. Nadi ITALY	A. Nadi ITALY	A, de Jong HOLLAND
1924	Paris	A. Posta HUNGARY	R. Ducret FRANCE	J. Garay HUNGARY
1928	Amsterdam	E. Tersztiansky HUNGARY	A. Petschauer HUNGARY	B. Bini ITALY

	Where Held	*First*	*Second*	*Third*
1932	Los Angeles	G. Piller HUNGARY	A. Petschauer HUNGARY	A. Kabos HUNGARY
1936	Berlin	A. Kabos HUNGARY	G. Marci ITALY	A. Gerevich HUNGARY
1948	London	A. Gerevich HUNGARY	E. Pinton ITALY	P. Kovacs HUNGARY
1952	Helsinki	P. Kovacs HUNGARY	A. Gerevich HUNGARY	T. Berczelly HUNGARY
1956	Melbourne	R. Karpati HUNGARY	J. Pawlowski POLAND	L. Kouznetsov USSR
1960	Rome	R. Karpati HUNGARY	Z. Horvath HUNGARY	W. Calarese ITALY
1964	Tokyo	T. Pezsa HUNGARY	C. Arabo FRANCE	U. Mavlikhanov USSR
1968	Mexico	J. Pawlowski POLAND	M. Rakita USSR	T. Pesza HUNGARY

THE WORLD CHAMPIONSHIPS

The first Championship of Europe was held in Paris in 1921, including an épée individual event only. Individual championships were held separately thereafter for various weapons, a foil team event for men being added in 1929. The first European Championships, with a full programme including team and individual events at all weapons for men and a ladies' individual event only, were held at Liège in 1930. These championships have continued in each non-Olympic year, a ladies' team event being added in 1933. The title of these championships was changed to World Championships in 1936. From 1932 a ladies' team World Championship was held as a separate event in each Olympic year, because no ladies' team event was included in the Olympic Games prior to 1960.

MEN'S FOIL: TEAMS

	Where Held	*First*	*Second*	*Third*
1929	Naples	Italy	Belgium	Hungary
1930	Liège	Italy	France	Belgium
1931	Vienna	Italy	Hungary	Austria
1933	Budapest	Italy	[Eq.] Austria Hungary	—
1934	Warsaw	Italy	France	Germany
1935	Lausanne	Italy	France	Hungary
1937	Paris	Italy	France	Austria
1938	Piestany	Italy	France	Czechoslovakia
1947	Lisbon	France	Italy	Belgium
1949	Cairo	Italy	France	Egypt
1950	Monte Carlo	Italy	France	Egypt
1951	Stockholm	France	Italy	Egypt
1953	Brussels	France	Italy	Hungary
1954	Luxembourg	Italy	France	Hungary
1955	Rome	Italy	Hungary	Great Britain
1957	Paris	Hungary	France	Italy
1958	Philadelphia	France	USSR	Italy
1959	Budapest	USSR	Germany	Hungary
1961	Turin	USSR	Hungary	Poland
1962	Buenos Aires	USSR	Hungary	Poland
1963	Gdansk	USSR	Poland	France
1965	Paris	USSR	Poland	France
1966	Moscow	USSR	Hungary	Poland
1967	Montreal	Roumania	USSR	Poland
1969	Havana	USSR	Poland	Roumania

MEN'S FOIL: INDIVIDUAL TITLE

	Where Held	First	Second	Third
1926	Budapest	G. Chiavacci ITALY	L. Berti HUNGARY	U. Pignotti ITALY
1927	Vichy	O. Puliti ITALY	P. Cattiau FRANCE	G. Guaragna ITALY
1929	Naples	O. Puliti ITALY	P. Cattiau FRANCE	G. Gaudini ITALY
1930	Liège	G. Gaudini ITALY	G. Marzi ITALY	G. Guaragna ITALY
1931	Vienna	R. Lemoine FRANCE	G. Marzi ITALY	J. Emrys Lloyd GREAT BRITAIN
1933	Budapest	G. Guaragna ITALY	G. Gaudini ITALY	J. Emrys Lloyd GREAT BRITAIN
1934	Warsaw	G. Gaudini ITALY	G. Marzi ITALY	G. Bocchino ITALY
1935	Lausanne	[Eq.] G. Bocchino ITALY E. Gardère FRANCE R. Lemoine FRANCE G. Marzi ITALY	—	—
1937	Paris	G. Marzi ITALY	E. Gardère FRANCE	R. Lemoine FRANCE
1938	Piestany	G. Guaragna ITALY	G. Bocchino ITALY	E. Gardère FRANCE
1947	Lisbon	C. d'Oriola FRANCE	M. di Rosa ITALY	E. Mangiarotti ITALY
1949	Cairo	C. d'Oriola FRANCE	R. Nostini ITALY	[Eq.] E. Mangiarotti ITALY G. Nostini ITALY
1950	Monte Carlo	R. Nostini ITALY	J. Buhan FRANCE	J. Lataste FRANCE
1951	Stockholm	M. di Rosa ITALY	E. Mangiarotti ITALY	J. Buhan FRANCE
1953	Brussels	C. d'Oriola FRANCE	E. Mangiarotti ITALY	M. di Rosa ITALY
1954	Luxembourg	C. diOriola FRANCE	E. Mangiarotti ITALY	G. Bergamini ITALY
1955	Rome	J. Gyurica HUNGARY	C. d'Oriola FRANCE	J. Lataste FRANCE
1957	Paris	M. Fulop HUNGARY	M. Midler USSR	A. L. N. Jay GREAT BRITAIN
1958	Philadelphia	G. Bergamini ITALY	F. Czvikovsky HUNGARY	B. Baudoux FRANCE
1959	Budapest	A. L. N. Jay GREAT BRITAIN	C. Netter FRANCE	M. Midler USSR
1961	Turin	R. Parulski POLAND	J. Kamuti HUNGARY	M. Midler USSR
1962	Buenos Aires	G. Svechnikov USSR	W. Woyda POLAND	J. Brecht WEST GERMANY
1963	Gdansk	J-P. Magnan FRANCE	R. Parulski POLAND	E. Francke POLAND
1965	Paris	J-P. Magnan FRANCE	D. Revenu FRANCE	G. Svechnikov USSR
1966	Moscow	G. Svechnikov USSR	J-P. Magnan FRANCE	V. Poutiatine USSR
1967	Montreal	V. Poutiatine USSR	J. Kamuti HUNGARY	B. Talvard FRANCE
1969	Havana	F. Wessel WEST GERMANY	V. Stankovich USSR	R. Parulski POLAND

LADIES' FOIL: TEAMS

	Where Held	First	Second	Third
1932	Copenhagen	Denmark	Austria	Germany
1933	Budapest	Hungary	Great Britain	Austria
1934	Warsaw	Hungary	Germany	[Eq.] Great Britain Italy
1935	Lausanne	Hungary	Austria	Germany
1936	San Remo	Germany	Hungary	Austria
1937	Paris	Hungary	Germany	Denmark
1947	Lisbon	Denmark	France	Italy
1948	The Hague	Denmark	Hungary	France
1950	Monte Carlo	France	Denmark	Great Britain
1951	Stockholm	France	Hungary	Denmark
1952	Copenhagen	Hungary	France	Italy
1953	Brussels	Hungary	—	Italy
1954	Luxembourg	Hungary	Italy	France
1955	Rome	Hungary	France	Italy
1956	London	USSR	France	Hungary
1957	Paris	Italy	Germany	Austria
1958	Philadelphia	USSR	Germany	France
1959	Budapest	Hungary	USSR	Germany
1961	Turin	USSR	Hungary	Roumania
1962	Buenos Aires	Hungary	USSR	Italy
1963	Gdansk	USSR	Hungary	Italy
1965	Paris	USSR	Roumania	Italy
1966	Moscow	USSR	Hungary	France
1967	Montreal	Hungary	USSR	Roumania
1969	Havana	Roumania	USSR	Hungary

LADIES' FOIL: INDIVIDUAL TITLE

	Where Held	First	Second	Third
1929	Naples	H. Mayer GERMANY	A. de Boer HOLLAND	M. Dany HUNGARY
1930	Liège	J. Addams BELGIUM	G. Schwaiger ITALY	M. A. Venables GREAT BRITAIN
1931	Vienna	H. Mayer GERMANY	B. E. Bogathy HUNGARY	E. Preiss AUSTRIA
1933	Budapest	G. Neligan GREAT BRITAIN	B. E. Bogathy HUNGARY	M. With DENMARK
1934	Warsaw	I. Elek HUNGARY	M. Elek HUNGARY	H. Hass GERMANY
1935	Lausanne	I. Elek HUNGARY	E. Preiss AUSTRIA	J. Addams BELGIUM
1937	Paris	H. Mayer GERMANY	I. Elek HUNGARY	E. Preiss AUSTRIA
1938	Piestany	M. Sediva CZECHOSLOVAKIA	C. Slabochova CZECHOSLOVAKIA	J. Addams BELGIUM
1947	Lisbon	E. Müller-Preiss AUSTRIA	S. Strukel ITALY	L. Malherbaud FRANCE
1949	Cairo	E. Müller-Preiss AUSTRIA	K. Lachmann DENMARK	R. Garilhe FRANCE
1950	Monte Carlo	[Eq.] R. Garilhe FRANCE E. Müller-Preiss AUSTRIA	—	F. Filz AUSTRIA
1951	Stockholm	I. Elek HUNGARY	K. Lachmann DENMARK	M. Nyari HUNGARY
1953	Brussels	I. Camber ITALY	R. Garilhe FRANCE	I. Keydel GERMANY
1954	Luxembourg	K. Lachmann DENMARK	I. Elek HUNGARY	R. Garilhe FRANCE
1955	Rome	L. Dömölki HUNGARY	B. Colombetti ITALY	I. Elek HUNGARY
1957	Paris	A. Zabelina USSR	H. Schmidt GERMANY	I. Camber-Corno ITALY
1958	Philadelphia	V. Kisseleva USSR	E. Gitnikova USSR	I. Rejto HUNGARY

	Where Held	First	Second	Third
1959	Budapest	E. Efimova USSR	G. Ghorokova USSR	T. Petrenko USSR
1961	Turin	H. Schmid WEST GERMANY	A. Zabelina USSR	V. Rostvorova USSR
1962	Buenos Aires	O. Orban-Szabo ROUMANIA	G. Gorokhova USSR	K. Juhaz HUNGARY
1963	Gdansk	I. Rejto HUNGARY	L. Sakovits HUNGARY	K. Juhaz HUNGARY
1965	Paris	G. Gorokhova USSR	O. Orban-Szabo ROUMANIA	V. Prudskova USSR
1966	Moscow	T. Samusenko USSR	A. Zabelina USSR	G. Gorokhova USSR
1967	Montreal	A. Zabelina USSR	A. Ragno ITALY	I. Bobis HUNGARY
1969	Havana	E. Novikova USSR	I. Drimba ROUMANIA	S. Cirkova USSR

ÉPÉE: TEAMS

	Where Held	First	Second	Third
1930	Liège	Belgium	Italy	France
1931	Vienna	Italy	France	Sweden
1933	Budapest	Italy	France	Sweden
1934	Warsaw	France	Italy	Sweden
1935	Lausanne	France	Sweden	Germany
1937	Paris	Italy	France	Sweden
1938	Piestany	France	Sweden	Italy
1947	Lisbon	Frnace	Sweden	Italy
1949	Cairo	Italy	Sweden	Egypt
1950	Monte Carlo	Italy	France	Sweden
1951	Stockholm	France	Italy	Sweden
1953	Brussels	Italy	France	Switzerland
1954	Luxembourg	Italy	Sweden	France
1955	Rome	Italy	France	Hungary
1957	Paris	Italy	Hungary	Great Britain
1958	Philadelphia	Italy	Hungary	France
1959	Budapest	Hungary	USSR	France
1961	Turin	USSR	France	Sweden
1962	Buenos Ayres	France	Sweden	USSR
1963	Gdansk	Poland	France	Hungary
1965	Paris	France	Great Britain	USSR
1966	Moscow	France	USSR	Sweden
1967	Montreal	USSR	France	Hungary
1969	Havana	USSR	Hungary	Sweden

ÉPÉE: INDIVIDUAL TITLE

	Where Held	First	Second	Third
1921	Paris	L. Gaudin FRANCE	E. Cornereau FRANCE	W. Daniels HOLLAND
1922	Paris	R. Heide NORWAY	R. Liottel FRANCE	E. Cornereau FRANCE
1923	The Hague	W. Brouwer HOLLAND	A. de Jong HOLLAND	R. Ducret FRANCE
1926	Ostend	G. Tainturier FRANCE	F. de Montigny BELGIUM	L. Tom BELGIUM
1927	Vichy	G. Buchard FRANCE	F. Jourdant FRANCE	X. de Beukelaer BELGIUM
1929	Naples	P. Cattiau FRANCE	F. Riccardi ITALY	M. Bertinetti ITALY
1930	Liège	P. Cattiau FRANCE	A. Pezzana ITALY	A. Rossignol FRANCE
1931	Vienna	G. Buchard FRANCE	B. Schmetz FRANCE	L. Rousset FRANCE
1933	Budapest	G. Buchard FRANCE	S. Ragno ITALY	B. Schmetz FRANCE
1934	Warsaw	P. Dunay HUNGARY	G. Dyrssen SWEDEN	H. Drakenberg SWEDEN

	Where Held	First	Second	Third
1935	Lausanne	H. Drakenberg SWEDEN	P. Deydier FRANCE	S. Ragno ITALY
1937	Paris	B. Schmetz FRANCE	J. Coutrot FRANCE	R. Stasse BELGIUM
1938	Piestany	M. Pécheux FRANCE	E. Mangiarotti ITALY	B. Schmetz FRANCE
1947	Lisbon	E. Artigas FRANCE	B. Ljungquist SWEDEN	R. Henkart BELGIUM
1949	Cairo	D. Mangiarotti ITALY	R. Bougnol FRANCE	P. Carleson SWEDEN
1950	Monte Carlo	M. Luchow　[Eq.] DENMARK	C. Forssell SWEDEN D. Mangiarotti ITALY	—
1951	Stockholm	E. Mangiarotti ITALY	C. Pavesi ITALY	S. Fahlman SWEDEN
1953	Brussels	J. Sakovicz HUNGARY	B. Berczenyi HUNGARY	F. Marini ITALY
1954	Luxembourg	E. Mangiarotti ITALY	C. Pavesi ITALY	F. Bertinetti ITALY
1955	Rome	G. Anglesio ITALY	F. Bertinetti ITALY	C. Pavesi ITALY
1957	Paris	A. Mouyal FRANCE	G. Baranyi HUNGARY	F. Bertinetti ITALY
1958	Philadelphia	H. W. F. Hoskyns GREAT BRITAIN	E. Mangiarotti ITALY	A. Tchernouchevitch USSR
1959	Budapest	B. Khabarov USSR	A. L. N. Jay GREAT BRITAIN	G. Delfino ITALY
1961	Turin	J. Guittet FRANCE	H. Lagerwall SWEDEN	T. Gabor HUNGARY
1962	Buenos Aires	G. Kausz HUNGARY	T. Gabor HUNGARY	I. Dreyfus FRANCE
1963	Gdansk	R. Losert AUSTRIA	I. Dreyfus FRANCE	G. Kostava USSR
1965	Paris	Z. Nemere HUNGARY	H. W. F. Hoskyns GREAT BRITAIN	G. Kostava USSR
1966	Moscow	A. Nikantchikov USSR	C. Bourquard FRANCE	B. Gonsior POLAND
1967	Montreal	A. Nikantchikov USSR	G. Kriss USSR	R. Trost AUSTRIA
1969	Havana	B. Andrzejewski POLAND	A. Nikantchikov USSR	C. von Essen SWEDEN

SABRE: TEAMS

	Where Held	First	Second	Third
1930	Liège	Hungary	Italy	Poland
1931	Vienna	Hungary	Italy	Germany
1933	Budapest	Hungary	Italy	Great Britain
1934	Warsaw	Hungary	Italy	Poland
1935	Lausanne	Hungary	Italy	Germany
1937	Paris	Hungary	Italy	Germany
1938	Piestany	Italy	France	Holland
1947	Lisbon	Italy	Belgium	Egypt
1949	Cairo	Italy	France	Egypt
1950	Monte Carlo	Italy	France	Egypt
1951	Stockholm	Hungary	Italy	Belgium
1953	Brussels	Hungary	Italy	Poland
1954	Luxembourg	Hungary	Poland	France
1955	Rome	Hungary	Italy	USSR
1957	Paris	Hungary	USSR	Poland
1958	Philadelphia	Hungary	USSR	Poland
1959	Budapest	Poland	Hungary	USSR
1961	Turin	Poland	USSR	Hungary
1962	Buenos Aires	Poland	Hungary	USSR
1963	Gdansk	Poland	USSR	Hungary
1965	Paris	USSR	Italy	France
1966	Moscow	Hungary	USSR	France

	Where Held	First	Second	Third
1967	Montreal	USSR	Hungary	France
1969	Havana	USSR	Poland	Hungary

SABRE: INDIVIDUAL TITLE

	Where Held	First	Second	Third
1922	Ostend	A. de Jong HOLLAND	M. Taillandier FRANCE	L. Tom BELGIUM
1923	The Hague	A. de Jong HOLLAND	M. J. Perrodon FRANCE	W. Daniels HOLLAND
1925	Ostend	J. Garay HUNGARY	E. Uhlyarick HUNGARY	A. Petschauer HUNGARY
1926	Budapest	A. Gombos HUNGARY	A. Petschauer HUNGARY	B. Bini ITALY
1927	Vichy	A. Gombos HUNGARY	E. Tersztiansky HUNGARY	A. Petschauer HUNGARY
1929	Naples	J. Glyckais HUNGARY	G. Marzi ITALY	A. Petschauer HUNGARY
1930	Liège	G. Piller HUNGARY	G. Marzi ITALY	G. Doros HUNGARY
1931	Vienna	G. Piller HUNGARY	G. Gaudini ITALY	A. Petschauer HUNGARY
1933	Budapest	A. Kabos HUNGARY	G. Marzi ITALY	G. Gaudini ITALY
1934	Warsaw	A. Kabos HUNGARY	G. Gaudini ITALY	L. Rajcsanyi HUNGARY
1935	Lausanne	A. Gerevich HUNGARY	E. Rajczy HUNGARY	L. Rajcszanyi HUNGARY
1937	Paris	P. Kovacs HUNGARY	T. Berczelly HUNGARY	L. Rajcsanyi HUNGARY
1938	Piestany	A. Montano ITALY	A. Masciotta ITALY	G. Perenno ITALY
1947	Lisbon	A. Montano ITALY	G. de Bourguignon BELGIUM	G. Daré ITALY
1949	Cairo	G. Daré ITALY	G. Pellini ITALY	V. Stagni ITALY
1950	Monte Carlo	J. Levavasseur FRANCE	E. Pinton ITALY	G. Daré ITALY
1951	Stockholm	A. Gerevich HUNGARY	P. Kovacs HUNGARY	G. Daré ITALY
1953	Brussels	P. Kovacs HUNGARY	A. Gerevich HUNGARY	R. Karpati HUNGARY
1954	Luxembourg	R. Karpati HUNGARY	P. Kovacs HUNGARY	T. Berczelly HUNGARY
1955	Rome	A. Gerevich HUNGARY	R. Karpati HUNGARY	R. Nostini ITALY
1957	Paris	J. Pawlowski POLAND	R. Karpati HUNGARY	T. Mendelenyi HUNGARY
1958	Philadelphia	I. Rylskyi USSR	D. Tychler USSR	J. Twardokens POLAND
1959	Budapest	R. Karpati HUNGARY	T. Mendelenyi HUNGARY	J. Pawlowski POLAND
1961	Turin	I. Rylskyi USSR	E. Ochyra POLAND	W. Zablocki POLAND
1962	Buenos Aires	Z. Horvath HUNGARY	J. Pawlowski POLAND	C. Arabo FRANCE
1963	Gdansk	I. Rylskyi USSR	J. Pawlowski POLAND	W. Calarese ITALY
1965	Paris	J. Pawlowski POLAND	M. Meszens HUNGARY	Z. Howvath HUNGARY
1966	Moscow	J. Pawlowski POLAND	T. Pezsa HUNGARY	Z. Horvath HUNGARY
1967	Montreal	M. Rakita USSR	J. Pawlowski POLAND	T. Pezsa HUNGARY
1969	Havana	V. Sidiak USSR	J. Kalmar HUNGARY	P. Bakonyi HUNGARY

AMATEUR CHAMPIONS OF GREAT BRITAIN

* After a barrage. For complete results of all other national team and individual championships, service championships and international events see the author's *Modern British Fencing* (1964 edition).

MEN'S FOIL

From 1898 to 1901 the championship was fought on the knock-out system and therafter on the pool system, so that a third place was only determined from 1902.

	First	*Second*	*Third*
1898	H. Turner	T. P. Hobbins	—
1899	B. C. Praed	T. P. Hobbins	—
1900	T. P. Hobbins	H. Evans James	—
1901	H. Evans James	R. Montgomerie	—
1902	*J. Jenkinson	*H. Evan James	[*Eq.*] H. Balfour T. P. Hobbins A. Rawlinson
1903	*J. Jenkinson	*H. Evan James	R. Montgomerie
1904	J. Jenkinson	R. Montgomerie	[*Eq.*] G. L. Jacobs H. Evan James
1905	*R. Montgomerie	*E. Seligman	A. Rawlison
1906	E. Seligman	P. M. Davson	R. Montgomerie
1907	E. Seligman	R. Montgomerie	[*Eq.*] E. M. Amphlett P. M. Davson
1908	R. Montgomerie	[*Eq.*] G. R. Alexander E. M. Amphlett P. M. Davson	—
1909	R. Montgomerie	P. M. Davson	E. M. Amphlett
1910	*R. Montgomerie	*P. M. Davson	[*Eq.*] E. Seligman R. M. P. Willoughby
1911	E. M. Amphlett	R. M. P. Willoughby	A. Rawlinson
1912	*P. G. Doyne	*P. M. Davson	*R. M. P. Willoughby
1913	G. R. Alexander	R. Sutton	P. G. Doyne
1914	R. M. P. Willoughby	G. R. Alexander	A. Rawlinson
1920	P. G. Doyne	S. Martineau	[*Eq.*] R. Sutton Maj. R. M. P. Willoughby
1921	R. Sutton	P. G. Doyne	[*Eq.*] E. Stenson Cooke Maj. R. M. P. Willoughby
1922	*R. Sutton	*E. Stenson Cooke	Ft-Lieut. F. G. Sherriff
1923	E. Stenson Cooke	T. E. Ryves	[*Eq.*] F. G. Davis R. Haigh
1924	*Ft-Lieut. F. G. Sherriff	*R. S. S. Meade	E. Stenson Cooke
1925	Ft-Lieut. F. G. Sherriff	*R. S. S. Meade	*M. J. Babington- Smith
1926	*S. R. Bousfield	*J. A. Obdam	*M. J. Babington- Smith
1927	Maj. A. D. Pearce	J. Emrys Lloyd	J. Winder
1928	*J. Emrys Lloyd	*Ft-Lieut. F. G. Sherriff	G. T. M. Gibson
1929	J. Evan James	C. A. Simey	Maj. A. D. Pearce
1930	J. Emrys Lloyd	T. E. Ryves	M. J. Babington- Smith
1931	J. Emrys Lloyd	M. J. Babington-Smith	F. E. Lloyd
1932	J. Emrys Lloyd	M. J. Babington-Smith	J. Winder
1933	J. Emrys Lloyd	H. D. H. Bartlett	Maj. A. D. Pearce
1934	H. D. H. Bartlett	G. V. Hett	B. P. Cazaly
1935	H. D. H. Bartlett	Maj. A. D. Pearce	J. Winder
1936	C. R. Hammersley	Maj. A. D. Pearce	G. V. Hett
1937	J. Emrys Lloyd	G. V. Hett	Dr R. F. Tredgold
1938	*J. Emrys Lloyd	*G. V. Hett	*A. R. Smith
1939	*H. Cooke	*P. M. Turquet	René Paul
1947	*René Paul	*Dr. R. F. Tredgold	H. Cooke
1948	*A. R. Smith	*René Paul	*U. L. Wendon
1949	René Paul	A. R. Smith	Raymond Paul
1950	René Paul	U. L. Wendon	Dr P. M. Turquet
1951	H. Cooke	Raymond Paul	René Paul
1952	U. L. Wendon	Raymond Paul	H. Cooke
1953	Raymond Paul	R. Cooperman	U. L. Wendon
1954	J. E. Fethers	Raymond Paul	René Paul
1955	Raymond Paul	E. O. R. Reynolds	René Paul
1956	René Paul	Raymond Paul	A. L. N. Jay
1957	Raymond Paul	A. L. N. Jay	H. W. F. Hoskyns
1958	Raymond Paul	H. W. F. Hoskyns	A. L. N. Jay

	First	Second	Third
1959	H. W. F. Hoskyns	Raymond Paul	René Paul
1960	D. Cawthorne	A. L. N. Jay	L. C. Cook
1961	A. M. Leckie	René Paul	R. A. Mackenzie
1962	René Paul	A. M. Leckie	A. R. Cooperman
1963	A. L. N. Jay	R. A. Mackenzie	M. Price
1964	H. W. F. Hoskyns	A. L. N. Jay	A. M. Leckie
1965	A. M. Leckie	A. L. N. Jay	P. J. Kirby
1966	G. R. Paul	A. M. Leckie	H. W. F. Hoskyns
1967	A. M. Leckie	A. L. N. Jay	V. Bonfil
1968	G. R. Paul	H. W. F. Hoskyns	N. Halstead
1969	M. J. Breckin	H. W. F. Hoskyns	B. Paul

LADIES' FOIL

	First	Second	Third
1907	Miss M. Hall	Miss D. Milman	Mrs Edwardes
1908	Miss M. Hall	[Eq.] Miss F. E. Carter Mrs Edwardes Miss J. Johnstone	—
1909	*Mrs C. E. Martin Edmunds	*Miss J. Johnstone	[Eq.] Miss M. Hall Miss A. B. Walker
1910	Miss J. Johnstone	[Eq.] Miss F. E. Carter Miss G. Daniell	—
1911	Miss G. Daniell	Miss J. Johnstone	[Eq.] Mrs Edwardes Miss A. B. Walker
1912	*Miss G. Daniell	*Miss C. A. Walker	*Miss A. B. Walker
1913	Miss A. B. Walker	Miss C. A. Walker	Mrs C. E. Martin Edmunds
1914	*Miss A. B. Walker	*Miss C. A. Walker	Miss D. Cheetham
1920	Miss C. A. Walker	Miss G. Daniell	Miss A. B. Walker
1921	*Miss G. Daniell	*Miss M. Hall	[Eq.] Miss G. M. Davis Miss J. Johnstone
1922	*Miss M. Hall	*Miss G. M. Davis	Miss J. Johnstone
1923	Miss G. M. Davis	Miss G. Daniell	Miss J. Johnstone
1924	Miss G. Daniell	Mrs M. Freeman	Miss O. B. Pearce
1925	Miss G. M. Davis	Mrs M. Freeman	Miss F. Bibby
1926	Miss G. M. Davis	Miss G. Daniell	Mrs M. Freeman
1927	Mrs M. Freeman	Miss G. Daniell	[Eq.] Miss M. M. Butler Miss G. M. Davis
1928	*Miss M. M. Butler	*Mrs M. Freeman	Miss G. Daniell
1929	*Mrs M. Freeman	*Miss W. Davis	Mrs G. Minton
1930	Miss M.M. Butler	Miss G. Daniell	Miss E. C. Arbuthnott
1931	*Miss M. M. Butler	*Miss G. Neligan	Miss E. C. Arbuthnott
1932	*Miss M. M. Butler	*Miss J. Guinness	*Miss G. Neligan
1933	*Miss J. Guinness	*Miss E. C. Arbuthnott	*Miss G. Neligan
1934	*Miss G. Neligan	*Miss J. Guinness	Miss M. M. Butler
1935	*Miss G. Neligan	*Miss J. Guinness	Miss M. M. Butler
1936	Miss G. Neligan	Mrs Penn Hughes	Miss E. C. Arbuthnott
1937	Miss G. Neligan	Mrs G. Minton	Miss K. Bartlett
1938	Mrs Penn Hughes	Miss P. Etheridge	Miss B. Puddefoot
1939	Miss E. C. Arbuthnott	Miss P. Etheridge	Miss B. Puddefoot
1947	Miss E. C. Arbuthnott	Miss L. M. Boyd	Mrs M. A. Glen Haig
1948	Mrs M. A. Glen Haig	Miss E. C. Arbuthnott	Mrs G. Minton
1949	Miss G. M. Sheen	Miss E. C. Arbuthnott	Miss M. Somerville
1950	Mrs M. A. Glen Haig	Miss E. C. Arbuthnott	Miss G. M. Sheen
1951	Miss G. M. Sheen	Mrs M. A. Glen Haig	Miss P. Butler
1952	Miss G. M. Sheen	Mrs M. A. Glen Haig	Miss C. Drew
1953	Miss G. M. Sheen	Mrs M. A. Glen Haig	Miss B. M. Screech
1954	Miss G. M. Sheen	Mrs M. A. Glen Haig	Miss J. Witchell
1955	Miss G. M. Sheen	*Mrs M. A. Glen Haig	Miss B. M. Screech
1956	*Miss G. M. Sheen	*Mrs M. A. Glen Haig	Mrs P. Ashmore
1957	Miss G. M. Sheen	Miss E. Berry	Miss M. Durne
1958	Miss G. M. Sheen	Miss E. Berry	Mrs M. A. Glen Haig
1959	Miss M. Stafford	Mrs M. A. Glen Haig	Miss J. Bailey
1960	Miss G. M. Sheen	Mrs M. A. Glen Haig	Miss M. Stafford
1961	Miss T. M. Offredy	Miss J. L. M. Pearce	Miss S. Netherway
1962	Miss T. M. Offredy	Miss J. Bewley-Cathie	Mrs P. Courtney-Lewis
1963	Miss M. A. Pritchard	Miss J. Bewley-Cathie	Miss J. Bailey
1964	Miss S. Netherway	Miss J. Bewley-Cathie	Miss R. Rayner

	First	*Second*	*Third*
1965	Miss J. Bewley-Cathie	Miss S. Netherway	Miss J. M. Davis
1966	Mrs S. Parker	Miss J. Bewley-Cathie	Miss J. M. Davis
1967	Mrs J. Wardell-Yerburgh	Miss J. Herriot	Miss M. Holmes
1968	Miss S. Green	Mrs J. Bain	Miss J. M. Davis
1969	Mrs J. Wardell-Yerburgh	Miss M. Holmes	Mrs J. M. Barkley

ÉPÉE

From 1904 to 1907 British fencer placed highest in the International Épée Competition organized
by the Épée Club was regarded as the Amateur Épée Champion for the year. From 1908, the
Amateur Fencing Association organized the Épée Championship as a separate event. The bouts in
his championship were for one hit only until 1932, when they were fenced for the best of three
hits. From 1956, bouts were for the best of nine hits. The final pool of the 1938 Épée Championship
was judged with the electrical judging apparatus for the first time in any British competition.

	First	*Second*	*Third*
1904	E. Seligman	—	—
1905	R. Montgomerie	—	—
1906	E. Seligman	—	—
1907	R. Montgomerie	—	—
1908	*C. L. Daniell	*M. D. Holt	R. Montgomerie
1909	*R. Montgomerie	*C. L. Daniell	[*Eq.*] A. G. Everitt
			S. Martineau
1910	E. M. Amphlett	[*Eq.*] S. Martineau	—
		E. Seligman	
1911	J. P. Blake	[*Eq.*] L. V. Fildes	—
		R. Montgomerie	
1912	R. Montgomerie	[*Eq.*] S. Beale	—
		W. A. Conduit	
		B. Leverson	
1913	*G. G. M. Vereker	*L. V. Fildes	[*Eq.*] G. Ames
			G. de Goldschmidt
			M. D. V. Holt
1914	R. Montgomerie	G. Cornet	A. G. Everitt
1920	*M. D. V. Holt	*J. P. Blake	Maj. C. B. Notley
1921	Capt. H. F. S. Huntington	[*Eq.*] H. E. Blaiberg	—
		J. P. Blake	
		R. Frater	
		Maj. C. B. Notley	
1922	G. M. Burt	[*Eq.*] J. P. Blake	—
		R. Frater	
		M. D. V. Holt	
		Ft-Lieut. F. G. Sherriff	
1923	M. D. V. Holt	[*Eq.*] G. M. Burt	—
		C. C. H. Drake	
		Maj. C. B. Notley	
1924	C. H. Biscoe	M. D. V. Holt	[*Eq.*] Hon. I. D. Campbell-
			Gray
			Maj. C. B. Notley
			T. E. Beddard
1925	Maj. C. B. Notley	C. H. Biscoe	[*Eq.*] H. E. Blaiberg
			G. M. Burt
			A. E. Pelling
1926	Hon. I. D. Campbell-Gray	Maj. R. E. Cole	[*Eq.*] L. V. Fildes
			Maj. C. B. Notley
			Maj. A. J.
			Whitehouse
			Maj. R. M. P.
			Willoughby
1927	*Maj. C. B. Notley	*B. Childs	D. D. Drury
1928	*B. Childs	*A. E. Pelling	C. C. A. Monro
1929	L. V. Fildes	[*Eq.*] Hon. I. D. Campbell-Gray	
		D. Dexter	
		C. C. A. Monro	
1930	*Hon. I. D. Campbell-Gray	*J. B. Armstrong	B. Childs
1931	B. Childs	[*Eq.*] Sir O. Mosley, Bt	—
		Maj. C. B. Notley	
1932	Hon. I. D. Campbell-Gray	Maj. C. B. Notley	Sir O. Mosley, Bt
1933	*A. E. Pelling	*D. Dexter	L. V. Fildes
1934	A. E. Pelling	Hon. J. C. Bampfylde	D. Dexter
1935	Hon. I. D. Campbell-Gray	B. Childs	C-L. de Beaumont

	First	Second	Third
1936	C-L. de Beaumont	T. E. Beddard	A. E. Pelling
1937	C-L. de Beaumont	B. Childs	A. E. Pienne
1938	*C-L. de Beaumont	*René Paul	A. E. Pelling
1939	*T. E. Beddard	*M. D. McCready	R. C. Winton
1947	P. C. Dix	C-L. de Beaumont	René Paul
1948	*Dr R. Parfitt	*U. L. Wendon	*C-L. de Beaumont
1949	P. C. Dix	René Paul	C. D. Grose-Hodge
1950	Dr R. Parfitt	René Paul	A. J. Payne
1951	A. E. Pelling	Dr R. Parfitt	Dr A. G. Signy
1952	A. L. N. Jay	Dr R. Parfitt	R. A. Harrison
1953	*C-L. de Beaumont	*Dr E. B. Knott	A. L. N. Jay
1954	P. A. Greenhalgh	A. L. N. Jay	Lieut.-Cmndr R. St. C. Sproul-Bolton
1955	R. A. Harrison	A. L. N. Jay	J. A. Pelling
1956	H. W. F. Hoskyns	A. L. N. Jay	Lieut.-Cmndr R. St. C. Sproul-Bolton
1957	*H. W. F. Hoskyns	*A. L. N. Jay	M. P. J. Howard
1958	H. W. F. Hoskyns	A. L. N. Jay	J. A. Pelling
1959	A. L. N. Jay	J. A. Pelling	H. W. F. Hoskyns
1960	A. L. N. Jay	M. J. P. Howard	I. R. Spofforth
1961	J. A. Pelling	R. A. Mackenzie	P. Jacobs
1962	P. Jacobs	M. J. P. Howard	J. A. Pelling
1963	J. D. Glasswell	P. Jacobs	J. A. Pelling
1964	P. Jacobs	H. W. F. Hoskyns	J. A. Pelling
1965	J. A. Pelling	E. O. Bourne	N. Halstead
1966	E. O. Bourne	G. R. Paul	C. B. Purchase
1967	H. W. F. Hoskyns	E. O. Bourne	G. R. Paul
1968	W. R. Johnson	H. W. F. Hoskyns	J. Fox
1969	G. R. Paul	W. R. Johnson	E. O. Bourne

SABRE

In 1898, 1900 and 1901 this championship was fought on the knock-out system, in all other years on the pool system.

	First	Second	Third
1898	Capt. W. Edgworth-Johnstone	W. P. Gate	—
1899	T. P. Hobbins	R. A. Poore	W. P. Gate
1900	Capt. W. Edgworth-Johnstone	A. D. Bell	—
1901	T. P. Hobbins	A. C. Murray	—
1902	T. P. Hobbins	[Eq.] A. D. Bell J. C. Newman	—
1903	H. Evan James	[Eq.] J. C. Newman C. A. Wilson	—
1904	C. A. Wilson	W. W. Marsh	E. R. McClure
1905	C. A. Wilson	J. Jenkinson	W. W. Marsh
1906	C. A. Wilson	[Eq.] J. Jenkinson W. W. Marsh A. Ridley Martin	—
1907	Lieut. F. E. B. Feilmann, RN	W. W. Marsh	A. G. Everitt
1908	W. W. Marsh	C. A. Wilson	[Eq.] A. V. Keene L. Leith A. C. Murray
1909	W. W. Marsh	A. C. Murray	Lieut. E. W. H. Brookfield, RN
1910	*A. Ridley Martin	*Lieut. F. E. B. Feilmann, RN	D. W. Godfree
1911	W. Hammond	W. W. Marsh	Lieut. F. E. B. Feilmann, RN
1912	Capt. C. Van der Byl	C. FitzClarence	A. Ridley Martin
1913	*A. Ridley Martin	*Capt. C. Van der Byl	C. FitzClarence
1914	W. Hammond	A. H. Corble	H. R. Butterworth
1920	Lieut. C. A. Kershaw, RN	[Eq.] Col. R. B. Campbell Capt. R. Dalglish, RN E. Seligman	—
1921	W. Hammond	[Eq.] Capt. H. F. S. Huntington *Lieut. C. A. Kershaw, RN	—
1922	*A. H. Corble	*Lieut. C. A. Kershaw, RN	E. Seligman
1923	*E. Seligman	Lieut. C. A. Kershaw, RN	Maj. R. M. P. Willoughby
1924	E. Seligman	Capt. R. Dalglish, RN	Cmndr E. W. H. Brookfield

	First	*Second*	*Third*
1925	Lieut.-Cmndr C. A. Kershaw, RN	[*Eq.*] Cmndr E. W. H. Brookfield Maj. G. N. Dyer D. W. Neilson	—
1926	*Lieut.-Cmndr C. A. Kershaw, RN	*J. A. Obdam	Col. R. B. Campbell
1927	A. H. Corble	Capt. G. L. G. Harry	Maj. C. B. Notley
1928	*Capt. G. L. G. Harry	*H. A. Forrest	C. G. Hohler
1929	Col. R. B. Campbell	O. G. Trinder	Maj. C. B. Notley
1930	*O. G. Trinder	*Capt. G. L. G. Harry	A. G. Pilbrow
1931	O. G. Trinder	Capt. G. L. G. Harry	A. G. Pilbrow
1932	A. G. Pilbrow	O. G. Trinder	C. G. Hohler
1933	O. G. Trinder	A. G. Pilbrow	C. G. Hohler
1934	O. G. Trinder	R. E. Brook	A. G. Pilbrow
1935	A. G. Pilbrow	O. G. Trinder	R. F. Tredgold
1936	R. E. Brook	Capt. G. L. G. Harry	A. G. Pilbrow
1937	Dr R. F. Tredgold	P. M. Turquet	O. G. Trinder
1938	A. G. Pilbrow	C-L. de Beaumont	Dr R. F. Tredgold
1939	Rr R. F. Tredgold	P. M. Turquet	O. G. Trinder
1947	Dr R. F. Tredgold	A. G. Pilbrow	O. G. Trinder
1948	*Dr R. F. Tredgold	*A. G. Pilbrow	*R. E. Brook
1949	Dr R. F. Tredgold	D. Shalit	A. G. Pilbrow
1950	*A. G. Pilbrow	*Dr P. M. Turquet	Dr R. F. Tredgold
1951	Dr P. M. Turquet	A. G. Pilbrow	W. M. Beatley
1952	O. B. Porebski	R. J. G. Anderson	Dr R. F. Tredgold
1953	*O. B. Porebski	*M. J. Amberg	*U. L. Wendon
1954	*A. R. Cooperman	*H. W. F. Hoskyns	*Dr W. M. Beatley
1955	Dr R. F. Tredgold	O. B. Porebski	A. R. Cooperman
1956	O. B. Porebski	Dr R. F. Tredgold	A. R. Cooperman
1957	*M. J. Amberg	*B. W. Howes	Dr W. M. Beatley
1958	M. J. Amberg	A. R. Cooperman	Dr E. M. Verebes
1959	M. J. Amberg	A. R. Cooperman	Dr R. F. Tredgold
1960	A. R. Cooperman	A. M. Leckie	B. S. McCarthy
1961	A. R. Cooperman	A. M. Leckie	G. T. Birks
1962	C. R. Fisher	A. R. Cooperman	G. T. Birks
1963	A. M. Leckie	M. J. Amberg	A. R. Cooperman
1964	A. M. Leckie	A. R. Cooperman	W. J. Rayden
1965	A. M. Leckie	W. J. Rayden	R. Oldcorn
1966	H. W. F. Hoskyns	R. Oldcorn	A. R. Cooperman
1967	A. M. Leckie	W. J. Rayden	D. L. Acfield
1968	A. M. Leckie	R. Craig	W. J. Rayden
1969	D. L. Acfield	R. Craig	H. W. F. Hoskyns